THE POLITICS OF EDITING

Hispanic Issues

HISPANIC ISSUES
VOLUME 8

THE POLITICS OF EDITING

NICHOLAS SPADACCINI AND JENARO TALENS
◆
EDITORS

UNIVERSITY OF MINNESOTA PRESS
MINNEAPOLIS

The editors of this volume gratefully acknowledge assistance from the Program for Cultural Cooperation between Spain's Ministry of Culture and United States' Universities, and the College of Liberal Arts and the Department of Spanish and Portuguese at the University of Minnesota.

Published by the University of Minnesota Press
2037 University Avenue Southeast, Minneapolis, MN 55414
Printed in the United States of America on acid-free paper.

Library of Congress Cataloging-in-Publication Data

The Politics of editing / Nicholas Spadaccini and Jenaro Talens, editors.
    p.   cm. — (Hispanic issues : v. 8)
  Includes bibliographical references and index.
  ISBN 0-8166-2028-8 (alk. paper). — ISBN 0-8166-2029-6 (pbk. : alk. paper)
  1. Spanish literature—Criticism, Textual. 2. Spanish American literature—Criticism, Textual. 3. Editing. I. Spadaccini, Nicholas. II. Talens, Jenaro. III. Series: Hispanic issues : 8.
PQ6039.P65   1992
860.9—dc20   91-32104
                                                     CIP

Hispanic Issues

Contents

◆ Introduction

Textual Editing, the Writing of Literature, and Literary History

Nicholas Spadaccini and Jenaro Talens

The essays that constitute this volume of Hispanic Issues are by recognized specialists who have had considerable experience in editing and interpreting Hispanic texts. The Afterword was written by a scholar outside the immediate field of Hispanism who nevertheless brings to his reflections an appreciation and knowledge of our field, a thorough command of the discipline of literary studies, and extensive work in Renaissance studies and contemporary critical theory. The reader will notice that several essays deal with issues concerning the editing of Spanish masterpieces or national monuments (the *Poem of the Cid, Conde Lucanor,* Garcilaso's poetry, *Lazarillo,* the Spanish *Comedia*), while others focus on areas heretofore neglected: the editing of texts written by nineteenth-century women and the problem of anthologizing twentieth-century women poets of Latin America. A common thread in these essays is an awareness of editing as an interpretative practice framed by the circumstances of the editor who mediates between the authority of the "author" or "text," the exigencies of the various institutions of literary production, and the horizons of expectation or, in some cases, even the requirements of readers of those texts.

In recent years it has become abundantly clear that traditional theories of textual criticism no longer retain the certainty that they once enjoyed. Perhaps nowhere have those theories been explored and questioned more poignantly than in the writings of Jerome McGann, who summarizes brilliantly the history of textual theory while developing arguments for "a socialized concept of authorship and textual authority" (*Critique* 8). McGann analyzes problems of modern textual theory, the copy text, authorial intentions, critical editions, etc., from a historical point of view, fully aware of the long-standing schism that has existed "between textual and interpretative studies" (11).

Broadly speaking, it may be said that modern textual criticism has been grounded in the ideology of the "authoritative text," i.e., the one representing the author's original intentions. Such a text will have been cleansed of the errors and corruptions that might have tainted the original document in the process of its transmission. Of course, the privileging of the original word as a vehicle for the transmission of meaning was part of the humanist philosophy of language. In Spain, people such as Antonio de Nebrija and Fray Luis de León, among others, are examples of the humanists' interest in the power of language to move individuals and States (in Nebrija's case) into action. That interest manifested itself in an intense desire to study the written word: to learn how it functioned and what it meant as a "concrete experience in the past." In short, humanist philological exegesis, which centered on the authority of the original word, approached the establishment of a text by means of grammatical and rhetorical erudition as opposed to the prevalent scholastic view of language, which was essentially ahistorical and "established meaning through traditional logical discussion" (Zamora 15–17).

When we deal with modern textual editing, and specifically with the ideology of the "authoritative text" and original intentions, we are talking about an ideology that can be said to have emerged largely with classical scholarship in the early nineteenth century, when such scholarship began to rationalize editorial procedures in what became known as the Lachmann method (McGann, *Critique* 15). This method presupposed that one could go back to a single exemplar, cleansed of errata, which Lachmann referred to as an archetype (Pasquali 15). In the Anglo-Saxon world the Lachmann procedures were refined and adapted to modern texts by Fredson Bowers (McGann, *Critique* 5), whose impact on the discipline has been, and continues to be, substantial.

In the case of Spain, the practice of textual editing since the turn of the century has had a somewhat different orientation. One thinks of the extraordinary legacy of the methodological syncretism effected by the great philologists who worked out of the famous Center for Historical Studies (El Centro de Estudios Históricos), among them Ramón Menéndez Pidal and Américo Castro. For these scholars, for others like them, and for their disciples it was not simply a question of returning a text to a pristine state but, just as important, it was a matter of understanding the text historically. Editing a text—according to Castro (1924)—"means understanding it and interpreting it. . . . Philology is essentially a historical science, consisting of lending the greatest possible meaning to the written monuments, and reconstructing the states of civilization that lie inert in the pages of the texts." The debt owed to these pioneers by contemporary editors and critics of Spanish classical texts is substantial, even if theoretical contradictions remain between the search for pristine original texts and critical exegesis—which, after all, implies an editor's ideological positioning within and toward the text (see Evangelina Rodríguez in this volume).

One of McGann's main lines of argumentation is that the methods of editing and interpreting ancient, classical, and early modern texts are not always productive or appropriate to "modern national scriptures," especially on the matter of authorial intentions. Thus, he says,

> the textual-critical theories which dominate our approaches
> to early-modern and modern works have failed to define
> properly either a) the status and nature of "the text," or
> b) the corresponding obligations which the critical editor
> has toward his work. My view is that editors cannot fol-
> low the guidance of a rule of final authorial intentions in
> determining the texts they will print because final authorial
> intention is a deeply problematic concept. Though this is
> evidently the case in relation to works produced in very
> early periods, the concept is especially treacherous in rela-
> tion to more recent works because it seems so clear and
> simple at the level of theory and method. (*Critique* 67–68)

If one agrees with the notion that a "fully authoritative text" must have been "socially produced," then one must also go along with the idea that "the critical standard for what constitutes authoritativeness cannot rest with the author and his intentions alone" (75). Thus, simply identifying individual author and work is not sufficient; one must also consider the dialectical relationship between "the historically located individual and the historically developing institutions of literary production" (80). Within this scenario, the location of authority becomes problematic since it could well reach "beyond the author" to undergo "dispersal and alteration from a number of directions" (84): multiple authors, ghostwriters, nonscriptural level of authority, authors' habits of composition and revision (85–87), and so on. In the final analysis, examples abound to sustain McGann's conclusion that, in dealing with modern texts, a critical editor "must be prepared to accept an initial (and insurmountable) limit: that a definitive text, like the author's final intentions, may not exist, may never have existed, and may never exist at any future time" (90).

While it is reasonable to assume that this argument may be more generally appropriate to modern texts, it can also be carried to certain texts of early national scriptures. An example is Spain's famous epic, the *Poem of the Cid*, which has come down to us in a single manuscript that was probably transcribed from an oral performance. In his essay for this volume, Colin Smith reviews the editorial fortunes of the *Poema* as it emerges from the shadow of the "nationalistic" construction of Ramón Menéndez Pidal, who as early as 1908–1911 had seen the Castilian epic—in its surviving text "of 1140"—as a largely autochthonous artifact, a position that he was to underscore again in 1961 when he saw the text of 1140 "as a reworking of an original composed about 1105—that is, within a few years of the death of the Cid of history in 1099." Smith surmises that Menéndez Pidal's "unspoken intention was to bring the *Poema* to within the period of the prime version of the *Chanson de Roland,* usually considered to belong to the years of the First Crusade," thus eliminating any major linkage between the two poems and reinforcing the notion of the Castilian epic's autochthonous emergence.

Menéndez Pidal's editorial construction of the *Poema*—a remarkable, scholarly tour de force by a major philologist to be sure— was institutionalized in Spain and elsewhere (the American university, for example) for some sixty years, enjoying a virtual monopoly in the widely distributed and accessible Clásicos Castellanos series until the early 1970s, when, in the waning years of the Franco regime, Spain's drive toward modernization had its peculiar repercussions in the publishing world. Continental scholars such as Colin Smith and Ian Michael were to publish their editions of the *Poema* in the Cátedra and Castalia series respectively, while a new generation of Hispanists from Spain and abroad began to reexamine the history of the reception of one of Spain's national monuments.

Clearly, the editorial fortunes of the *Poema* began to undergo a vibrant renewal, which continues to this day. Smith alludes perceptively to these changes and, in the process of doing so, underscores his own philosophy of editing: "the editor's objective is to rerepresent the poem in a way that shows due respect for previous editors but also demonstrates that there is something new to say, not, perhaps, strictly in relation to the text, but at least in relation to new modes of analysis consistent with the editor's times and with what he or she has learned from contemporaries." Within this line of thinking about editing, it is clear that the choice of editorial method used or the editorial operations performed by the scholar in the process of establishing a text are choices and activities that cannot be separated from hermeneutics. Editing is ultimately an art that is practiced for a purpose within a certain set of historical circumstances. Here one might think, for example, of another Spanish national classic—the Castilian poet from Toledo, Garcilaso de la Vega, whose editorial good fortunes in the sixteenth century were tied to the projection of Spanish as a "national" hegemonic language (see Iris M. Zavala in this volume).

In the case of both Garcilaso's poetry and the *Poem of the Cid,* the elucidation of the works' textual history and the explication of their receptive histories are two dialectically related historical processes. McGann (*Beauty* 84) makes use of an excellent example from Thucydides's *The History of the Peloponnesian War* (Bk. II, Sec. 54, 122) to prove exactly this point, showing that Thucydides's "interest lies in the meaning of scholarship and criticism rather than in the meaning of [a] line of ancient verse" (89). That line ("A Dorian War shall come and with it death") was commented by Thucydides as follows:

> A dispute arose whether dearth and not death had not
> been the word in the verse; but at the present juncture it
> was of course decided in favour of the latter; for the peo-
> ple made their recollection fit in with their sufferings. I
> fancy, however, that if another Dorian war should ever af-
> terwards come upon us, and a dearth should happen to ac-
> company it, the verse will probably be read accordingly.
> (Cited by McGann, *Beauty* 88–89).

What emerges from all of this is that authorial intention cannot
always be readily ascertained and that, in any case, meaning and
authority cannot be disconnected from the social practice of reading. As if to underscore this very point, Elias L. Rivers (in this
volume) points to the problematic nature of a classic national text—
Garcilaso's poetry. He cites as an example lines 229–232 of the
Third Eclogue, which describe the death of the nymph Elisa. (See
Rivers and Conley respectively in this volume.) Rivers shows how
a controversy has raged during the past 450 years among the editors
of Garcilaso regarding the reading of a word that refers to Elisa's
lifeless body. This word has been taken variously as *degollada*
(beheaded), *ygualada* (equaled or leveled), *yugulada* (jugulated),
de Gollada (of Gollada). Rivers goes on to conclude that the history
of the work's reception ultimately privileges the reading of *degollada* regardless of what the poet's final intention may have been.

We know the importance of the history of a work's reception,
and it has been shown that the editing of texts has responded to
different exigencies during the past several hundred years. Iris M.
Zavala (in this volume) reminds us, correctly, that the origins of
editing in Spain are connected with the political project of
Charles V in the same manner that the systematization of Castilian
grammar in Antonio de Nebrija's *Gramática* (1492) is offered as a
strategy for the practical deployment of language, which would
serve as "companion of the Empire." For Nebrija, the process of
consolidation and union "in a body and unity of Kingdom"—which
was the "work of divine goodness and providence"—coincided with
the development of the Castilian language (Gómez Moriana 98).
In the case of Garcilaso, Zavala states, the various editions and
commentaries available in the sixteenth century also show that "the
canonization of the soldier-poet from Toledo coincides with the
establishment of the imperial humanist *doxae*, the institution-

alization of literature, and the constitution and articulation of a 'national' hegemonic cultural language: Castilian Spanish." In the sixteenth century, therefore, a modern author is raised to the status of a classic as the editing of his work becomes part of the "conceptualization of the modern Imperial State."

In this line of thinking, the value of the text can be said to respond to specific conditions and needs. Yet we know that Garcilaso has never ceased to be a canonical figure and that his works have been, and continue to be, edited and read. One need only glance at the various histories of Spanish literature over time, at the curricula of secondary schools in Spain, or at university catalogs wherever courses are taught on the Spanish Golden Age (including American universities), to see that centuries after the "conceptualization of the modern Imperial State," and indeed, even now in Spain, when the languages of other nationalities (Catalan, among others) contest the hegemonic role of Castilian Spanish, Garcilaso remains a national monument. One might say, then, that a politics of textual editing—which involves literary scholars and interpreters, publishing houses, schools, academies, and other agencies—might indeed emerge out of a certain institutional consensus or convenience that, in turn, does not guarantee the same degree of certainty when it comes to the other end of the communicative process: the receiver or reader of the text. That is, there may be a politics of textual editing, but what happens to that politics when specific readers, who operate in concrete historical circumstances, confront the text?

Here one might recall a 1971 seminal essay by Roland Barthes ("From Work to Text"), in which he distinguishes between "the work," which "is concrete, occupying a portion of book-space" and "the text," which, according to Barthes, "exists only as discourse" and never as concrete object. Whereas "works" are called "objects of consumption," "the text is experienced only as an activity, a production." For Barthes and for a large number of contemporary critics, literature is seen as a process of production rather than consumption, and readers of texts become active collaborators in the production of meaning. McGann sees no problem in giving the reader a certain flexibility to engage in imaginative forays, pointing out that in disvaluing a critical method that seeks to treat artistic works as objects, Barthes appeals to a tradition of aesthetic criticism that "emerges with Kant and Coleridge and continues into our own day" (*Beauty* 93). But McGann also argues for acknowledgment of the presence and relative authority of the traditional text, "for there can be no production process, no continuous act of generation, except within the limits of those specific means and relations of production which the present must accept as its continuing inheritance. This necessity exists because all literary products descend into immediate experience; that is, they come to the reader in determinate forms" (95). While the philological text and the poststructuralist text are said to aspire, respectively, toward science and knowledge and toward art and experience (94), in both instances "the generation of the text is . . . a perpetually renewed historical process of specific and concrete events" (96). In the final analysis, "the 'discourse' of literature . . . is not an undifferentiated linguistic stream, but a continuing set of finite relationships that develop in a valley of Dry Bones between an author, printers, publishers, readers of various sorts, reviewers, academicians, and— ultimately—society at all levels, and perhaps even international society" (96–97).

We have come a long way in this discussion from the matter of the authoritative text and authorial intentions, which we have tried to problematize (and polarize) with a brief detour through the poststructuralist emphasis on the reader as producer of "texts" rather than consumer of "works" as concrete objects. In the process of doing so, we have also taken the position held by most of the contributors to this volume (let us recall the words of Colin Smith cited earlier) that editing a text, any text, always involves a process of interpretation and that such an interpretation is contingent upon factors as varied as the critic's academic training and political disposition, the stipulations of the series and / or publishing house to which the text is destined, the intended readers of the text, previous editions and studies, changes in the academy, national upheavals, international conflicts, and so on.

One of us recalls how in 1969 he came across an essay written by the Spanish novelist Juan Goytisolo (1967) on the Spanish picaresque novel entitled *La vida y hechos de Estebanillo González, hombre de buen humor* (1646). Goytisolo called it the second most important Spanish novel of the Golden Age after *Don Quijote*, because, among other reasons, *Estebanillo* engaged the reader into reflecting upon a world that was totally secularized, devoid of idealisms, and circumscribed by the mercenary tenor of the Thirty Years' War, an international conflict fought less for religious reasons than for the economic self-interest of the powers involved—the Spanish and Austrian wings of the Hapsburgs, France, Sweden, etc. Goytisolo had read *Estebanillo* as an antiwar novel, arguing that it exposed the mechanisms of war and the brutality committed in the name of certain institutions of power. The reading of the Goytisolo essay happened to coincide with the writing of a dissertation on the same novel, and the preparation of an edition of *Estebanillo* for the Clásicos Castalia series. These activities were taking place during the last stages of the Vietnam War, and Goytisolo's essay obviously had struck a chord.

A more recent experience concerns the teaching of a class in English for nonmajors on the picaresque novel during the height of the scandals of the televangelists who were accused of bilking millions of dollars from the faithful to amass personal fortunes and luxurious life-styles. We recall the classes on *Lazarillo* and the facility with which students could relate the theatrical performance of the seller of indulgences in the novel's fifth chapter, or *tratado,* to the soap opera that was played out daily on television by the husband-and-wife team of Jim and Tammy Bakker. A responsive chord is also struck for contemporary American readers of *Lazarillo* when the issues of indigence and social welfare are highlighted in terms of the responsibility of the individual and/or society. Students are amazed to find that an Erasmian humanist of *Lazarillo's* time could frame the issue of social welfare in institutional and individual terms and that the reading of a Spanish text of the mid-sixteenth century could instigate a reflection on Reaganomics and its diatribes on the modern "welfare state."

Most editions of *Lazarillo* have indeed highlighted the connections between Lázaro's story of indigence and dishonor and the story of Spain during the times of Charles V. Joseph V. Ricapito (in this volume) reviews the editorial history of this text since the mid-nineteenth century and points out the various interpretative strategies to which it has been subjected during the past 150 years. One of the constants of those strategies has been an emphasis on social satire, although, as Ricapito indicates, with the advent of stylistics and New Criticism there emerged an emphasis on the text's aesthetic dimensions. Ricapito's own essay—which includes an analytical section on the story and discourse of *Lazarillo* and which reaffirms the thesis that he held in the introduction to his edition in the Cátedra series—is proof that a textual editor is ultimately engaged in an activity that can be described as hermeneutic. Ricapito's edition (1976), which, ironically, was purged from Cátedra's Letras Hispánicas collection by the series editor (who managed to replace it with his own edition), highlighted the Erasmian traits of the novel, placing the text squarely within the discussion of sixteenth-century Erasmian humanism that criticized the selling of religion and the abandonment of the spiritual and physical needs of the poor by the institutional Church and the early modern State.

One cannot underestimate the power of a well-marketed edition in shaping interpretative attitudes, nor can one minimize the importance of well-marketed series in the area of canon formation or canon validation and/or revision. As opposed to scholarly books and monographic studies, which generally receive limited circulation, editions in series such as Cátedra's Letras Hispánicas, Castalia's Clásicos Castalia, and Espasa-Calpe's Clásicos Castellanos—to mention some of the most prominent—are reprinted regularly and the volumes in circulation can be counted in the tens of thousands. As Ricapito states (in this volume), introductions in these series are often used to "polemicize with competing literary theories" or to disqualify the work of previous editors and interpreters of the same text. Ricapito's own edition was replaced by another that was neither better nor worse but which definitely highlighted literary sources and structural analysis.

As an institutionalized activity textual criticism is inseparable from literary criticism and interpretation and, in any case, "cannot be reduced to a set of rules: each new problem calls for new thought" (West 9). Some of the essays in this volume problematize precisely this question. Susan Kirkpatrick, for example, emphasizes the idea that literary production is essentially a historical and social activity. She then focuses on the Romantic notion of authority (*male* authority) and the concept of authorial autonomy and on the manner in which those notions were used by influential nineteenth-century literary critics and editors such as Valera and Hartzenbusch in order to exclude women's voices from the canon or, in some cases, to operate an effective marginalization of those voices within the canon. Evangelina Rodríguez, on the other hand, problematizes the very idea of a science of editing when she points to the enormous task facing the textual critic who sets out to edit Spanish Golden Age plays—even plays by well-known play-wrights—without taking into account the concrete circumstances of textual transmission of works, which, frequently written for specific theater companies (who often traded copies among them-selves), most likely journeyed to the printer through such groups (Reichenberger 78). Both Kirkpatrick and Rodríguez, from their own vantage points and areas of concern, call for more creative and meaningful ways of editing texts for the contemporary reader and argue, implicitly, for a rewriting of literary history.

That textual editing and literary history are complementary ac-tivities can be gathered from the essay of Pere Ferré (in this volume) which deals with the political strategy of Almeida Garrett, the Portuguese liberal intellectual who edited a corpus of traditional ballads, using "ancient popular knowledge" as he sought to project "the idea of nation." Thus the leader of the Romantic movement in Portugal used editing in the drive to build a national identity, and, through a particular practice of editing collections of ballads, he sought to provide a generation of poets with national models, i.e., with examples from the culture and wisdom of the people. It is clear, then, that for Garrett establishing the text of a *romance* was not a scientific undertaking but a political move tied to the literary sphere of the Romantic revolution in Portugal. In later historical periods different criteria were to be used in editing these texts. Those criteria revolved around the notion of authenticity: the text was either corrupted by the influence of the "common people" or, on the opposite side of the spectrum, it entailed an appropriation of the poem-song on the part of the learned minor-ities, an appropriation that "masked" the very "being" of the poem (Catalán 452, cited by Ferré). One can see from these positions how textual editing is a complex activity involving, ultimately, the editor's own presuppositions and biases, i.e., his or her own agenda or project. One might argue, of course, that editing texts that were transmitted orally has its own peculiar set of circumstances and problems, but, as we have seen, so does editing other types of texts. What does a present-day editor do, for example, with a play from the Spanish Golden Age that, in addition to having gone through substantial tribulations in the process of its transmission, was written (as most plays were) not only for the *eye* (with the idea that it would be represented on stage) but also for the *ear?* That being the case, how does a modern editor capture the phonic rhythm prevalent in the seventeenth century, especially of texts that lacked punctuation signs in the autograph manuscripts, even if those signs are present in printed versions that may or may not have been revised by the author (Cañedo and Arellano 348–349)?

The modern editor of such texts is faced with modernizing orthography, accents, and punctuation in order to make the text accessible to the contemporary reader. But we know that even after completion of these operations the textual editor's task is not finished, for most editions (especially the widely distributed, annotated editions that circulate in the accessible series mentioned earlier) do not begin and end with an activity that is considered to be largely *ecdoctic*. The textual critic's operation, as we have said earlier, also entails a movement into the sphere of hermeneutics. Everything—from the notes to the introduction to contextual elements (dedications, prologues, iconographic sign, etc. [Spang 319–338]) to the select bibliography that is provided to the reader—is an attempt to communicate with the latter in a certain way about the text. The reader, of course, is not merely a passive consumer, for he or she too tries to make sense and produces meaning in line with his or her horizon of expectations. From this perspective both editor and reader become writers of literature.

Having come full circle, we might ask now what happens under this scenario to the notions of "authoritative text" and final intentions. We might even ask, with Foucault (1979), if "given the historical modifications that are taking place it does not seem necessary that the author function remain constant in form, complexity, and even in existence," and we might muse on his idea that "the author function will disappear, and in such a manner that fiction and its polysemous texts will once again function according to another mode, but still with a system of constraint—one which will no longer be the author, but which will have to be determined or, perhaps, experienced" (160).

Literary production is a social activity that operates within identifiable institutional settings. Today, perhaps more than at any other time in recent history, editorial activities function in a web of relationships that transcend traditional disciplines and national boundaries. Universities, publishing houses, journals, theoretical "schools," scholarly conferences, and symposia serve to stimulate and to validate a vigorous reexamination of the traditional canon. All of this is having some disquieting effects on certain segments of the profession. One thinks of the debate within academia and, more recently, in the national press about the sins of political correctness or apocalyptic discussions concerning the demise of the Eurocentric, male-dominated canon. Within the context and scope of these discussions traditional notions about editing are increasingly called into question, perhaps more than ever before.

It may be appropriate to end this introduction with a quote from the stimulating essay in this volume by Myriam Díaz-Diocaretz as she explains her approach to editing an anthology of Latin American women writers. Such an anthology is defined as "the meeting place not of single authors, but of *author-functions* and discursive phenomena, constituted as social formations, *out of which the very important construction of gender originates,* unfolding potential social influence." In a poststructuralist, postmodern world, where most traditional notions and loci of authority have come increasingly into question, authoritative texts and authors' final intentions were bound to suffer the same fate. Editing is no longer what it used to be, nor, one might add, is the writing of literary history.

Works Cited

Anonymous. *La vida y hechos de Estebanillo González, hombre de buen humor.* 2 vols. Ed. Nicholas Spadaccini and Anthony Zahareas. Madrid: Castalia, 1978. [Clásicos Castalia 86, 87.]

———. *La vida de Lazarillo de Tormes.* Ed. Francisco Rico. Madrid: Cátedra, 1987.

Barthes, Roland. "From Work to Text." In *Textual Strategies: Perspectives in Post-Structuralist Criticism.* Ed. Josué V. Harari. Ithaca: Cornell Univ. Press, 1979. 73–81.

Bowers, Fredson. *Textual and Literary Criticism.* Cambridge: Cambridge Univ. Press, 1959.

Cañedo, Jesús, and Ignacio Arellano. "Observaciones provisionales sobre la edición y anotación de textos del Siglo de Oro." *Edición y anotación de textos del Siglo de Oro.* Pamplona: Univ. de Navarra, 1986. 339–355.

Castro, Américo. *Lengua, enseñanza y literatura.* Madrid: V. Suárez, 1924.

Catalán, Diego. "El romancero medieval." *Comentario de textos, IV. La poesía medieval.* Madrid: Castalia, 1983.

Foucault, Michel. "What Is an Author?" In *Textual Strategies: Perspectives in Post-Structuralist Criticism.* Ed. Josué V. Harari. Ithaca: Cornell Univ. Press, 1979. 141–160.

Gómez Moriana, Antonio. "Narration and Argumentation in the Chronicles of the New World." In *1492–1992: Re/Discovering Colonial Writing.* Ed. René Jara and Nicholas Spadaccini. Minneapolis: Prisma Institute, 1989. 97–120. [Hispanic Issues, Vol. 4.]

Goytisolo, Juan. "Estebanillo González, hombre de buen humor." *El furgón de cola.* Paris: Editions Ruedo Ibérico, 1967. 59–76.

McGann, Jerome. *A Critique of Modern Textual Criticism.* Chicago: Univ. of Chicago Press, 1983.

———. *The Beauty of Inflections. Literary Investigations in Historical Theory and Method.* Oxford: Clarendon Press, 1985.

Pasquali, Giorgio. *Storia della tradizione e critica del testo.* Florence: Felice Le Monnier, 1952.

Reichenberger, Arnold G. "Editing Spanish *Comedias* of the XVIIth Century: History and Present-Day Practice." In *Editing Renaissance Dramatic Texts.* Ed. Anne Lancashire. New York: Garland, 1976. 69–96.

Spang, Kurt. "Hacia una terminología textológica coherente." In *Edición y anotación de textos del Siglo de Oro.* Ed. Jesús Cañedo and Ignacio Avellano. Pamplona: Univ. de Navarra, 1986. 319–338.

Tanselle, G. Thomas. "The Editorial Problem of Final Authorial Intentions." *Studies in Bibliography* 29 (1976): 167–211.

Thucydides. *The History of the Peloponnesian War.* Ed. and Trans. Sir Richard Livingstone. Oxford Univ. Press, 1973.

Zamora, Margarita. *Language, Authority, and Indigenous History in the "Comentarios reales de los indios."* Cambridge: Cambridge Univ. Press, 1988.

◆ Chapter 1
Poema de mio Cid

Colin Smith

The *Poema* is a very special case, and the task of editing it has a variety of diplomatic and, one might say, almost political undertones. "The more archaic the text the stronger the passions that it may arouse today": not a bad question, perhaps, to set in an examination for advanced students ("Discuss"). My motive in accepting the invitation of Oxford University Press to edit the poem in the late 1960s was very practical. Having taught the poem and related matters for some years on the basis of the then utterly established canons and critical text and reference works of Ramón Menéndez Pidal, I slowly became aware that something had to be done both to modernize the theoretical base and to improve the presentation of the text for student use. I spent two fascinating and intense years on the work, and when Oxford produced the edition in 1972 I waited with trepidation for reactions and reviews. Should I be dismissed from my post, banned from Spain, anathematized from academic pulpits?

In the outcome there was no need to have worried, but my fears had not been groundless either. On the one hand, Spaniards might resent this intrusion by a foreigner into a national preserve. The tradition that linked the *Poema* to so much that followed—in other epic verse, ballads, Golden Age plays, the whole chronicle tradition that evolved into national printed historiography in the sixteenth and seventeenth centuries, and geographically with Burgos, Valencia, and many other places—is I think much stronger than that which proceeds in other countries from the *Roland* or the *Nibelungenlied*, and English-speaking nations feel no sort of link at all with *Beowulf* and its congeners. Menéndez Pidal had after all headed a substantial section of the introduction to his popular edition "Valor nacional del poema": the text had played a part in the very formation of the national ethos. One must add to this the fact that the Cid is the national hero, at least of Castile, for so long the motor of Peninsular politics and of a unity that many in the seventeen *autonomías* of Spain may no longer accept but which was firm enough still in the early 1970s. The poem is also the first full literary text to survive in Castilian or any of the other Romance vernaculars of the Peninsula, and is thus a cornerstone of what became a major world literature (in practical terms, it is required reading for university students of Spanish literature in Spain, members—very numerous—of the *intelectualidad* of the future, so the way in which the work is presented in editions and lectures influenced by them is very significant). In prose form when incorporated into the Alphonsine chronicles it, with the other epic texts, was influential in the very formation of Castilian prose discourse: how to tell a story, how to handle the diverse tones of direct speech, how to balance this against narrative, what elements of poetic diction could be useful in prose, and so on.

On the other hand, Spanish critical thought about the *Poema*, the epic in general (including that of France), ballads, chronicles, and all related matters, was still in the 1960s and early 1970s dominated by the work and, indeed, until his death in 1968, the person, of Menéndez Pidal. His edition and concomitant studies had appeared in his great three-volume work of 1908–1911 (Vol. II having both "paleographic" and critical texts), and the poetic text with introduction and notes in more popular form that he published in the Clásicos Castellanos series in 1913 is still in print today, virtually unchanged. It was in this form that the *Poema* was read by students and many others, almost exclusively, over sixty years and beyond. Menéndez Pidal's authority—still being developed in the 1950s and 1960s in further important contributions, concerning French as well as Spanish—was reinforced by distinguished pupils, constituting a "school" in Spain, the United States, and elsewhere in the 1930s. After 1939, though far from being Franco supporters, they were among the few intellectuals active within the general poverty of university and intellectual life in Spain, a sort of "establishment" that had not willed itself into this position[1] but which enjoyed the respect of Hispanism world-wide and which could be sure that its doctrines were taken as unquestioned truths in the first chapter of manuals of literary history.[2] If ever it did seem that there was any such thing as a "definitive" edition, Menéndez Pidal's version of the *Poema* was it.

To challenge all this was therefore a bold and delicate task, as I explained briefly, with a sort of apology to any Spaniard who might feel offended, in the preface to my 1972 edition. I need not have worried, however. Despite the fact that most Francoist institutions remained firmly in place, Spain was strongly on the move toward change and modernization and, after her long semi-isolation, toward internationalization, too. All manner of cultural contacts were rapidly increasing. Spanish authorities were well aware of the immense growth of university populations in Europe and the Americas since 1945, and of the strength of Hispanism in non-Spanish-speaking countries. There was in Spain a genuine feeling that if any work of art, whether *Don Quijote* or a painting by Velázquez, was a human and universal possession, as was obviously true, the foreign scholar might have insights worth considering. An edition by a foreigner even of the national epic could be thought of as a stimulus and a renovation rather than as a piece of hostile iconoclasm. This openness was expressed in practical terms by a willingness, even an eagerness, to publish the work of foreigners either for the first time or in Spanish translations of books previously available in English or other languages; thus Cátedra published the Spanish version of my 1972 *Poema* in 1976, much reprinted, and then a completely revised second edition in 1985. The case of Ian Michael's edition of the *Poema* is closely parallel: it appeared in 1975 from Manchester University Press, accompanied on facing pages by the English translation of Rita Hamilton and Janet Perry, and was immediately produced in much expanded form (naturally without the English version) by Castalia in Spanish in 1976, with a revised edition in 1978. There are great advantages for authors in seeing their work transformed from the small print-run of a prestigious university press into the much cheaper and larger print-runs of Spanish paperback series; they will probably earn as much in royalties, their work circulates much more widely in student and other hands, and their ideas gain currency in Spanish. The same is true of monographs; my 1983 book for Cambridge University Press, *The Making of the "Poema de mio Cid,"* was welcomed in translation by Editorial Crítica of Barcelona in 1985 (*La creación* . . .), to the honor of an influential director who had made it plain that he strongly disagreed with the whole approach. The dependence of foreign Hispanists on the goodwill of Spanish publishers is great, a vital factor in much that we do; it is a pleasure to record a large personal debt to them and to acknowledge their friendly and positive help.

Some of my remarks might suggest that I claim a great deal of originality, a revolution, in my approach to the *Poema* and to the task of editing it. This is hardly so. A bibliography records works that have been used or are generally important, but discussion in an introduction and notes gives a better guide to the author's formation and tendencies. Even when the author argues against a view or tries to make another's factual information more precise, the negation has been a stimulus to thought and study. On the *Poema,* several surveys cover the ground and remove the need for discussion here.[3] More than is the case with most texts, however, it must be noted that the practical problem of how one handles manuscript readings—right down to obscure letters, corrections, possible erasures, smudges, concluding words that may or may not be part of the text proper—is conditioned by one's ideas about the whole nature of this kind of epic, which places the editor instantly in the realm of controversy. The danger of offending Spanish national susceptibilities has already been mentioned, with the conclusion that this was no longer a real factor.[4] More recently, in epic and related studies, a sort of transatlantic divide has opened up, since Menéndez Pidal's "(neo)traditionalism" is powerfully represented in American Hispanism, and has been reinforced since the 1960s by the "oralist" approach with its seemingly scientific methods of analysis. (Significant differences remain between the two, despite efforts to gloss these over; Menéndez Pidal in a study published in 1965–1966 made clear his reservations about the early application of oralist methods to Romance epic.) Many in Europe adopt an approach that is called by Americans, pejoratively, "(neo)individualism." Some have gone so far as to dub this the approach of a "British School," but while I hope it can reasonably be said that the British contribution to medieval Hispanic studies—in history as well as literature, and not forgetting the Arabist side—has been a worthy one in recent decades, this much overstates the matter, and such a school does not exist.[5] It is true that two articles by Peter Russell in 1952 and 1958 contained the essence of a view of the *Poema* radically different from that of Menéndez Pidal, and that papers by William J. Entwistle in the 1930s and 1940s already had seeds of this; but it is equally true that Menéndez Pidal's established doctrine about the date and geography of the poem was under overt attack by A. Ubieto Arteta in 1957, within Spain, and that already remarks of Martín de Riquer in the late 1950s and the 1960s and Dámaso Alonso (in general, a staunch "traditionalist") in the early 1970s again in Spain showed a substantial independence of view.[6] From all these I began to learn and to think that a new edition of the *Poema* was necessary and likely to be viable.

There was much to be learned too from nineteenth-century editors of the poem. Their work had been overlaid and almost relegated to obscurity by Menéndez Pidal's, not because this was willed by him—he made good use of it, naturally with every acknowledgment—but simply because he acquired so much authority and published his text in readily available form for so long. The poem had been brought to light and published by Tomás Antonio Sánchez in Madrid in 1779, in the first of a set of remarkable volumes entitled *Colección de poesías castellanas anteriores al siglo XV;* the magnitude of this achievement of the Enlightenment has perhaps still not been fully appreciated, but for a variety of good reasons it was not followed up by critical scholarship. From 1810 to 1829 the Venezuelan Andrés Bello worked at intervals on the *Poema* in the Sánchez edition and on French epic manuscripts held in the British Museum, London, and it seemed natural enough to him to associate the poem—of relatively late date, he thought—with the corpus of these French texts. His edition of the *Poema,* with notes and comments often still of great interest, was not published when he finished it or during his lifetime, chiefly because on leaving London he went to Chile and became a founding father of that Republic in many civic aspects; the work was eventually published in 1881. One may conjecture that the history of Cidian scholarship would have been very different if Bello had been able to go to Spain to meet colleagues and work on manuscripts there, or even if his edition had been published early. When for my edition I reread Bello and took a good deal from him, I little knew how warmly this would be greeted in Caracas, particularly by D. Pedro Grases and the Casa de Bello Institute, for there was a feeling that at last a proper justice was being done by a European specialist to an important part of Bello's early work.[7] Other editions preceding Menéndez Pidal's of which account was taken for textual readings and notes are those of Hinard (1858, with French translation), Vollmüller (1879), Lidforss (1895), and Huntington (1897–1903), while sections of the poem were edited by Milá y Fontanals (1874) and Restori (1890). Since these were respectively French, German, Swedish, American, Catalonian, and Italian, one could say that on the one hand the poem was becoming internationally known (as well as at home in Janer's Volume LVII of the Biblioteca de Autores Españoles, 1864), while on the other hand no trepidation about national susceptibilities was being felt among foreign editors, which was true; however, the notion that the author of the *Poema* might have learned something of his craft from French, a constant in the work of Hispanic Bello and natural enough to French Hinard, was a matter of bitter controversy in the Peninsula.[8]

This leads to another awkward aspect of the "nationalistic" kind. In Menéndez Pidal's view the Castilian epic was an almost wholly autochthonous product. Its metrics and language had developed over the centuries and its themes and attitudes were native ones stemming from, and in some cases closely dependent upon, events of Peninsular history, the whole flowing in an unbroken tradition (with a change of language, naturally) from early Germanic epic, that is, in Spain, that of the Visigoths. Only at a late stage, in the *Poema* held to have been composed in about 1140, did Menéndez Pidal think that a few very superficial elements of phraseology (specified in the Clásicos Castellanos introduction) had been adopted by the author-minstrel from French poems. When in a study published in 1961 Menéndez Pidal saw the surviving text "of 1140" as a reworking of an original composed about 1105—that is, within a few years of the death of the Cid of history in 1099—his unspoken intention was to bring the *Poema* to within the period of the prime version of the *Chanson de Roland,* usually considered to belong to the years of the First Crusade.

That is to say, in general, the two great western Romance cultures had to run side by side, and more or less independently. I have described this as a nobly nationalistic endeavor by the Spaniards, deserving study by a scholar competent to trace this important aspect of the cultural renaissance that the thinkers of the 1898 Generation tried to stimulate. One can well sympathize with the need of a backward Spain to assert itself beside its often all-too-dominant neighbor, not forgetting Napoleonic and some later memories either. (The fixation of some 1898 thinkers, including important non-Castilian ones, upon Castile similarly calls for further study.) But it seems to me as a noncontinental medievalist that the facts of cultural history on a broad scale impose the view that, particularly in the twelfth and thirteenth centuries, a France that was booming in intellectual matters and many of the arts and crafts was bound to influence Christian Spain profoundly, just as it did other countries. When we can trace royal and ecclesiastical connections, trade, the movement of persons, and the development of architectural styles, often in quite full detail, this becomes no mere assumption but a documented assertion. If Spaniards have never tried to deny the imitation of French styles of architecture and decoration at this time in northern Spain, I see no reason why they should have doubts about the influence of French models on their nascent literature. In the case of the *Poema* I have gone further, arguing that it was the first Castilian epic, the initiator of a new genre, the work of a man who in the early years of the thirteenth century wished to provide his homeland—Castile, specifically Burgos—with a national epic to rival the best French *chansons de geste.* I add, not as a sop to any nationalistic opinion but as a considered aesthetic judgment on a text that is a part of me as few others are, that he triumphantly succeeded. All this is argued in parts of my 1983 book, where earlier articles and, of course, vital contributions by others are drawn together into a coherent thesis (which includes such further elements as the use by the learned poet of certain Latin texts, archival materials, etc.). This has partially convinced a few and been condemned by more: for a hostile but well-reasoned view, with full bibliography, the reader should consult the recent book by Joseph J. Duggan. Naturally, the demonstration of how French texts influenced the *Poema* does not depend on asserting the view that the work was the first of its kind. At least the debate is no longer conducted along "decimonónico" nationalistic lines, however nobly inspired.

The foregoing is a somewhat lengthy consideration of generalities, but is by no means irrelevant to the editing of the *Poema*. In any introduction much will need to be said about Romance epic as a whole, the relationship of poetic plot to the events of history and of personages to their real-life prototypes. If we consider the text as having survived by a happy accident—that a scribe recorded a performance and that his manuscript was copied and a copy preserved—from a long series of variable and unrecorded orally generated versions, we shall take one view of its art. If we consider it as a new work of relatively late date by a cultured author, in writing, we shall take a very different view of its sources and its art and may well try to see aspects of its plot and moral messages as directly relevant to an audience at a particular time and in an identifiable (if conjectured) place. In either event, any editor may now be subject to deconstructive analysis for the bias that he or she will inevitably have given to all elements of his or her work. Even notes may be affected by one's critical stance, for example when a turn of phrase is equated with one found in French or in a Latin legal document of the Peninsula (traditionalists would regard such similarities as merely coincidental or insignificant). Within the broadly similar approaches that Americans designate as "neoindividualist" there are many differences of emphasis, so that whereas a particular strength of Ian Michael's edition is its interest in geographical matters, based on his earlier studies, mine might be said to have neglected this in favor of literary aspects and the history of the law. Professor Duggan's 1989 book shows that if he should proceed to edit the *Poema*—as all will surely hope—he would have much to say on economic and social aspects. The present new power of Arabist studies in and about the Peninsula may lead to renewed efforts to show that the poem was influenced by Arab modes.[9]

Finally, among these general remarks, one should say that if modernists face the peril that their still-living author may tell them they are simply wrong in their analysis (though faulty memory and self-justification by retrospective correction on the author's part can be factors too), the corresponding danger for the medievalist is that some document may come to light that will disprove his statement or theory. This is especially true of Spain, where minor archives and libraries may remain unexplored or be in an agreeably inviting chaos. A good recent illustration of this concerns Juan Ruiz studies.[10] After all, somewhere in Spain the missing first folio of the *Poema* manuscript may lie concealed (see Smith, "The Lost Literature"). Meanwhile, one crosses the fingers or invokes an appropriate saint (Saint Anthony of Padua?), or perhaps does both, and hopes for the best, informing one's students at the start of each course that "the pleasure of medieval studies is that because documents are few, and often forged, conjecture is endless." If I should find that lost first folio, I suppose I could always reconceal it, rather than face academic ruin if it should show me up as a fraud.

That the poem survives in a unique manuscript both simplifies and complicates the task of the editor. It simplifies, because one does not have to take account of other manuscripts with variant readings (as happens in French; for some French epics several or many manuscripts survive, the variants being so substantial in some cases that the term *remaniement*, complete reworking, has to be used). We do not get involved in the task of constructing hypothetical stemmata, as has to be undertaken for, for example, the *Libro de buen amor*, of which there are three manuscripts plus fragments. If our footnotes are not filled with variant manuscript readings, however, they contain at least some of the readings and corrections proposed by earlier editors, the purpose being partly to show respect for honored predecessors but more to provide the user with a series of choices so that he may decide for himself. The true complexity in our case stems from the fact that while the manuscript is not nearly so defective as some used to make out, it is less than perfect. This "perfection" is not a matter of regular metrical structures (itself a debated matter; see below) but of sense and grammar, acceptable forms of place-names, etc.: the copyist of the surviving manuscript in the later fourteenth century has made or inherited some obviously unsatisfactory readings. The editor attempts to restore these to acceptable forms, basing himself where possible on evidence within the text—an earlier or later

mention of a place-name, a good majority of grammatical usages—
but has to use informed guesswork at times. This guesswork may
depend on the editor's view of the logic of an itinerary or of how
a word was pronounced and then represented in writing at a date
(itself the subject of controversy) when he or she thinks the poem
was composed or when this version of it was first fixed on parchment. However, since by the fourteenth century some modernization of forms and spellings had inevitably crept in—for example,
las sus fijas in place of *las sues fijas, sus vassallos* in place of *sos
vassallos*—and since so little written Castilian of (say) early-thirteenth-century date is available to us for comparison, we are likely
to be making a rather messy kind of restoration even with the
most careful work. Not only date but place too comes into it, since
the speech of Medinaceli was probably not that of Burgos, and it
is proposed by Ubieto Arteta that the surviving Castilian version
was made from an original composed in Navarre or Aragon with
their very different dialects and reasons for interest in the Cid (81–
85). No recent editor has cared to follow Menéndez Pidal in the
kind of wholesale archaizing of the text in which he indulged,
confident in the view that the poem had been composed in or near
Medinaceli in about 1140 (and, of course, strengthened by his
immense command of Romance philology).

The metrical structures of the *Poema*, in association with those
of other epic texts and fragments and portions reconstructed from
chronicles, are not well understood and may never be. I think it
fair to say that critics are approaching agreement on the idea that
the epic line was built on a series of stresses natural enough to all
varieties of Spanish and probably emphasized further in performance by the voice of the presenter and by any musical accompaniment; but the stress system was still a fairly free one, and we
do not know enough about it to propose any textual corrections
based on any such analysis. (Even restoration of the syllable-based
Libro de Alexandre and *Libro de buen amor* is a highly controversial
matter, as recent editions show.) The contrast with French is thus
absolute: in French a poem might have a basis of lines that were
octosyllabic (rarely) or decasyllabic (4 + 6 or 6 + 4) or dodeca-
syllabic—alexandrines—but which was in all cases fairly regular
and which may invite correction of miscopyings with some con-
fidence. This remains true even if, as I have proposed, the author

of the *Poema* in creating a new system learned much from French metrical models (since he was at the same time adapting common formulae and other phraseology from French) and was seeking to adjust these to very different Spanish speech-rhythms. We may ourselves perceive stresses or rhythms and feel tempted to adjust a manuscript line accordingly, but we cannot be sure what the author intended or how a presenter of the poem in, let us say, Burgos in 1208 would have pronounced his lines, or whether some artificial stress was allowable beyond what ordinary speech imposed. In how many different ways has *To be or not to be* been delivered?

What is sure is that at some point, in a way all too visible in the surviving manuscript, line divisions were seriously disturbed: some lines were unduly shortened, others extended, that is in writing, in ways not intended by the author. Various reasons for this have been proposed; for example, that the text was dictated from memory to a scribe, an artificial process in which the performer's sense of rhythm and pause was upset in the absence of a musical accompaniment. This is an explanation favored by oralists and traditionalists. My proposal is that at some stage a scribe who was economizing on parchment wrote the text down in full lines of prose, as happened with other Peninsular poems (see *The Making* 107) and that a successor scribe who tried to reconstitute verse lines did not wholly succeed, either because by his time the public presentation of epic had lapsed, and with it the sense of rhythm, or because for the copyist's purpose—historical, genealogical, service to local pride?—the text was adequate as it stood.[11]

Editors try to restore reasonable line lengths, agreeing about obvious cases but not about others. An instance of the latter involves lines 1275–1277. The Cid is instructing Alvar Fáñez about his embassy to Alfonso VI; in the manuscript, with punctuation added and abbreviations expanded,

> Kiss his hand for me and urgently beg him
> that he, of his grace, may allow me to bring forth
> from there my wife and my daughters;

> Desi por mi besalde la mano efirme gelo Rogad

> Por mi mugier & mis fijas, si fuere su merçed,
> Quenlas dexe sacar;

Line 1275 presents no problem. Line 1276 is structurally acceptable but its eccentric rhyme (*é* in a laisse rhymed in *á*) is suspect, though this alone might not be a reason for correcting it; 1277 will not do at all. What most readers knew over so many years in Menéndez Pidal's edition was the neat and expressive version:

> Kiss his hand for me and urgently beg him
> that he, of his grace, may allow me to bring from there
> Doña Jimena, my wife and my natural daughters.

> desí por mí besalde la mano e firme gelo rogad
> por mi mugier *doña Ximena* e mis fijas *naturales,*
> si fore su merçed quenlas dexe sacar.

That is to say, a scribe omitted words as superfluous to the basic sense—which is true, but no way to proceed with a poetic text—and Menéndez Pidal put them back. When one glances at earlier editions other possibilities emerge: that the phrase *si fuere su merçed* was a gloss by a scribe who thought the Cid should show further deference to the monarch. Restori and Lidforss thought so, and in 1972 I followed them, leaving two lines in place of three. Earlier, Bello in a different way had made two lines only. Michael's solution, in accordance with his generally very conservative principles, is to retain all the words of the manuscript but to place *si fuere su merçed* as a first hemistich of line 1276b–1277, which leaves *por mi mugier e mis fijas* as a first hemistich of an incomplete line (indicated in his text by a series of points). The matter is obviously minimal, and the progress of the plot is unaffected whichever view we take; but there are scores of such instances, and the problem as a whole is far from minimal. We shall never know the answer, and in most cases recourse to the chronicle accounts provides no outside help. In some instances this kind of textual disturbance really does affect one's view of a personage or the progress of the plot, these cases having to be argued by editors at greater length; examples will be found in the episode of the Count of Barcelona.

There is worse to come. A copyist may have omitted a line, for one of a number of mechanical reasons that apply equally to us today. One may become aware of this by a gap in the sense of the text; for example, a few lines have dropped out after 441, as editors agree by suspension points and a footnote, while Menéndez Pidal supplies four lines of *restauración arbitraria* in italics. Similarly, a line might be repeated not immediately but after a few lines, the copyist perhaps realizing his error but failing to erase the superfluous material. Here, however, within a rhetoric that allowed or encouraged insistence and repetition, it can sometimes be argued that the repetition of a line had an artistic purpose and that no error was involved (e.g., 97/99, 1042/1045). Sometimes a line may have been misplaced, as Menéndez Pidal believed when removing 398 to a new place after 415, but others have not accepted this, while recognizing that in its original place the line is not free of problems that require lengthy annotation.

All this is complicated and only partially helped by the existence in the chronicles of prose versions of the *Poema*. The text that best represents the poem is the *Crónica de veinte reyes*, its Cid section now available in an excellent edition (Powell). Sometimes other chronicles have sections or details of interest, not, in my view, because they had access to variant versions of the *Poema* (as traditionalists, believing in a multiplicity of poems each separately available to chroniclers as they updated their materials, think), but because the chroniclers exploited a single prose version in differing ways (Smith, "The First Prose Redaction"). The extent to which the chronicle accounts can be used to restore missing or damaged parts of the poetic manuscript is much contested. In view of a continuation of the Cid's exclamatory line 14 present in the *Primera Crónica General,* Menéndez Pidal saw the need to create on its basis a new poetic line, 14b:

We shall come back to Castile laden with honor.

Mas a grand ondra tornaremos a Castiella.
(*Cantar de mio Cid* III, 1026)

He explained that this is a "verse that is necessary to complete the meaning" ("verso necesario para completar el sentido"). But there is really nothing to complete, and although the great editor's line is an excellent one, recent versions have rejected or disregarded this and similar additions, or have relegated them to notes or appendices. The same applies to the major lacuna—one folio, about fifty lines—that all recognize as existing after line 2337. Menéndez Pidal did not create verse here, but reasonably printed the prose text of the *Crónica de veinte reyes*. Two factors, however, now make this a much more uncertain process. First, it is now realized that the chroniclers were perfectly capable of making their own adjustments or interpolating passages of their own invention, without necessary dependence on some poetic manuscript superior to the one we have. Second, the major lacuna after 2337 may have developed at an early stage in purely poetic transmission, and the chronicle team may have filled it from memory of the story in outline or by deduction from what they knew about earlier and later parts of the plot. Other considerations apply to the lacuna caused by the loss of the first folio. Editors from Bello to Menéndez Pidal have reconstructed here from the *Crónica de Castilla* up to twelve lines of verse that fit end-on to the first line of the surviving manuscript (linking the object pronoun *los* of line 2 to a restored *palaçios* in the last of the new lines), and this seems to me to be reasonably assured. We still do not know what went before, however, and it is possible that the statement about the reason for the Cid's banishment and other preliminaries were in prose form anyway, a possibility heightened by the fact that the chronicles give no hint of verse rhythms or poetic diction here.

The lacunae were naturally not of the poet's making. He did suffer a few small confusions (another reason, incidentally, for regarding this text as tentative or as existing for us only in draft or preliminary form, as argued further below). Editors draw attention to these small errors without attempting to correct them. An example concerns the duplicated mention of two knights in very different roles in lines 1994, 1996, and then 1999.

So much for major adjustments. Corrections to line endings, if any, depend also on general arguments about the poem's metrics. Menéndez Pidal thought that the poet's system involved unity of rhyme within each laisse. Where this was not present in the manuscript, which is often, he assumed the fault was the result of mishearing or miscopying (e.g., when a common formula or epithet was involved) and corrected to produce regularity of rhyme. But it can be argued that the poet's system permitted an occasional unrhymed line or an ending that shared the stressed vowel of the laisse but not its accompanying unstressed vowel (e.g., in laisse XXVII, *nasco* preceded by *posadas-agua* and followed by *agua-carcava,* and also occasional couplets whose rhyme might not accord with that of the laisse [e.g., 124–125]). Such variations are especially visible at points where a laisse is ending and a new one starting. A further consideration, naturally unacceptable to those of contrary general views, is that if the *Poema* was a first work of its kind and the initiator of a new genre (in 1207?), its technical aspects might have had a tentative or experimental quality, including metrical practices that deviated from the norm in French *chansons* known to the poet and from what was to become the norm in Spanish. It is also possible that what we have is the poem in a draft form that was copied and circulated before the poet was able to give it a finishing touch. One concludes this aspect by repeating the remark about "conjecture is endless": indeed it is, but one adds, when addressing one's students, that "my conjectures are likely to be better than yours, simply because I've been around longer." After all, there are two centuries' worth of critical reading to be mastered first.

To what extent does all this matter? We may take respect for the poem, its hero, his values (but not any nationalistic overlay imposed in our own times), and much else, for granted. The editor's objective is to rerepresent the poem in a way that shows due respect for previous editors but also demonstrates that there is something new to say, not, perhaps, strictly in relation to the text, but at least in relation to new modes of analysis consistent with the editor's times and with what he or she has learned from contemporaries. Thus María Eugenia Lacarra's edition of 1982 adopts my edition of the text but has materials based on her important book of 1980, with its novel analysis in terms of early-thirteenth-century politics and rivalries. I have already stated the hope that Professor Duggan will base an edition of the poem on his 1989 study. Even the interpretation of the poem may depend on a view of textual detail. My essay on "Tone of Voice" was a subjective reading of passages in which all did indeed depend on the emphasis given to certain words and phrases, that is, on whether one regarded these as rich in irony or sarcasm or some other quality, or as plain unweighted communication. Here, as any deconstructionist would be the first to observe, the reader is going to be influenced in his or her interpretation not so much by the editor's comments in the notes, or by such essays as "Tone of Voice," but by the very punctuation of the poetic text. The original naturally has none. If the text is to be at all presentable, modern norms must be introduced. There will be some disagreement, but not much, about what constitutes a sentence and where points and capitals should be used. There will be more debate about what is properly narrative and what direct speech, and, within what is obviously direct speech, about the personage to whom it should be attributed (see, e.g., lines 1240–1242, 1818–1820, 2552). Sometimes it is unsure what is a question and especially what is an exclamation. My tendency, following remarks in my introduction designed to stimulate the imagination of modern readers and lessen the gap of the centuries, to view the poet as a sort of theatrical author composing for a society that had no stage, was to invest the poem with dramatic qualities by liberal use of exclamation marks, specially in contexts of appeal, scorn, indignation, irony. Key passages about the moneylenders, the Count of Barcelona, and the Infantes come to more vivid life in this way, but, admittedly, with results that—as in my "Tone of Voice" essay—may lead the reader along a particular path signposted by the editor in the direction of a personal interpretation; for example, that it is in parts not merely humorous but cruelly so, the medieval public being, like the Shakespearean and Cervantine one, less squeamish than the modern one.[12]

Here one cannot avoid mentioning a problem that has aroused not nationalistic feelings but worse, racist and religious ones. Although they are not so defined in the text, the moneylenders Rachel and Vidas are taken by nearly all critics to be Jews, as the *Crónica de Castilla* already did about 1300. On any reading, the Cid succeeds in cheating them, and in the subsequent text as we have it, he never repays them, compensates them, or even apologizes for what he did (Menéndez Pidal of course held that the poet "forgot" to include a scene of repayment, mentioning this among other "Olvidos del juglar," but most more recent students have not supported this). That there is humor in this episode—a minidrama in itself, perhaps with notes of farce—is agreed by most,[13] but the quality and force of this humor is much debated, together with the degree of anti-Semitism—if any—involved. One has to proceed partly by conjecture, regarding the author's intentions and the nature of the audience's predisposition and expectations in (say) Burgos in 1207, but also on a basis of what one can learn about Jews and moneylending and the law and the attitude of the Church in Castile and more widely in western Europe at the time, not forgetting the literary antecedents that this tale of deception had in a variety of cultures. The bibliography of this theme is now immense and the passions aroused by it all too strong.[14] If any modernist imagines that medieval studies represent a haven safe from unpleasant intrusions, an ivory tower barricaded against the "real world," he or she should spend a few hours viewing this battlefield—from a safe distance.

Whether one should see the manuscript before producing a valid new edition is unsure. Ian Michael did, as he explains in the introduction to his edition, in order to look closely at disputed readings of passages damaged by the application of a cocktail of reagents over the centuries. Anecdotal evidence of recent years suggests that such viewing is not easy. I confess that I should like to see and briefly touch the sacred object one day. For most scholarly purposes it is sufficient to use one of two good facsimile texts now available.[15]

Finally, much depends on the public intention of the editor and his publisher, on whether the edition is completely independent or is conditioned by the requirements of an existing series. Menéndez Pidal was able to produce an ideal solution: a scholarly edition embracing both "paleographic" and critical texts, together with two other volumes of relevant materials in the same set, followed by his popular version in Clásicos Castellanos. In recent times I think it fair to say that editions have been "semipopular," that is, in relatively cheap form and designed to be used on several levels from the scholarly to that of the general reader and college student. Modern production techniques and type fonts enable a quite amazing amount of diverse materials, carefully organized, to be included in one modestly priced book.[16]

"Modestly priced" yes, and I hope that our opinions and our proposals about the text are modestly, even humbly, expressed too. Our role is minor compared with that of the poet, whom I call Per Abbat, author of one of the best epics ever written. Burgos has justly given him his facsimile but not as yet that statue that (as I said at the end of *The Making*) he deserves.

Notes

1. One of the first to comment publicly on this was probably Juan José Carreras Ares in a lecture entitled "Función del tema y mito cidiano en la Generación del 98 y el franquismo," part of a "Ciclo cidiano" given in the University of Saragossa in February-March 1977. I do not know if this was published. See then María Eugenia Lacarra, "La utilización del Cid de Menéndez Pidal en la ideología militar franquista," and now Richard Fletcher, 202–205. The Cid as represented in Menéndez Pidal's *La España del Cid* and other works, an amalgam of the figures of history and literature, is under discussion in these studies.

2. The first dissenting section of such a manual was probably that by Alan Deyermond in Vol. I of the Benn series, *A Literary History of Spain*, published in 1971 and thus nearly coincidental with my edition. Deyermond's book was translated at once into Spanish (Barcelona, 1973) and in both forms has been very influential.

3. One might start with Charles B. Faulhaber, and Alan Deyermond, "Tendencies," in *"Mio Cid" Studies.* For a longer view see Michael Magnotta, which is valuable despite the author's formulaic (self-parodying?) reassertion of all Menéndez Pidal's opinions. Francisco López Estrada's *Panorama crítico sobre el "Poema del Cid"* is a generous survey by a Spaniard.

4. Occasional anecdotal evidence reached us in a contrary sense, however. In the late 1970s a candidate for a university post in Spain who had absorbed recent dangerous foreign notions and was beginning to allude to them in his *oposiciones* exercise was interrupted by a member of the tribunal: "Please, sir, express yourself in accordance with our national school" ("Por favor, señor, explíquese de acuerdo con nuestra escuela nacional").

5. Its existence was reluctantly accepted by Alan Deyermond in deference to American colleagues he was addressing at the 1985 MLA meeting (see published version, "British Contributions to the Study of Medieval Spanish Epic," with full bibliography).

6. On Riquer, see references in Colin Smith, *The Making* 157 and note 15. For Alonso, see his *Obras completas*, II (Madrid, 1972), 145–161, a survey of Menéndez Pidal's *La epopeya castellana a través de la literatura española* first published in 1947; a few apparently very slight remarks in the long footnote 29 to page 161 are quite fundamental. So far as I am aware, very little attention has been drawn to these points.

7. This resulted in an invitation to Caracas in 1981 and a paper, "Los trabajos de Bello sobre el *Poema de mio Cid,*" published in *Bello y Chile.* Bello's edition of the *Poema* is republished, with an extensive preliminary study by Pedro Grases, in Vol. VII of Bello's *Obras completas* (Caracas, in progress).

8. Sometimes the discussion was on patriotic rather than scholarly grounds (summarized by Magnotta, 90–106).

9. See Francisco Marcos Marín, *Poesía narrativa árabe y épica hispánica* and Alvaro Galmés de Fuentes, *Epica árabe y épica castellana.* The evidence is reviewed very skeptically by Jules Horrent, "Reflexiones sobre las relaciones árabo-hispano-francesas en la épica."

10. Henry Ansgar Kelly's original and well-argued book, *Canon Law and the Archpriest of Hita*, was almost at once, and of course unintentionally, put out of court at least with regard to dates by Francisco J. Hernández, "The Venerable Juan Ruiz, Archpriest of Hita."

11. Even this text, however, seems to have been used for at least one public reading by a professional for reward, since at the end we find the note "El romanz es leido, dat nos del vino." The implication of *es leido* is that "I the presenter have read this text out to you (from the manuscript I am holding before me)."

12. When I had said in the conclusion to "Tone of Voice" by way of frank apology that "in the difficult instances discussed above, I suggest or propose, without asserting; in the last analysis, all I can say is that 'This is the way in which I hear it,'" it was a trifle hard to find an experienced bibliographer commenting that "the notion of tone is unacceptably subjective" (18–19) (see *The Year's Work in Modern Languages* 298).

13. The exception is Miguel Garci-Gómez, *El Burgos de mio Cid: Temas socio-económicos y escolásticos, con revisión del antisemitismo*. For a balanced and partly sympathetic review of this aggressive book, see John Edwards's review in *Olifant*.

14. A good survey with much bibliography is that of Nicasio Salvador Miguel, "Reflexiones sobre el episodio de Rachel y Vidas en el *Cantar de mio Cid*." The discussion has continued since then with undiminished vigor. For Garci-Gómez, interpretations with which he disagrees have often been influenced by Spanish attitudes to, and treatment of, the Jews in the later Middle Ages, and if foreign critics are involved, the anti-Spanish "Leyenda negra" may come into it too.

15. A good two-volume set containing Menéndez Pidal's "paleographic" edition and the facsimile was published in Madrid in 1961. In 1982 the Excelentísimo Ayuntamiento de Burgos issued an extremely handsome two-volume set with a superb facsimile and accompanying studies.

16. The then recent editions of Miguel Garci-Gómez, María Eugenia Lacarra, Jules Horrent, José Manuel Ruiz Asensio (1982, in the Burgos set previously mentioned), José Jesús de Bustos Tovar (1983), Emilia Enríquez Carrasco (1984), and Francisco Marcos Marín (1985) are compared on a number of criteria by Smith, "On Editing." Among these the Horrent edition, the fruit of a lifetime's work on French and Spanish epic themes, merits special consideration, and has been so reviewed.

Works Cited

Alonso, Dámaso. *Obras completas*. Vol. II. Madrid: Gredos, 1972.

Anonymous. *Poème du Cid. Texte espagnol accompagné d'une traduction française....* Ed. D. Hinard. Paris: Imprimerie Impériale, 1858.

———. *Poema del Cid*. Ed. Karl Vollmüller. Halle, 1879.

———. *La gesta del Cid*. Ed. Antonio Restori. Milan: U. Hoepli, 1890.

———. *Los cantares de Myo Cid*. Ed. Volter Edvard Lidforss. 2 vols. Lund, 1895.

———. *Poem of the Cid*. Ed. Archer Milton Huntington. 3 vols. New York: G. P. Putnam's Sons, 1897–1903.

———. *Cantar de mio Cid*. Ed. Ramón Menéndez Pidal. 3 vols. Madrid: Imprenta de Bailly-Bailliere e Hijos, 1908–1911.

———. *Poema de mio Cid*. Ed. Ramón Menéndez Pidal. Madrid: Clásicos Castellanos, 1913.

————. *Poema de mio Cid.* Ed. Colin Smith. Oxford: Oxford Univ. Press, 1972. Spanish version, Madrid: Cátedra, 1976.

————. *Poema de mio Cid.* Ed. Ian Michael. Manchester: Manchester Univ. Press, 1975.

————. *Poema de mio Cid.* 2nd ed. Ed. Ian Michael. Madrid: Castalia, 1978.

————. *Poema de mio Cid.* Ed. María Eugenia Lacarra. Madrid: Taurus, 1982.

————. *Poema de mio Cid.* Ed. Andrés Bello. Intro. Pedro Grases. *Obras completas de Andrés Bello.* Caracas (in progress).

Carreras Ares, Juan José. "Función del tema y mito cidiano en la Generación del 98 y el franquismo." University of Saragossa, February-March 1977.

Deyermond, Alan. *A Literary History of Spain.* Vol. I. London and New York: Barnes and Noble, 1971. [Spanish trans. Barcelona: Ariel, 1973.]

————. "Tendencies in 'Mío Cid' Scholarship, 1943-1973." *"Mío Cid" Studies.* Ed. Alan Deyermond. London: Tamesis, 1977. 13-47.

————. "British Contributions to the Study of Medieval Spanish Epic." *La Corónica* 15 (1986-1987): 197-212.

Duggan, Joseph J. *The "Cantar de mio Cid": Poetic Creation in Its Economic and Social Contexts.* Cambridge: Cambridge Univ. Press, 1989.

Edwards, John. Book review of *El Burgos de "Mio Cid,"* by Miguel Garci-Gómez. *Olifant* 13 (1988): 57-64.

Entwistle, William J. "My Cid—Legist." *Bulletin of Spanish Studies* 6 (1929): 9-15.

————. "Remarks Concerning the Order of the Spanish Cantares de Gesta." *Romance Philology* 1 (1947-1948): 113-123.

Faulhaber, Charles B. "Neo-traditionalism, Formulism, Individualism, and Recent Studies on the Spanish Epic." *Romance Philology* 30 (1976-1977): 83-101.

Fletcher, Richard. *The Quest for El Cid.* London: Hutchinson, 1989.

Galmés de Fuentes, Alvaro. *Epica árabe y épica castellana.* Barcelona: Ariel, 1978.

Garci-Gómez, Miguel. *El Burgos de mio Cid: Temas socio-económicos y escolásticos, con revisión del antisemitismo.* Burgos: Diputación Provincial de Burgos, 1983.

Hernández, Francisco J. "The Venerable Juan Ruiz, Archpriest of Hita." *La Corónica* 13 (1984-1985): 10-22.

Horrent, J. "Reflexiones sobre las relaciones árabo-hispano-francesas en la épica." *Homenaje a Alvaro Galmés de Fuentes.* Vol. III. Oviedo: Univ. of Oviedo, 1987. 665-684.

Kelly, Henry Ansgar. *Canon Law and the Archpriest of Hita.* Binghamton, N.Y.: Medieval and Renaissance Texts and Studies, 1984.

Lacarra, María Eugenia. *El "Poema de mio Cid": Realidad histórica e ideología.* Madrid: J. Porrúa Turanzas, 1980.

————. "La utilización del Cid de Menéndez Pidal en la ideología militar franquista." *Ideologies and Literature* 3 (1980): 95-127.

López Estrada, Francisco. *Panorama crítico sobre el "Poema del Cid."* Madrid: Castalia, 1982.

Magnotta, Michael. *Historia y bibliografía de la crítica sobre el "Poema de mio Cid" (1750-1971).* Chapel Hill: Univ. of North Carolina, Dept. of Romance Languages, 1976.

Marcos Marín, Francisco. *Poesía narrativa árabe y épica hispánica.* Madrid: Gredos, 1971.

Menéndez Pidal, Ramón. *La España del Cid.* 2 vols. Madrid: Plutarco, 1929.

————. *La epopeya castellana a través de la literatura española.* 1947. 2nd ed. Madrid: Espasa-Calpe, 1959.

————. "Dos poetas en el *Cantar de mio Cid.*" *Romania* 82 (1961): 145–200. Rpt. in *En torno al* Poema del Cid. Barcelona: E.D.H.A.S.A., 1963. 109–162.

————. "Los cantares épicos yugoeslavos y los occidentales. . . ." *Boletín de la Real Academia de Buenas Letras de Barcelona* 31 (1965–1966): 195–225.

Milá y Fontanals, M. *De la poesía heroico-popular castellana.* Barcelona: Vedaguer, 1874.

Powell, Brian. *Epic and Chronicle: The "Poema de mio Cid" and the "Crónica de veinte reyes."* London: Modern Humanities Research Association, 1983.

Russell, Peter E. "San Pedro de Cardeña and the Heroic History of the Cid." *Medium Aevum* 27 (1958): 57–59. Spanish trans. in *Temas de* La Celestina *y otros estudios del* Cid *al* Quixote. Barcelona: Ariel, 1978. 73–112.

————. "Some Problems of Diplomatic in the *Cantar de mio Cid* and Their Implications." *Modern Language Review* 47 (1952): 340–349. Spanish trans. in *Temas de* La Celestina. . . . 15–33.

Salvador Miguel, Nicasio. "Reflexiones sobre el episodio de Rachel y Vidas en el *Cantar de mio Cid.*" *Revista de Filología Española* 59 (1979): 183–223.

Smith, Colin. *The Making of the "Poema de mio Cid."* Cambridge: Cambridge Univ. Press, 1983.

————. "Los trabajos de Bello sobre el *Poema de mio Cid.*" *Bello y Chile: Tercer Congreso del Bicentenario.* Vol. II. Caracas: Fundación la Casa de Bello, 1981. 61–73.

————. "The Lost Literature of Medieval Spain." *Guillaume d'Orange and the Chansons de geste: Essays Presented to Duncan McMillan.* Ed. Wolfgang van Emden and Philip E. Bennett. Reading, England: Société Rencesvals, 1984. 137–150.

————. "Tone of Voice in the *Poema de mio Cid.*" *Journal of Hispanic Philology* 9 (1984–1985): 3–19.

————. "On Editing the *Poema de mio Cid.*" *Iberoromania* 23 (1986): 3–19.

————. "The First Prose Redaction of the *Poema de mio Cid.*" *Modern Language Review* 82 (1987): 869–886.

Ubieto Arteta, A. "Observaciones al *Cantar de mio Cid.*" *Arbor* 37 (1957): 145–170.

————. *"El Cantar de mio Cid" y algunos problemas históricos.* Valencia: Anubar, 1973.

————. *"El Cantar de mio Cid* y algunos problemas históricos." *Ligarzas* 4 (1972): 5–192. Book published in Valencia, 1973.

The Year's Work in Modern Languages. 47 (1985): 298.

◆ Chapter 2

Critical Editions and Literary History
The Case of Don Juan Manuel

Reinaldo Ayerbe-Chaux

Before I examine the subject of this essay, I would like to point out some disturbing facts about textual scholarship. First, the proliferation of modern editions that reprint an already published text, with no variants or explanatory notes, has served to undermine the value of textual scholarship. The work of creative scholarly editions of early texts, even when done with seriousness and care, rarely receives the credit it deserves, as witnessed in negative tenure and promotion decisions when a candidate presents textual editions as evidence of his or her scholarship. Furthermore, critical editions receive very few reviews as the complex task of editing requires thorough dedication and not many reviewers have the preparation and the time necessary to assess the value of such editions. Moreover, critics and students alike either ignore the existence of critical editions or disregard them in favor of the noncritical and cheaper editions commonly available. Finally, despite the investment of dedication and time on the part of the scholar, a critical text, once published, becomes easy prey for veiled acts of piracy, and its illegitimate reprints can pass unnoticed. Charges of plagiarism do not seem to be applicable in text editing.

All these facts notwithstanding, textual scholarship continues to occupy an important place in literary studies. Editing ancient texts is one of the most demanding and serious tasks a scholar can undertake. The chapter written by G. Thomas Tanselle in *Introduction to Scholarship in Modern Languages and Literatures* duly places textual scholarship on the same level as linguistics, literary theory, or other forms of serious criticism.

For some theorists of textual editing the ideal edition would be the facsimile reproduction of the ancient manuscript followed by its paleographic transcription. Facsimile reproduction of manuscripts, however, is costly, and most editors can publish only the paleographic transcription of the text. The Hispanic Seminary of Medieval Studies at the University of Wisconsin-Madison has excelled in paleographic microfiche editions of an enormous corpus of Hispanic medieval texts. I myself have contributed to those editions.

Whereas the only objective of the paleographic edition is to preserve the text, the essential aim of the critical edition is to construct the text. The main reason for a construction of the text is that paleographic editions are difficult to read, and therefore critical editing seeks to present a more readable text. The critical editor puts his or her critical acumen to the service of historical reconstruction of the text. The main problem emerges when one tries to determine the extent of such critical reconstruction, which depends on the role that literary history is allowed to have in text editing. Using as a point of reference my critical editions of Juan Manuel's *Libro del Conde Lucanor* and of his *Cinco Tratados* I would like here to examine text editing and literary history from two specific angles: (1) The history of the manuscripts of a given work and the relationship of such history to the edited text. This aspect will be examined in the *Libro del Conde Lucanor;* and (2) The editing of an only extant manuscript, as in *Cinco Tratados,* and the writing of the literary history of the text.

I

Alberto Blecua in his study *La transmisión textual de "El Conde Lucanor"* has written a literary history of the text. José Manuel Blecua (Alberto's father) then edited the text of *El Lucanor* (see

Juan Manuel, *Obras completas*). José Manuel Blecua based his edition on manuscript S, transcribing it thoroughly and carefully and only making a few and necessary corrections. At the end of each *exemplo* he published all the variants of the other manuscripts. The criteria followed are the same as those used by Hermann Knust, the first critical editor of the text, in 1900. It is imperative to point out though that Blecua's 1983 edition greatly surpasses Knust's in care and accuracy. J. M. Blecua accepts Alberto's conclusion that manuscript S is the *codex optimus et antiquior*. Alberto wrote: "In the case of *El Conde Lucanor* the best criterion is to edit -S- which is both the *codex optimus* and the *codex antiquior*, provided that mistakes are amended by using the other manuscripts, and anaphoric variants are taken into consideration" ("Editar en el caso de *El Conde Lucanor* el *codex optimus* que es, a su vez, *el codex antiquior* -S- es el mejor criterio, siempre que se subsanen sus errores con las lecciones de otros testimonios y se tengan en cuenta las variantes adiáforas" [115]). To consider S the *codex antiquior* is questionable to say the least (see Funes, and Ayerbe-Chaux, "Manuscritos"). Nevertheless, for the purpose of the present essay it is important to realize that this editorial attitude establishes, to a certain point, a separation between the text and the history of the text. The history of the text written by Alberto Blecua does not dare affect the six texts of *El Lucanor*, which remain static and engraved forever in stone. One of them, S, becomes the idol or icon that we all must revere.

My critical edition of *El Lucanor* represents a totally different attitude toward the text and its history. While the introduction carries an abbreviated history of the text, because of the limits imposed by the publishers, the brevity is only apparent because the guidelines established by the introductory history of the text extend beyond the introduction. As a result, the critical text becomes text and history at the same time, thus eliminating the dichotomy between text and its history that characterized the other editorial policy. The manuscripts are samples of the transmission process of the text and the critical text becomes also a living part of such a process.[1] The kind of editing that I am describing uses literary history whenever the editor traces a word in other texts in order to determine its phonetic or morphological changes and choose the preferable reading among several variants. Literary history comes into play each time the meaning of a word is studied in other works of different periods and genres. Similarly, all notes establishing sources or relationships of the edited text with other literary texts constitute literary history.[2]

This open attitude toward the text stimulates the proposal of corrections and frequently allows the critic to look into some of the interesting enigmas that a text may present about the process of its composition without fear of desecrating the icon. While my critical edition was still in press in Alhambra, I raised some historical questions about the text and the way Juan Manuel wrote it in my essay "Don Juan Manuel y la conciencia de su propia autoría." Granted that the matter of the authenticity of the 1335 prologue, which I then defended, is still debatable,[3] a fundamental question remains. I asked in the article whether the shorter *Lucanor* found in the Puñonrostro codex might not be an earlier version by Juan Manuel himself. The prologue of 1335 refers to a version that he later corrected. It does not specify the extent of such corrections or elaborations. Couldn't the Puñonrostro text reflect that earlier work and not simply be explained as a variant made different by the copiers? We may never know the answer, but by asking the question we make of the text a more flexible, less fixed entity. It is the breakdown of the concept of textual rigidity that interested me then and still entreats me today.

Both Alberto Blecua and I arrived by separate ways to the conclusion that the manuscript of Puñonrostro represents a unique line of the text. Perhaps I was more categorical than Blecua in this respect. Now, while thinking about critical editions and literary history, we can ask ourselves again: does the Puñonrostro manuscript belong to a textual line derived from a first and initial writing of the text that later was expanded by the author himself? Does manuscript S belong to the revised line, or second writing of the text? This question, which was not really solved in the critical edition, is worth examining for it touches on the basic literary history of the text. Since Ramón Menéndez Pidal's time, the politics of editing has been so strongly set in favor of a consecrated and untouchable manuscript S that the question has been kept in limbo. An affirmative answer may not be as preposterous after all.

I would like to examine two major variants in manuscript P (Puñonrostro). The question that is under examination was implied in the manner in which I edited the first and most important variant in the Alhambra edition. The two texts were edited side by side, giving them equal value. The variant occurs in the second *exemplo* that contains the well-known story of the farmer and his son who go to the market leading a donkey. Because of the comments of people they meet, the son rides the donkey. A remark they hear afterward makes them change their minds, and the father rides the donkey. A new disapproving comment prompts them both to ride the poor beast. A final condemning word from those concerned for the wretched ass that has to carry two people brings father and son back to what they were doing in the first place.[4] The five manuscripts (six, if one counts the edition of Argote de Molina) contain normal variants in the beginning of the tale, up to the point where the farmer and his son encounter the first critics. From then on the manuscript of Puñonrostro offers a much more concise text, in some instances almost cutting the narrative to its bare bone. I must point out that the Puñonrostro text as a whole is more sober than the others, lacks unnecessary narrative details, and avoids the superfluous use of "very," "much," and "great" (*muy, mucho,* and *grand*).

Let me quote a small portion of the Alhambra critical edition on the right, juxtaposed with the Puñonrostro text on the left (84.50–84.62):

Puñonrostro edition	Alhambra critical edition
And they encountered some men who were coming from the village that they were going to.	
And, while talking	And after they spoke and departed from one another, those men they met began to talk among themselves
they said that the good man and his son did not seem too bright,	and said that the good man and his son did not seem too bright,
since the donkey went unladen and they went on foot.	because they took the donkey unladen while they both went on foot.
And on seeing this, the good man said:	And the good man, after he heard this, asked his son

-Son: what do you think of what those men say?	what he thought of what they were saying.

Et encontraron unos omnes que venían daquella villa do ellos yvan

E en departiendo	Et de que fablaron en uno et se partieron los unos de los otros, aquellos omnes que encontraron començaron a departir ellos entre sí
dixieron que aquel omne bueno et su fijo non paresçían omnes de buen recabdo,	et dizían que non les paresçían de buen recabdo aquel omne bueno et su fijo,
yendo el asno vazío et ellos yr de pie.	pues levavan la vestia descargada et yr entreamos de pie.
Et esto visto, dixo el omne bueno	Et el omne bueno, después que aquello oyó, preguntó a su fijo
-Fijo, ¿qué te paresçe de aquel dicho de aquellos omnes?	que quel paresçía daquello que dizían.

The two texts join again in the direct discourse of the father when for the second time he stresses to his son what has happened (89.130).

There are clearly two versions of the text. The main and most obvious difference is that in the Puñonrostro text father and son are criticized face to face, while talking with those they meet on the way. The critics in the other version gossip, criticizing the pair after they leave. The father overhears them, and wants his son to react to the collective judgment.[5] In this case we do not have just simple variants that may be attributed to medieval text copying or explained by incompetence of the scribe, or by the latter's religious and doctrinal biases and prejudices. Since the more expanded version is commonly considered to be authentic, it is difficult to conceive that the more laconic version of the Puñonrostro manuscript is the result of successive contaminations of the text in the copying process. Scribes were known to gloss and to expand; they seldom abbreviated the text. The aesthetic or literary preferences or elaborations of scribes never go in such direction, especially in the *Lucanor* text. There are no abbreviations of the text to such an extent.

As one convinced of the literary acumen of Juan Manuel it is easy for me to speculate that in the first place, back-stabbing is more difficult to take than a direct suggestion, thus prompting the self-confident son to say that the comments are right.[6] In the second place, if the father was going to reprove his son by summarizing twice what had happened to them on the road, then it was necessary for the basic narrative to be expanded. These are two good reasons for Juan Manuel to change the text, and it does not seem adventurous to state that his literary awareness made him rework the narrative here. The Puñonrostro manuscript thus could belong to a textual line that would represent a first writing of the book.

A second major variant occurs in *exemplo* XXIX, with the fox that plays dead in the street of a town. The passersby scalp its fur, plug one of its nails, and pull out one of its teeth. The fox does not move. Only when someone wants to cut its heart out does the fox run for its life.

Again I quote:

Puñonrostro edition	Alhambra critical edition
and they took so much hair that they sheared him totally	And so many men said this that they sheared him totally.
and in spite of all this he never moved.	And in spite of all this, the fox never moved because he understood that it did him no harm to lose his hair.
And another man came and said that the fox's nail was good to cure whitlows, and he pulled it out.	Afterward, another man came and said that the thumbnail of the fox was good to cure whitlows, and he pulled it out. And the fox did not move.
And another man came and said that a fox's tooth was good as a toothpick, and pulled it out with a stone.	And afterward, another man came who said that a fox's tooth was good for toothache; and pulled it out. And the fox did not move.
And a shoemaker came and said that the fox's tail was good as a shoehorn, and he	

cut it. And another man came and said that the fox's eye was a good medicine, and he pulled it out. And in spite of all this he never moved.

And a physician went by and said that the fox's heart	And afterward, after some time, another man came and said that the heart

was good for heartache, and he took hold of a knife to cut the heart out.

et tanto le tomaron fasta quel trasquilaron todo	Et tantos dixieron esto fasta que lo trasquilaron todo
et nunca por todo esto se movió.	Et por todo esto nunca se movió el rraposo, porque entendía que aquellos cabellos non le fazían daño en los perder.
Et vino otro et dixo que la uña del rraposo era buena para sanar panarizos et sacógela.	Después vino otro et dixo que la uña del polgar del rraposo que era buena para guaresçer de los panarizos et sacógela. Et el rraposo non se movió.
Et vino otro et dixo quel diente del rraposo era bueno para mondar los dientes, et sacógelo con una piedra.	Et después vino otro que dixo que el diente del rraposo era bueno para el dolor de los dientes: et sacógelo. Et el rraposo non se movió.
Et vino un çapatero et dixo que rrabo de rraposo era bueno para calçar, et cortógelo. Et vino otro e dixo que el ojo del rraposo era bueno para melezina e sacógelo e nunca por todo esto se movió.	
Et desque pasó por y un físico dixo quel coraçón del rraposo	Et después, a cabo de otra pieça, vino otro que dixo que el coraçón

era bueno paral dolor del coraçón et metió mano a un cochiello para sacarle el coraçón. (297.34–298.46)

As both María Goyri and Germán Orduna have pointed out, the added lines of a cut tail and a plucked eye, which are also found in a similar and more extended variant of manuscript M, may derive from the *Libro de buen amor,* stanzas 1415–1416 (184, note 9). Scribes perhaps at one point added these extra details, either influenced by the powerful and popular verses of Juan Ruiz, the Arcipreste de Hita, or because everyone knew the story of the fox in such a picturesque way. The matter would end there if the text were simply expanded, as it happens in manuscript M. It would be an interesting case of text contamination due to the popularity of another text or to the oral tradition that influenced the scribe to make a substantial change. Nevertheless, in the Puñonrostro manuscript the same passage contains not just a considerable expansion but a simplification or reduction of the text as well, and therefore it becomes more difficult to explain *all* the variants as progressive textual contaminations. I have emphasized "all" because some of the differences may be contaminations, such as "to cure whitlows" ("sanar panarizos") and "a physician went by" ("pasó por y un físico").

If we can consider the theory proposed here, that Juan Manuel may have possibly corrected and revised a first version of his book, we have new evidence of his keen literary awareness. Ian Michael has said that the differences of the *exemplo* in the Arcipreste de Hita and in Juan Manuel are due to the distinct lesson that each writer wants to convey: "These distinct moral points extracted from the tale by the two authors serve to indicate that the popular tale, although it often has an implicit moral lesson, need not possess a lesson at all and, indeed, may frequently be capable of imparting quite different lessons" (181).[7]

With this in mind we can reexamine the two texts. First, all the additions in the possibly "revised" version stress Patronio's lesson: one should be patient in trivial things that can be tolerated without great harm or ignominy, but "in defence of one's rights or honour or estate it is better to be defeated or die than to live and tolerate these affronts dishonourably" (England 197). The first addition says that the fox did not move "because he understood that it did him no harm to lose his hair" ("porque entendía que aquellos cabellos non le fazían daño en los perder") and then the "revised" text adds twice that "and the fox did not move" ("et el rraposo non se movió"), thus stressing tolerance of harmless injuries.

If the additions highlight the lesson, so do the omissions. Having a tooth smashed with a stone and not just extracted, a sort of pain that human beings sooner or later in life must suffer, and having the bushy tail cut and one eye plucked are no minor injuries indeed. To endure them without moving would be totally contrary to the main lesson Patronio intends to convey. All in all we have strong indications that Juan Manuel may have revised the story, submitting it to major changes.

A third variant is closely related to the one just examined because it occurs in an *exemplo* also used by the Arcipreste de Hita in the *Libro de buen amor:* the thief who makes a pact with the Devil (stanzas 1453–1476). The Arcipreste creates a very funny final scene and develops a witty dialogue between the Devil and the thief in stanzas 1464–1476. This is poorly reflected in the Puñonrostro variants to say the least. Here most surely we have a case of text contamination due to the enormous popularity of the Arcipreste's *exemplo.* The two versions read:

Puñonrostro edition	Alhambra critical edition
and thinking he would find the money, he found inside a folded rope;	and thinking he would find the five hundred *maravedís,* he did not find the money but a rope in the purse.
and on seeing this, he ordered him to be hanged.	And as soon as he saw this, he ordered him to be hanged.
Don Martin arrived and told him that he helped his friends in such need; and told him that he would support him on his back as long as he could; and that he should rest his feet on top of him and he would support him until all the others had left, if he could, otherwise he would leave him. And after the devil supported him a little, he told the man: Friend, how heavy you are! I can't support you any longer. And thus he died and lost his body.	And as they were putting him on the gallows, don Martin came, and the man told him to help him. And don Martin told him that he always helped all his friends until he brought them to this point. (412.122)

et cuydando fallar los dineros, falló una soga dentro rebuelta;

et desquesto vio mandólo enforcar.

Llegó don Martín et díxole que a tales priessas acorría él a sus amigos; et díxole que le sosternía a cuestas en cuanto él pudiesse et que pusiesse los pies ençima dél, et quel sosternía fasta que se fuessen todos los otros, si pudiesse, et synon quel dexaría. Et desque el diablo le sostuvo un poco, díxil al omne: Amigo, ¡commo pesas! Non te puedo sostener más. Et assí murió et perdió el cuerpo.

et cuydando fallar los quinientos maravedís, non falló los dineros, mas falló una soga en la limosnera.

Et luego que esto vio mandól enforcar.

Et poniéndolo en la forca, vino don Martín et el omne le dixo quel acorriesse. Et don Martín le dixo que sienpre él acorría a todos sus amigos fasta que los llegava a tal lugar. (412.122–413.128)

This portion of the Puñonrostro manuscript, much more clearly than the other two that have been quoted, shows the signs of possible successive contaminations of the text. The omission of "quinientos maravedís, non falló" and the change "soga dentro rebuelta" have all the characteristics of scribal errors. Besides, the expanded portion lacks the clarity and precision of Juan Manuel's style, as when the Devil says to the thief that "he would support him until all the others had left, if he could, otherwise he would leave him" ("et quel sosternía fasta que se fuessen todos los otros, si pudiesse, et synon quel dexaría"). It just does not make sense either in Spanish or in English.

Of course, in regard to the variants of the *exemplos* of the farmer, his son, and the donkey, and of the fox that plays dead, one can always say that the incompetent medieval scribes made all these major changes in successive versions. After all, they did not read the text as intelligently as we do now in our academic circles. Nevertheless, what matters most is that the Alhambra critical edition of the text raises these questions and presents these enigmas and, regardless of the answer we may give, the matter constitutes a crucial and fascinating aspect of literary history that does not surface when we have only one of the manuscripts to revere.

There are other major variants in the rest of the manuscripts, especially in H (Spanish Academy of History) and M (National Library, Madrid), but these variants have all the characteristics of successive contaminations of the text in the scribal transmission process. Manuscript H sometimes seems to draw from the "primitive" line and the "revised" line as well.

I cannot close this section without noting that the scribe of the Puñonrostro text at the end of *exemplo* XLVIII adds a different and lengthy interpretation of the lesson of the *exemplo*, but warns that it is his own addition by saying: "And this exemplum is also told in another way" ("En otra manera se dize este exemplo" [439.180]). Because this is obviously spurious, Blecua does not print it in the variants of the manuscripts. Nevertheless, in the first place, this attests to the thoroughness of the scribe, and in the second place it constitutes a precious piece of literary history since it indicates another form of interpreting the story of the *exemplo*, based on another version (*relato paralelo*) found in the medieval collections of exempla.

II

With the exception of *El Conde Lucanor*, Juan Manuel's other works have come to us in a single manuscript which most probably dates from the second half of the fifteenth century (Ayerbe-Chaux, "Manuscritos" 89). In 1986 I finished the paleographic transcription of all the works of Juan Manuel that we have today (see *Textos y concordancias*). Most recently (summer of 1989), I published a critical edition of five of his treatises (*Cinco Tratados*), which José Manuel Blecua had also published in the first volume of his *Obras completas* (1982). The two editions differ, among other things, in the distribution of paragraphs and in punctuation, important characteristics that determine the ease with which the text is read. The two editors also make different corrections. My edition, which was based on the paleographic transcription of 1986, gives Blecua credit each time his correction of the text or his reading has been adopted in my critical text (not a very common practice in Spanish text editing).

The two editions represent again two different concepts of the role of critical editors in regard to literary history. No doubt that scholars who edit ancient texts can be content with just the sphinx-like presentation of the text, leaving to the reader the pleasure or the agony of answering questions and solving enigmas. According to some theoreticians, simply establishing the basic text is the task of critical editors. On the other hand, should not we be especially thankful to the editor who also helps the reader in the intellectual journey with notes and references? In *Cinco Tratados*, for example, the text of *El libro del cavallero et del escudero* is accompanied by numerous quotations and references to Alfonso X el Sabio's works, especially to his *Siete Partidas*. Other Spanish medieval works are also amply quoted such as *Los Lucidarios* and the *Castigos e documentos del rey don Sancho*. In addition, the writings of Ramon Llull, and San Isidoro's monumental work, his *Etimologías*, contribute greatly to establish the intellectual framework of the text.

There are cases in which the text has been contaminated beyond repair in the scribal transmission. Intellectual history can then be most illuminating. I want to give an example from the *Libro de los estados* (chapter XXVII, 48.24), where Juan Manuel talks about the creation of man. The text is irreparably incomplete. The idea of the passage is that because God created man in his image and likeness (Genesis 1:26), the human soul participates in God's spirituality, and God, in his turn, participates in the corporeality of man in the incarnation. The first part of the statement was a well-known element of Aquinas's doctrine (*Summa Theologica*, I, Q. 3, Art. 1 ad 2um). But St. Thomas had never based any of the reasons for the incarnation of the Son of God on the very familiar verse of Genesis: "Let us make man in our image and likeness" ("Fasciamus hominem ad imaginem et similitudinem nostram"), because the theological basis of the incarnation could only be the redemption of man, not his creation. It is quite understandable that the heterodox concept of Juan Manuel, the layman, would be crossed out and amended by subsequent scribes of his work, who thus left us with a defective text.

We must come to terms with the ancillary role of literary history in text editing. It is important that the editor give the general historical background of the work in question in a thorough and scholarly introduction. It is also most desirable that the reader find useful references that elucidate the meaning of the work. The editor is usually the only one, or one of the few scholars, who has battled with the text, transcribing it word by word, sentence by sentence. He or she has looked for the best ways of expressing its meaning while dividing sentences and placing periods and commas. Why, one might ask, not take the process of editing a step further and investigate the relationship of the text with other contemporary texts and determine its place in the intellectual history of the times? Since there is no better qualified person than the conscientious editor for this task, we would all be grateful indeed if this knowledge were made available in the critical edition.

As I am about to close this contribution to *The Politics of Editing*, I realize how impossible it is to have a final word in this matter. No one can determine the precise boundaries of textual reconstruction in critical editions. Blecua, for example, uses modern punctuation but omits orthographic accents. How far are we going to allow literary history to intervene in textual scholarship? I for one advocate a greater role because a more flexible attitude may be quite beneficial. One important mission of scholars is to transmit knowledge, and by making the ancient texts more readable and understandable we are increasing their exposure. Not only the general public but other scholars as well may benefit. Texts that would seem to be engraved in stone are brought to life by historical annotations which, presented by the critical editor, are just one of many readings of the text. Yet, with his or her reading, the editor opens the text to discussion and further research—no minor benefit indeed.

Notes

1. I pointed out the polarization of the two editorial policies in the reprint of the Alhambra critical text by Taurus: "There are two positions in textual scholarship nowadays. One is very conservative, the other more audacious and adventurous. The former, on facing the complexity of the variants in the manuscripts and in the Argote edition, has decided to continue editing the text found in manuscript S, subjecting it to minimal corrections, absolutely indispensable. It would seem that María Goyri de Menéndez Pidal's harsh reprimand to Eugenio Krapf, 'the bookseller,' because he edited the Puñonrostro manuscript in Vigo in 1902, continues to intimidate editors. The other position, the one I have adopted, subjects the text to corrections and emendations, taking into consideration the study of variants and proceeding step by step with philological principles. I do respect José Manuel Blecua's careful work in his recent edition of the *Complete Works* of Juan Manuel. Nevertheless, I have preferred to offer a text that has been labored, can still be corrected, and is opened to philological research and discussion" ("La crítica

textual está hoy más o menos dividida en dos actitudes: la una muy conservadora, la otra más audaz y aventurera. La primera, ante la complejidad de las variantes de los manuscritos y la edición de Argote, se decide a seguir editando el texto del manuscrito S, sometiéndolo a mínimas correcciones, absolutamente indispensables. Parecería que la dura reprimenda de María Goyri de Menéndez Pidal a Eugenio Krapf, 'el librero', por haber editado el manuscrito de Puñonrostro en Vigo en 1902 (RABM, VII [1902], 320–321), siguiera intimidando a los editores. La otra actitud, la que yo adopté, basándose en los estudios de las variantes y llevando de la mano a la madre filología, somete el texto a correcciones y enmiendas. Respeto el trabajo cuidadoso de José Manuel Blecua en su reciente edición de las *Obras completas* de don Juan Manuel. Sin embargo, he preferido brindar un texto trabajado, susceptible de correcciones y abierto a la investigación y a la discusión filológica" [Don Juan Manuel, *Libro del Conde Lucanor,* ed. Ayerbe-Chaux, 39]).

2. Barbara Kiefer Lewalski, in "Historical Scholarship," has written: "Most students of literature spend a good deal of time practicing historical scholarship. Whenever a scholar checks the Old English Dictionary for the meanings a particular word may have carried in an earlier era, or seeks out a possible source for a literary work, or pursues an allusion within the text to some contemporary event or earlier work of literature, or considers the impact of contemporary politics or philosophy upon a particular novel or poem, that scholar is using historical resources to understand literature better" (53).

3. Francisco Rico has raised the most serious objection to the authenticity of the short prologue in "Crítica del texto y modelo de cultura en el Prólogo General de don Juan Manuel." I am indebted to him for sending me a *separata* of his important study.

4. Juan Manuel masterfully develops this simple narrative to stress the lesson the farmer wants to give his son and vicariously the writer to the reader. This was highlighted in Ayerbe-Chaux, *Materia tradicional* 35–39. Not only Ayerbe-Chaux, but also Ian Michael in "The Function of the Popular Tale" stressed the link between the didactic lesson of a fable or exemplum and the turn a narrative takes in Juan Manuel or the Arcipreste de Hita. Therefore it is quite surprising to hear Aníbal Biglieri's cry of eureka claiming discovery of this aspect of Juan Manuel's criticism in his recent book, *Hacia una poética del relato didáctico: ocho estudios sobre El Conde Lucanor.* According to Biglieri, the critics who have preceded him are "naive realists" ("realistas ingenuos") who overlooked the didactic intentions of the medieval writer.

5. John England has captured this overhearing in his recent English translation of *El Conde Lucanor:* "They spoke for a while and then went on their way, and the men they had met began to talk among themselves and say that they considered the man and his son foolish to go on foot when the donkey was unladen. When the good man overheard this, he asked his son what he thought about what they were saying" (47).

6. See Ayerbe-Chaux, *Materia tradicional:* "I must point out another detail: those who comment and criticize are not people who simply go by (as in the other versions) but persons they know, with whom they stopped to talk, and once separated, criticize them behind their backs. One cannot deny how well conceived this detail is: as the son criticizes his father, friends and acquaintances now criticize the son's conduct. Ironically the young fellow, who always contradicts his father, is the

one who now follows blindly the suggestions of common people" ("Debo señalar un detalle más y es el hecho de que aquellos que comentan y critican no son gente que simplemente pasa [como en las demás versiones], sino personas conocidas con quienes se paran a conversar y al separarse critican por la espalda. No se puede negar lo acertado del detalle: como el hijo critica al padre, así los amigos y conocidos son los que ahora critican su conducta. Irónicamente, el joven que siempre contradice a su progenitor es quien ahora sigue ciegamente las sugerencias del vulgo" [39]).

7. Based on Michael's unquestionable point, I emphasized Juan Manuel's consciousness of the lesson Patronio wants to give to Count Lucanor: "Thus, it is not a matter of omitting unlikely details, as Lecoy writes, but of insisting at every turn of the narrative on the lesson to be drawn. The importance of the lesson that the author has in mind conditions thus the development of the narrative. This seems extremely important to me to vindicate the creative freedom of medieval writers who may take the anecdote from an oral or written source but in reality transform it at their liking and according to their particular purposes" ("No se trata, pues, de omitir detalles inverosímiles, como apunta Lecoy, sino de insistir a cada viraje de la anécdota en la lección que se va a sacar. La importancia de la moraleja que el autor tiene en la mente condiciona, pues, el desarrollo de la anécdota. Esto me parece sobremanera importante para reivindicar la libertad creadora de los autores medievales que pueden tomar la anécdota de fuente oral o escrita, pero en realidad la transforman a su manera y de acuerdo a sus propósitos particulares" [Materia tradicional 68]).

Works Cited

Ayerbe-Chaux, Reinaldo. *El Conde Lucanor: materia tradicional y originalidad creadora.* Madrid: Porrúa Turanzas, 1975.

———. "Don Juan Manuel y la conciencia de su propia autoría." *La Corónica* 10 (1982): 186–190.

———. "Manuscritos y documentos de don Juan Manuel." *La Corónica* 16 (1987): 88–93.

Biglieri, Aníbal. *Hacia una poética del relato didáctico: ocho estudios sobre El Conde Lucanor.* University of North Carolina Studies in Romance Languages and Literatures 233. Chapel Hill: Univ. of North Carolina Press, 1989.

Blecua, Alberto. *La transmisión textual de "El Conde Lucanor."* Barcelona: Universidad Autónoma, Bellaterra, 1980.

Funes, Leonardo. "La capitulación del *Libro de los estados.* Consecuencias de un problema textual." *Incipit* 4 (1984): 71–91 and 6 (1986): 3–26.

Goyri de Menéndez Pidal, María. Review of *El Conde Lucanor.* Ed. Eugenio Krapf. Vigo, 1902. *Revista de Archivos Bibliotecas y Museos* 7 (1902): 320–321.

Juan Manuel. *Cinco Tratados.* Ed. Reinaldo Ayerbe-Chaux. Madison: Hispanic Seminary of Medieval Studies, 1989.

———. *El Conde Lucanor: A Collection of Medieval Spanish Stories.* Ed. and Trans. John England. Warminster, England: Aris and Phillips, 1987.

———. *El libro de los enxiemplos del conde Lucanor et de Patronio.* Text and notes from the unpublished works of Hermann Knust. Ed. Adolf Birch-Hirschfeld. Leipzig: Dr. Seele and Co., 1900.

———. *Libro de los estados.* Ed. R. B. Tate and I. R. Macpherson. Oxford: Oxford Univ. Press, 1974.

————. *Libro del Conde Lucanor et de Patronio.* Ed. Germán Orduna. Buenos Aires: Huemul, 1972.

————. *Libro del Conde Lucanor.* Ed. Reinaldo Ayerbe-Chaux. Madrid: Alhambra, 1982.

————. *Libro del Conde Lucanor.* Ed. Reinaldo Ayerbe-Chaux. Madrid: Taurus, 1986.

————. *Obras Completas.* Vols. I and II. Ed. José Manuel Blecua. Madrid: Gredos, 1982–1983.

————. *Textos y concordancias de la obra completa de Juan Manuel.* Ed. Reinaldo Ayerbe-Chaux. Madison: Hispanic Seminary of Medieval Studies, 1986.

Lewalski, Barbara Kiefer. "Historical Scholarship." In *Introduction to Scholarship in Modern Languages and Literatures.* Ed. Joseph Gibaldi. New York: Modern Language Association of America, 1981. 53–78.

Michael, Ian. "The Function of the Popular Tale." In *Libro de buen amor: Studies.* Ed. G. B. Gybbon-Monypenny. London: Tamesis, 1970. 177–181.

Rico, Francisco. "Crítica del texto y modelo de cultura en el Prólogo General de don Juan Manuel." *Studia in honorem Prof. M. de Riquer,* vol. I. Barcelona: Quaderns Crema, 1986. 409–423.

Tanselle, G. Thomas. "Textual Scholarship." In *Introduction to Scholarship in Modern Languages and Literatures.* Ed. Joseph Gibaldi. New York: Modern Language Association of America, 1981. 29–52.

◆ Chapter 3

A National Classic
The Case of Garcilaso's Poetry

Elias L. Rivers

How does a group of poems become a classic, a national monument? And what is the status of such monuments today? Questions such as these must be posed if we wish to understand the historical process of canon formation and literary history as traditionally practiced, and perhaps even to modify this tradition. The archetypal case, for Western literature, is the Homeric corpus. A tradition of oral composition and performance, that is, a system for producing rhythmically controlled but evanescent poetic happenings with innumerable variants in the presence of different audiences, was transformed, after the invention of the Greek alphabet had made possible the transcription of a virtuoso performance, into a canonical written tradition with a minimal infiltration of oral variants (Lord, Havelock). This fixed text was then taught in schools to literate students who memorized passages, but who no longer had the ability to compose traditional poetry orally. Closer to us are the cases of Virgil and Horace, who composed less traditional, that is, more eclectic or "original," poetry with writing instruments instead of musical instruments in their hands. They established their own texts and controlled, for a while at least, the reproduction and circulation of these texts. In a parallel situation in Spain, we have a text such as the single manuscript of the *Poema de mio Cid*, which seems to represent the transcription of an oral performance (whether or not this performance ultimately derived from a written composition), followed later by manuscripts of works deliberately written by Don Juan Manuel, for example, and deposited in a monastery as the authorized sources for all future copies.

The invention of the printing press, combined with the new humanistic methods of reconstructing from many derivative copies the lost original texts of classical authors, made the whole process both more public and more self-conscious. Garcilaso de la Vega (1501?–1536) was born into this early modern world of literary editions; before the end of the sixteenth century his posthumously published works were generally acclaimed as the major national poetic monument. How did this come about? What have been the subsequent developments? And what is the present situation of Garcilaso's poetry?

What Jerome McGann has called "the originary textual moment" (82) has been rather well defined for Garcilaso's poetry by historical and biographical scholars, above all by Rafael Lapesa, the senior Spanish philologist. After dating each poem as precisely as possible, Lapesa has reconstructed a "trajectory" or sequence of different stylistic models and tendencies within which to place Garcilaso's literary production. There can be no doubt that early in his life Garcilaso not only read Spanish courtly poetry of the type prevalent during the fifteenth century (what Lapesa calls his "Hispanic roots") but also received humanistic training in the reading of classical Latin poetry. His Spanish readings had an immediate influence on his earliest writings, but his Latin readings had a more delayed influence, mediated by his later readings and imitations of Italian poetry, which were first encouraged in 1526 by his older Catalonian friend Juan Boscán and which became more intensive after he was ordered in 1532 by the Emperor Charles V to the Spanish viceroy's court in Naples. In Naples he also wrote some Latin poetry for local circulation among humanist friends. Unless a great deal of earlier production has been lost, his four years in Naples constitute virtually his whole poetic career, cut short by his early death in battle.

Few scholars have tried to document more precisely the original social circumstances of Garcilaso's production of poetry, but some further speculation is justified by the occasional character of many of the poems. The least historically circumstantial in this sense are the Petrarchan sonnets and *canzoni;* as Inés Azar has recently shown, the sonnets are not linked together to form a love-life sequence, but are isolated, detached fragments with no portrait of a lady at their center. (The historical identity of the Portuguese lady Isabel Freyre is more directly relevant to the eclogues than to the fragmentary *Canzoniere.*) It seems likely that these Petrarchan poems were circulated in manuscript copies among groups of Garcilaso's friends, Spanish and Italian ladies and gentlemen, centered in Naples, perhaps also in Barcelona and at the Emperor's court. There are non-Petrarchan sonnets addressed, and hence presumably sent, to individuals: to Boscán, to Giulio Cesare Caracciolo and to Mario Galeota, to two Italian ladies, to a nobleman. One sonnet is an epitaph written for the tomb of his brother in Naples, telling how he died; it must have circulated within the family, at least. (Garcilaso's mother belonged to an aristocratic family with strong literary traditions.) Two of the three eclogues are dedicated in their opening lines to two specific individuals: one is the Viceroy of Naples and the other is probably the Viceroy's wife. Four of his classical poems are epistolary in form: his Horatian epistle and his elegy addressed to Boscán, another elegy addressed to the Duke of Alva, and a Horatian ode addressed to Violante Sanseverino, a Neapolitan lady. In these four cases the poetic genres, the addressees, and the historical circumstances are made explicit and are inseparable from one another.

There is no indication that Garcilaso himself ever intended to publish any of his poetry. Most of what we have might well have disappeared had it not been for his friend Juan Boscán, who upon Garcilaso's death became his literary executor. As Boscán's widow was later to write, "Boscán took charge of Garcilaso's poetic remains because of the great friendship that had united them for so long, and because after Garcilaso's death people sent Boscán his poems so that he might take proper care of them" (Rivers, *Obras completas con comentario* 19). More than five years after Garcilaso's death, in March of 1542, Boscán and his wife signed a contract with a printer for the publication of a volume entitled *The*

Works of Juan Boscán with some works by Garcilaso de la Vega.
According to the contract, it was to be an edition of one thousand
copies on good paper. But while it was being printed, at the rate
of one gathering a day, and being proofread by Boscán, the latter
was ordered to Perpignan, with the Duke of Alva, and there con-
tracted an illness that turned out to be fatal; he died in September
of 1542. In the following year his widow supervised the rest of the
printing, and the volume was published in Barcelona in 1543. Despite royal copyrights, at least two pirated editions were published
in rapid succession, in Lisbon and in Barcelona. In 1544 two authorized editions were published, in central Spain and in Antwerp;
during the following thirteen years there was at least one edition,
or reprint, each year. This sequence of editions indicates a highly
significant readership throughout the Spanish Empire: in the Neth-
erlands, Italy, and the American colonies, as well as in the Iberian
Peninsula. It is important to note that what people were reading
was not Garcilaso's works alone, but the more voluminous works
of Boscán as well, consisting of old-style Castilian courtly poetry,
a formal Petrarchan *canzoniere,* and other Italianate and neoclassical poetry, prefaced by Boscán's aggressive manifesto emphasizing
the classical superiority of an innovative combination, in Spanish,
of Italian-style versification with Italian and neoclassical genres of
poetry. In poetry, as we know, the acoustic (and graphic) form of
the material signifier is fully as important as the more conceptual
and idealistic structure of the signified. From the beginning, then,
this volume was presented as marking a revolution in Spanish
poetry: the combined works of Boscán and Garcilaso developed a
new social capacity to read and write verse in a different way.

At the same time, from the beginning, readers made a distinction
between Boscán's poetry and Garcilaso's; already in 1546 Ambrosio
de Morales emphasized the latter's superior imitation of Latin models, especially Virgil and Horace (Rivers, "Garcilaso divorciado"
121). After 1557 the number of editions of the poetry of Boscán
and Garcilaso together in one volume began to decline, and in
1569 an enterprising publisher in Salamanca finally brought out a
much slimmer volume of Garcilaso's poetry alone, with new textual
revisions. (As this publisher, the bookseller Simón Borgoñón, remarks in his dedication of the volume to the Rector of the University
of Salamanca, readers had already been separating Garcilaso's

works from those of Boscán, a fact that had encouraged his publication of a smaller book.) Borgoñón's edition was not copyrighted;
the following year a Madrid publisher reprinted it.

The scholar who had revised the Borgoñón text was Francisco
Sánchez de las Brozas (known in Latin as Sanctius Brocensis, whose
grammatical theories, according to Noam Chomsky, were to influence the Cartesian linguistics of Port Royal). One of Spain's
greatest and most outspoken humanists, Sánchez was elected Professor of Rhetoric at the University of Salamanca in 1573, and that
same year he put together a new edition of Garcilaso's poetry, with
several previously unpublished sonnets and other short poems, as
well as brief but substantial humanistic notes on Latin and Italian
sources and models (including without name of author some recent
Spanish translations of Horatian odes, actually written by his famous Salamancan colleague and ideological ally the Augustinian
friar Luis de León, who at that time was being tried by the Inquisition). Sánchez was careful to consult with the royal authorities
in Madrid before applying for permission to publish his new edition;
he had his printer take his manuscript to Juan Vázquez del Mármol,
the King's chaplain and censor, inviting him to suggest any revisions
in advance. Vázquez objected to some of the more radical changes
in the familiar text, and Sánchez was careful to follow his advice,
at least for his first edition (Rivers, "Garcilaso divorciado" 123).
When they brought out their first scholarly edition in 1574, Sánchez
and the printer had in mind a local market of university students
and other academics, that is, readers of Latin; Garcilaso's text was
being given the sort of learned attention that had been previously
reserved for the Latin classics. This slim and inexpensive volume
became the standard scholarly edition for the next forty years,
being reprinted at least six times between 1577 and 1612, with two
revisions. In his preface to the reader Sánchez explains the literary
importance of Renaissance *imitatio*, or what we would now call
intertextuality, and its usefulness, along with the collation of manuscript variants, for the emendation of unintelligible passages. In
later editions he cites an antischolarly opposition in his vigorous
defense of humanistic attitudes.

In 1580 a competing scholar in southern Spain, the cleric and poet
Fernando de Herrera of Seville, brought out another scholarly edition of Garcilaso's poetry, with much longer notes and commentaries.

This monumental, expensive volume constituted in effect a full-length course in Renaissance poetic theory, with definitions of classical rhetorical terms, with mythological and technical information, and with sixteen encyclopedic discourses, or lectures, on various related topics, all somehow made relevant to Garcilaso's poems. Whenever possible, Herrera tried to establish a text that was different from Sánchez's; he accepted only six of the nine unpublished sonnets discovered by Sánchez. Without mentioning Sánchez by name, he opposed his ideas frequently and occasionally even criticized Garcilaso's own stylistic choices. Herrera added a few new Latin and Italian sources, as well as subsequent imitations of Garcilaso by later Spanish poets, mostly Andalusian. He systematically changed certain of Garcilaso's third-person clitic object pronouns, to make them conform to Andalusian (and Spanish American) usage. Herrera's edition was not published again, but with its reformed spelling and precision in typographical details, its pedantic criticism and Spanish nationalism, it represents an attempt to set a deluxe standard for annotated critical editions. The volume provoked a controversy between two scholarly groups, one associated with the innovative humanism of certain faculty members at the University of Salamanca, under attack by the Inquisition but supported by some lay members of the royal government in Madrid, and another rival humanistic group located in the provincial capital of Seville, the center of colonial wealth, and supported by some local aristocrats; Herrera was asserting the cultural superiority of an area liberated by Castile from Arab rule and now closer to the new frontier in America. This controversy produced at least one substantial document of an overtly polemical sort. This document, recently edited with scholarly precision for the first time and explicated in detail by Juan Montero, consists of a series of commentaries in which "Prete Jacopín" (Juan Fernández de Velasco, a Castilian nobleman and amateur scholar) satirically criticizes specific aspects of Herrera's edition and in which Herrera responds, defending himself point by point and occasionally counterattacking.

In the subsequent revisions of his edition, Sánchez ignored Herrera's criticisms and the whole controversy. Less discreet was the only other editor of the period, Tomás Tamayo de Vargas, who published his derivative edition and commentaries in Madrid in

1622; as Antonio Alatorre has shown, Tamayo made secret use of "Prete Jacopín" and his ideas in criticizing Herrera.

During the second half of the sixteenth century, given the wide accessibility and popularity of Garcilaso's poetry as a cornerstone of high culture in Spain, its influence may be detected in many different texts, both in verse and in prose. The pastoral novel, from Montemayor's *Diana* (1558?) on, is filled with echoes of Garcilaso's eclogues. His Horatian ode, written in a peculiar five-line stanza taken from Bernardo Tasso, set the pattern for Fray Luis de León and other Spanish translators and imitators of Horace's poetry. Not always approved of by ecclesiastical censors, Garcilaso's rather pagan poetry was parodied line for line by a certain devout Sebastián de Córdoba (Granada, 1575); these Christian "contrafacta" influenced the mystic poetry of St. John of the Cross. Cervantes, thoroughly familiar with Garcilaso's poetry, echoes his lines both in verse and in prose, not only in his pastoral novel but in *Don Quijote* as well. Góngora's poetic revolution too would have been impossible without its roots in Garcilaso's. Scholarly editions and popular imitations combined to make Garcilaso's poetry a living part of sixteenth-century Spanish elite culture, and in the seventeenth it was still used as a touchstone both to defend and to attack Góngora's controversial new poetry. Garcilaso was still universally hailed as "the prince of Castilian poets"—but, as we shall see, his sales were declining.

In 1612 the final reprint of Sánchez's edition appeared, and Tamayo's 1622 edition was the last edition of Garcilaso to appear for almost 150 years. This is in itself a remarkable phenomenon: the scholarly editions (1574–1622) had definitively established Garcilaso's reputation as the unique classical poet of Spain, but once this cultural "fact" had been asserted and fully accepted (it seems never to have been questioned during this period), his works apparently no longer had much of a reading public. It is true that poets continued to read them "professionally," as is obvious from the echoes of Garcilaso that recur from time to time in major writers such as Lope de Vega, Góngora, and Quevedo; but the latter two poets generally wrote in a very different style, which today is labeled as Baroque. We can thus surmise that there had been a radical change in poetic taste; lip service was still paid to Garcilaso, but his poetry had become an archaic monument, exercising an influence that concealed a certain anxiety and even antagonism. Perhaps Cervantes can be seen as the best example of this, and as the link between Renaissance and Baroque tastes: a slavish imitator of Garcilaso in his youthful verse and continually echoing him in his prose, the mature Cervantes developed another burlesque style, especially in his *Viaje del Parnaso* (1614), in which verse is used to make fun of all poetry, even by implication Garcilaso's.

In 1765, José Nicolás de Azara, a diplomat and classical scholar, published at long last a new edition of Garcilaso's complete poetry, of which only selections had been available in anthologies. He also published editions of Horace and Virgil. Azara, as Spanish ambassador in Rome and Paris, had of course rejected his country's Baroque literature as being in bad taste and, by returning to Garcilaso and his major Latin antecedents, was asserting that Spain too had a civilized, classical tradition, worthy of the Enlightenment. Azara's edition is essentially based on that of Francisco Sánchez, with a discreet selection from the latter's humanistic notes. Azara made one significant change concerning presentation to the reader: his edition began, not with Garcilaso's Petrarchan sonnets, often medieval or witty in style, but with his Virgilian eclogues, clearly belonging to the classical humanistic tradition. Azara's edition, frequently reprinted during the nineteenth century, became the new standard; even the best-known edition in the twentieth century, that of Tomás Navarro Tomás, published in 1911 as the third volume in the Clásicos Castellanos series, followed Azara's order of poems, giving special prominence to the eclogues. Navarro, however, based the text of his edition on Herrera's, which he took to be the most carefully corrected and printed of the classical editions. Navarro's new annotations were the first to be written for the modern student and general reader.

Meanwhile, of course, nineteenth-century Germanic philology had been developing a more scientific level of textual criticism, in an attempt to separate, in a positivistic way, the material transmission of texts from their literary interpretation. The first scholar to apply modern methods in a radical way to the critical study of Garcilaso's poetry and texts was the North American Hispanist Hayward Keniston, whose solid biographical and literary study was published in New York in 1922 and whose critical edition of Garcilaso's works was published in New York in 1925, with a rigorous apparatus of bibliographical descriptions and variants based on the collation of many early editions and manuscripts. Keniston chose the first edition (Barcelona, 1543) as his copy text, assuming that in substance it was more directly related than any other to Garcilaso's own (lost) original manuscripts; at the same time, he considered the spelling of the first edition to be too idiosyncratic and replaced it with the spelling of the Antwerp (1544) edition. Although the latter decision is certainly debatable, Keniston's edition set a high new level of positivistic textual restoration. Outside of a few scholarly libraries, however, his edition was virtually unknown and inaccessible in Spain and most other countries; thus it had almost no effect on the popular or scholarly reading of Garcilaso's poetry. Conversely, the accessibility of the Navarro edition, revised and kept in print without interruption in a popular series of classical Spanish texts, perpetuated the prestige of the Herrera text, although with new notes and with Azara's order of presentation.

In Spain a twentieth-century rereading of Garcilaso's poetry begins not so much with Navarro's edition as with appreciative essays by Azorín, a representative of the so-called Generation of 1898, who like Azara felt akin to Garcilaso as an intellectual poet who was cosmopolitan and European, not narrowly Spanish. This point of view was still valid for the Generation of 1927; we have, as examples of Garcilaso's influence, Salinas's love poetry and Alberti's eclogue. Margot Arce's book, published in Madrid in 1930, is based on a similar attitude, with her analysis of Garcilaso's ideology as typical of the Renaissance. The most influential reading of Garcilaso by a member of that generation was undoubtedly that which Dámaso Alonso, invoking the name of Azorín, published in his *Poesía española* of 1950, a subtle stylistic analysis of the complex interplay of run-on lines and vocabulary that evokes an aesthetic landscape that is both mythological and Spanish. At the same time we must also take into account the Franco regime's endorsement of Garcilaso as the ideal soldier-poet and classical escapist. In 1943 a group of poets founded a magazine entitled *Garcilaso*, which combined in an ambiguous way neoclassical lyricism and the fascistic triumph of nationalism (Rubio), converting the name of our poet into an ideological slogan. This slogan was opposed by an existentialist ("anti-Garcilaso") movement known as "tremendismo," in which Dámaso Alonso also took part as the author of *Hijos de la ira* (1944). Politics was clearly involved, but did not produce a new edition of Garcilaso's poetry.

The Herrera tradition, as renewed by Navarro's edition, was reinforced in 1966 and 1972 by Antonio Gallego Morell's edition of the Herrera text with the classical commentaries of Francisco Sánchez, Fernando de Herrera, and Tomás Tamayo de Vargas; this edition of the commentaries has become the standard source of quotations. But at about the same time, in 1964, Elias L. Rivers followed the example of Keniston in returning to the first edition as the basis for both substance and accidentals of a new edition of Garcilaso's text; a few press variants were discovered in the process. Since 1969 this has been the basis of a new popular edition, with minimal notes, in the well-distributed Clásicos Castalia series, which has successfully competed with the Navarro edition. More important, in 1970 Alberto Blecua published a study of the textual problems involved in editing Garcilaso; he reevaluated the older editions and surviving manuscripts, finding Sánchez's text preferable to Herrera's and the first edition as the necessary point of departure for any new edition. His most important advance over Keniston and Rivers was to establish the premise that Garcilaso could not have written metrically defective lines and that hence such lines required emendation. Blecua's study was fully taken into account by Rivers in 1974 when the latter published a critical edition of Garcilaso's complete works (including prose and Latin poems) with a comprehensive commentary, both classical and modern (Sánchez complete, including his revisions, and selections from Herrera, Tamayo, Azara, Navarro, Mele, Keniston, Lapesa, and Blecua, as well as from many other modern studies). This edition has been widely used by scholars and advanced students and has influenced most subsequent popular editions, including the recent (1989) edition by Angel L. Prieto de Paula for beginning students in the Castalia Didáctica textbook series.

From this brief history of Garcilaso's poetry, of its origins and its reproduction and its present status, we may draw some conclusions about the timeless permanence of a classic national text. One concrete example will illustrate the historically problematic nature of such a text. The climactic lines (229–232) of Garcilaso's

Third Eclogue, describing the death of the nymph Elisa, were published in 1543 as follows:

> Near the water, in a flowery spot,
> she lay among the grass with severed throat
> as the white swan lies when he loses
> his sweet life among the green grasses.

> Cerca del agua, en un lugar florido,
> estava entre las yervas *degollada*
> qual queda el blanco cisne quando pierde
> la dulce vida entre la yerva verde.

Francisco Sánchez was the first to draw attention to the word *degollada*, the basic meaning of which is quite violent (with throat cut, beheaded). He had found another reading in a good manuscript and was convinced that Garcilaso had written *ygualada* instead. In a letter to the royal secretary Vázquez before publishing his first annotated edition, Sanchez had written that he did not dare insist on this new reading because of Vázquez's objection: "Even though I know quite certainly that Garcilaso had written 'ygualada,' I have left that brutal word 'degollada'; and I have removed the note, for I prefer to err in the direction of being obedient rather than being obstinate" (Rivers, "Garcilaso divorciado" 123). In fact Sánchez does keep the reading *degollada* in his 1574 edition, but he draws attention in a note to the manuscript reading *igualada*. He revised this in his 1577 edition by changing his text to read *igualada* and by expanding his note. Herrera in 1580 kept the reading *degollada*, defending it explicitly against Sánchez's objections. In 1970 Alberto Blecua reviewed the problem in detail (172–176), citing the many defenses of the *degollada* reading and concluding on the basis of sound textual arguments that *igualada* is the correct *lectio difficilior*. But Porqueras Mayo and Martínez López presented further arguments in favor of *degollada*, and Rivers in his 1974 edition accepted this reading. More recently Lapesa has argued that Garcilaso may well have written *degollada* in a first draft, but that later he revised his text, writing not *ygualada* (an unusual Spanish word that had been hard for Sánchez and Blecua to define) but *yugulada*, a Latinism or Italianism that fits the passage with semantic precision ("Apéndice III" 209). From a classical point of view, it seems to me that when Blecua's arguments are combined with Lapesa's emendation, we have the best solution to the problem of what the poet's final intention was. Not all scholars have been convinced, however. Olga Tudorica Impey has subsequently argued for *igualada* as a semantic Latinism equivalent to "aequata" in the sense of "allanada" (159). Conversely Mario di Pinto has discovered a Toledan place-name "Val de la Gollada" that makes possible an entirely new reading of line 230: "estava entre las yervas de Gollada" (139). We may conclude that, in any case, from a historical point of view, the poet's final intention has no ultimate privilege: he did, it seems, at one point write *degollada* (or *de Gollada*), and that reading has been the most widely circulated during the history of his different editions. This reading cannot be silently suppressed. Whether or not *ygualada* will ever prevail, as a hapax legomenon that is unique not only in Garcilaso's own poetry but in the history of Spanish literature, depends on the future dynamics of the politics of editing.

Works Cited

Alatorre, Antonio. "Garcilaso, Herrera, Prete Jacopín y don Tomás Tamayo de Vargas." *Modern Language Notes* 78 (1963): 126–151.

Alonso, Dámaso. *Poesía española: ensayo de métodos y límites estilísticos.* Madrid: Gredos, 1950.

Arce Blanco de Vázquez, Margot. *Garcilaso de la Vega: contribución al estudio de la lírica del siglo XVI.* Madrid: Centro de Estudios Históricos, 1930.

Azar, Inés. "Tradition, Voice and Self in the Love Poetry of Garcilaso." In *Studies in Honor of Elias Rivers.* Ed. Bruno Damiani and Ruth El Saffar. Potomac, Md.: Scripta Humanistica, 1989. 24–35.

Azara, José Nicolás de, ed. *Obras de Garcilaso de la Vega, ilustradas con notas.* Madrid: Imprenta Real de la Gaceta, 1765.

Azorín [José Martínez Ruiz]. Four essays on Garcilaso published in *Lecturas españolas,* 1912; *Al margen de los clásicos,* 1914; *Los dos Luises y otros ensayos,* 1921; *Los clásicos redivivos,* 1945.

Blecua, Alberto. *En el texto de Garcilaso.* Madrid: Insula, 1970.

Chomsky, Noam. *Cartesian Linguistics.* New York: Harper and Row, 1966.

Di Pinto, Mario. "Non sgozzate la ninfa Elisa." *Studi Ispanici* (1986): 123–143.

Gallego Morell, Antonio. *Garcilaso de la Vega y sus comentaristas.* Granada: Univ. de Granada, 1966.

Havelock, Eric. *Preface to Plato.* Cambridge: Harvard Univ. Press, 1963.

Herrera, Fernando de, ed. *Obras de Garcilasso de la Vega con anotaciones de Fernando de Herrera.* Seville: Alonso de la Barrera, 1580.

Keniston, Hayward. *Garcilaso de la Vega: A Critical Study of His Life and Works.* New York: Hispanic Society, 1922.

———, ed. *Garcilaso de la Vega, Works: A Critical Text with a Bibliography.* New York: Hispanic Society, 1925.

Lapesa, Rafael. *La trayectoria poética de Garcilaso.* Madrid: Revista de Occidente, 1948.

———. "Apéndice III. Poesía y realidad: destinatarias y personajes de los poemas garcilasianos de amor—Isabel Freyre, la ninfa 'degollada.'" *Garcilaso: Estudios completos.* Madrid: Istmo, 1985. 197–210.

Lord, Albert. *The Singer of Tales.* Cambridge: Harvard Univ. Press, 1960.

Martínez López, Enrique. "Sobre 'aquella bestialidad' de Garcilaso (Egl. III, 230)." *PMLA* 87 (1972): 12–25.

McGann, Jerome J. *The Beauty of Inflections: Literary Investigations in Historical Method and Theory.* Oxford: Clarendon Press, 1985.

Montero, Juan, ed. *La controversia sobre las "Anotaciones" herrerianas.* Seville: Ayuntamiento, 1987.

Navarro Tomás, Tomás, ed. *Garcilaso, Obras.* Madrid: Espasa, 1911, 1924, 1935. [Clásicos Castellanos 3.]

Porqueras Mayo, Alberto. "La ninfa degollada de Garcilaso (Egloga III, versos 225–232)." In *Actas del tercer congreso internacional de hispanistas.* México: El Colegio de Mexico, 1970. 715–724.

Prieto de Paula, Angel L. *Garcilaso.* Madrid: Castalia, 1989.

Rivers, Elias L., ed. *Garcilaso de la Vega, Obras completas.* Madrid: Castalia, 1964.

———. "Garcilaso divorciado de Boscán." *Homenaje al Profesor Rodriguez-Moñino.* Madrid: Castalia, 1966. 121–129.

———. ed. *Garcilaso de la Vega, Obras completas con comentario.* Madrid: Castalia, 1974.

———. *La poesía de Garcilaso: ensayos críticos.* Barcelona: Ariel, 1974.

Rubio, Fanny. *Las revistas poéticas españolas (1939–1975).* Madrid: Turner, 1976. 108–117.

Sánchez de las Brozas, Francisco [El Brocense], ed. *Obras del excelente poeta Garci Lasso de la Vega, con anotaciones y enmiendas del licenciado Francisco Sánchez.* Salamanca: Pedro Lasso, 1574, 1577, 1589.

———. Personal correspondence with Juan Vázquez del Mármol concerning *Obras. Ensayo de una biblioteca española de libros raros y curiosos.* Vol. IV. Ed. Bartolomé José Gallardo. Madrid: Tello, 1889. 449–459.

Tamayo de Vargas, Tomás, ed. *Garcilasso de la Vega, natural de Toledo, príncipe de los poetas castellanos.* Madrid: Luis Sánchez, 1622.

Tudorica Impey, Olga. "El entorno clásico y filológico de la muerte en la última égloga de Garcilaso, vv. 229–32." *Romanische Forschungen* 99 (1987): 152–168.

◆ Chapter 4

The Art of Edition as the Techné of Mediation: Garcilaso's Poetry as Masterplot

Iris M. Zavala

Good letters have come to Spain with the Empire.

Mas ya han entrado en España las buenas letras con el imperio.

—Fernando de Herrera 1580

The focus of my inquiry is that there are crucial patterns of interplay between editing and mediation, and that these patterns, though historically varied, are to a surprising degree quite definite in the modes of organizing experience.[1] What I will discuss is the mediating function of editing in the creation of a unifying, totalizing discourse: editing as a form of interpretive practice that advances master narratives. In the sixteenth century editing appears as an active construct of forces of language, intended to influence the production of meaning within a universalist State, and also as an instrument of social mediation aimed at institutionalizing the monosemy and appropriating textual production. As a signifying realm of modern literary science, editing is linked to the humanism of the Renaissance and the emergence of the *doxae*.

In order to present a working hypothesis for the study of the role and function of specific texts, I will limit myself to a few lines of questioning, examining the mediating forces that bear on the work. Those forces are: (1) the relationship between literary styles and their articulation in the context of development of a uniform national language; (2) editorial technologies as mediators in the organization and institutionalization of meaning; (3) editing as a form of political exercise for the use of hegemonic appropriation of discourse, as a necessary precondition for the formation of a modern imperial State. Accordingly, the editors of Garcilaso inaugurate a distinctive ideology and politics of language, in which local dialects are discouraged in favor of a uniform language that constitutes the official vehicle of communication.

We know by now that neither writing nor language is innocent or neutral, and that both inscribe a considerable number of presuppositions that are inseparable from ideology as a system of signification. Ideological discourses are both the object and the limiting conditions, what Macherey called the inscription of "otherness" in the work (79). Along a similar line of inquiry, Althusser described his conception of "social totality" (whose limitations I will not discuss now) as constituted by distinct and relatively autonomous levels or instances articulated in particular relations of domination and subordination. He also describes "theoretical practice" as a structure of production that elaborates its object of knowledge in accordance with its own law. Thus, knowledge is inscribed in the structure of the real object, and theoretical production is based on an intertextual relation (Althusser and Balibar 94).[2]

My purpose here is to extend these lines of inquiry into the area of editing as a form of signifying practice or speech genre, to suggest a link between literary production and scientific forms of theorization, as an intertextual form of mediation by which the editor produces a reading of what was missing in the text, a reading that divulges the absent event in the text it reads and at the same time relates it to a different text present as a necessary absence in the first. The uses to which the editor may put a text within the social process constitute a privileged mode of reproduction of the imperial myths of universality and hegemony and the affirmation of specific moral and ethical values, thus dispersing and displacing competing signifying practices and different modes of production. Editing is a form of *metacommentary* that questions the function of the text in relation to its interpretations; editing works a form of mediation to inscribe the historical master code, despite the heterogeneity of the specific historical experience. Through the mediation of editing, institutionalized meaning and value are constructed from a process of reorganization that embeds networks of relationships.

It is perhaps worth noting here that the influential contribution of members of the Bakhtin circle has been an indispensable aid to the theorization of my approach, since they highlight the fact that social relations of production, power, and systems of discourse are linked by ideology (Voloshinov). Ideology understood as the totality of conventionalized forms of semiotic systems is thus an important factor relating knowledge and the subject; a theory of ideology is a theory of semiotic value, since the sign signifies by virtue of social consensus, and every utterance is in principle dialogic, open to contradictory uses. The semiotic involves the concrete exchange of signs in society and history. Language is thus placed in concrete social situations to establish a typology of speech genres that depend on usage. Finally, within this broad generalization, the production of meaning or the signifying process is a function of speech genres, structured normatively through formal, contextual, and thematic (ideologeme) features, or ways of speaking in particular situations (Voloshinov 20). Each genre is then a distinct social practice, a situational utterance in the shared event of discourse in which the ideological is always inscribed.[3]

Before pursuing my line of inquiry, a working definition of *mediation* may be in order, one that is grounded in the fact that in all disciplines materials are mediated by discourse and that genres are split by the mediations of enunciating subjects. In a more general sense, mediation consists of those elements of the production process that mark the object's historicity. In other words, it is an established relationship in a complex structure between autonomous levels of organization. In a social formation, mediation is the influence that a "situation (economic, for example) exercises in the development of another situation (political, ideological)" (Angenot 127). My suggestion is that editing, as an instrument of literary production, mediates between meaning and social evaluation in the historically concrete and varying model in which signifying practices are appropriated.

A history of editions is linked to these decisive questions; mediation, in this domain, would correspond to the overdetermination of genres and language production by a set of literary norms in the attempt to reappropriate literary discourse for structures of hegemony or for the institutions governing cultural production. As a speech genre, editing should then be linked to new information technologies or new semiotic modes of scientific production that are the result of the communicative work of an extending political system. This argument is significant, since the origins of editing in the Hispanic world are closely connected with the Imperial Spain of Charles V, in the same way that the institutionalization of grammar is closely related to Peninsular unity through the patronage given by Queen Isabella I to Antonio de Nebrija's *Gramática* (1492). While specialists in the theories of signifying practices (grammarians and rhetoricians) offered more systematizing instructions out of their own political practices, the pedagogical apparatuses encoded the ideological theories for practical deployment. The rhetorical theories of antiquity, as well as widespread and highly sophisticated translations and annotations, enriched the efficacy of signification, doing so through metacommentaries that mediated the specific uses of language toward the legitimation of a modern society where literature became a question of social category, denoting a privileged access to reading and writing practices.

What I have just said, in a general way, is privileged in the edition and commentaries of Garcilaso de la Vega, which sustain the fiction of one language. A few reminders are in order. The works of the poet from Toledo were first published together with those of Juan Boscán (in Catalonian, Joan Boscán) in the posthumous edition *Las obras de Boscán y algunas de Garcilaso* (1543), whose dissemination prompted the independent publication of Garcilaso's poetry in 1569. This edition, in turn, was the basis for several other editions: the magnum edition and commentary of the prestigious rhetorician Francisco Sánchez de las Brozas, El Brocense (1574), the monumental edition of the rhetorician and poet Fernando de Herrera (1580), and those of Tomás Tamayo de Vargas (1622) and José Nicolás de Azara (1765). My purpose is not to make evaluative comments on these editions or editing practices (on this see Gallego Morell, and Rivers), but to stress that the canonization of the soldier-poet from Toledo coincides with the establishment of the imperial humanist *doxae,* the institutionalization of literature, and the constitution and articulation of a "national" hegemonic cultural language: Castilian Spanish. Simultaneously, three areas of discursive formation coincide: the institutionalization of literature and literary history; that of a "national" classic; and that of a privileged courtly speech genre (lyrical poetry, the sonnet, the "lira," the eclogue). In a preliminary way, I also wish to suggest that the modes of organization of Garcilaso's cultural text reveal—particularly in El Brocense's and Herrera's annotations—two polemics: one about the process by which institutional meanings are assigned and another regarding how symbolic meaning and value are acquired through social agreement.

What seems important is that, at this juncture of the sixteenth century, a modern or contemporary poet is raised by a Salamancan rhetorician and grammarian to the status of a *classic* through the same hermeneutic instruments used to establish the signifieds of the authoritative voices of the Latin past, specifically that of Virgil, whose prestige had grown since the fifteenth century. In contrast, Herrera ceases to take for granted that organizing frame; he adds additional angles of perception by drawing attention to divergent centers of analogies and connections, mainly aspiring to introduce the alternative Andalusian poetics into the hegemony of the imperial civil society. Herrera's conceptual framework struggles to contest the subordination of "heteroglossia" (Bakhtin) to a totalizing Castilianization during that phase of developing centralization that saw Seville as the center of power for political hegemony: an "Andalusian Castile" (see Chaunu). Herrera seemed to frame his poetics with an eye toward the aims and activities of other areas with which he had a partisan (though perhaps not uncritical) identification. For such a purpose, he employed categories and explanatory models that revealed the successful use of poetic language other than Garcilaso's. At this historical juncture, a very particular tension of the interpretive situation is indexed. To restate the most critical point, editing is a practice that seeks to disclose the truth of the present by uncovering the essential attributes of the past, constructing a comprehensive view of history. The history of editing in the emergent humanism is constructed as a canonization of classics into monolithic formations that later—in the eighteenth and nineteenth centuries—will be accepted without challenge, as literature becomes an object of the historical sciences.

Though there are numerous refinements and qualifications to be made, in what follows I suggest that on the basis of these presuppositions of the transmission and extension of a totalizing culture, another crucial event plays a vital role in this conjuncture: the emergence of humanism. Through it, the theorization of language as a system of meaning constituting an interrelated set of norms and beliefs is encouraged and specified. Language (and writing) comes to stand metonymically for modern existence at large and the point of departure for all attempts to project social relations. Humanism, which has been at present recognized and challenged as a logocentric discourse, sets itself up as a form of metanarrative or scientific discourse aligning itself with the processes of cultural production. The humanist universal project is questioned on account of its various contradictory commitments in the built-in aporias, one of which is the interplay of linguistic and cultural differences. This "Italianized" (thought as humanist and universal), self-authorized source of meaning as a totality, was challenged by some (poets, humanists) on the basis of that most rooted binary distinction—the regional, as opposed to the universality of the modern *doxa*.[4] In Imperial Spain, the rise of humanism is interrelated with the expansion of the Empire and the establishment of Charles I, King of Spain (1516–1556) as Holy Roman Emperor (1519–1556) and with his abdication in favor of his son Philip II (1556–1598). Warfare gives way to the bureaucratization of the Empire and to multidirected hegemonic problems both within and outside the Empire: court factions, the Black Legend (the Antonio Pérez affair), "heresy," and the wars with the Turks, the Dutch, England, and France, among others (on this see Elliott).

Two adjacent yet crucial problems are implicit in the sort of inquiry I am proposing: Joan Boscán—a Catalonian and the translator of Castiglione's *Il cortegiano,* a friend of Garcilaso and his first editor—is marginalized (although the joint 1543 edition is still reprinted) and never reaches the status of a canonical figure. At the same time, as part of an attempt to create a unified Spanish (Castilian) national literature, Garcilaso's poetry is raised to the uncontested category of a monument of classical literature, becomes a "best-seller," and is mythicized in an ontological realm of universality, while Garcilaso becomes the "Prince of Castilian Poets." Of particular interest in this line of inquiry is the 1580 edition by the rhetorician Fernando de Herrera, a native of Seville, whose erudite and polemical annotations served as a pretext for the development of a poetics and a theory of language authorizing Andalusian poetics (see Gallego Morell for many examples), thus remapping marginal areas toward the discourse of the center. In order to include universal facts of human experience, Herrera's polemical empirical fieldwork chose the markers of Lepanto in the historical area, Thomas More in the religious-political sphere, and Garcilaso on the matter of national language. Editing Garcilaso was not just a technical problem of poetics, then, but a whole systematic conceptualization of the modern Imperial State, militant and triumphant with its inheritance of the Roman (Imperial) classical world. The models and extensions of stabilized cultural norms are informed by that identification and interest. The specific appropriation of Imperial Rome and classical antiquity was, at that specific juncture, a return to ideals of political and social organization and cultural values as a construct of a master narrative that justified the ruling function of Castile, as the legitimate descendant of the Visigoths and chosen by God against the infidel to restore the original Peninsular unity (well noted by Gil Fernández). It was an urge to recover suppressed possibilities of totalizing ideals, with claims to a metanarrative or higher order of knowledge based on the suppression of heteroglossia. A world dominated by monoglossia expresses itself in the epistemological mode of monolithic notions of truth; a quest for both ideological hegemony and a totalizing unity played an important role as subtext of the canonical editions of the founding discourses. No less important, editing as a form of scientific discourse objectified and naturalized to a great extent male rhetorical tradition and the paradigms of "nationality" through gendered relationships (femininity or masculinity of languages, basic to Herrera). Gender and genre are both bound in this founding *doxae*.

In what follows, I propose to relate this appropriation of the new humanistic science of editing to (1) an "ideological" mediation with regard to the masked conflict of hegemonic discourse, and (2) a "solution" to the internal conflicts of the Empire through a form of unified Castilianization. Specifically, these conflicts were with the Andalusians (e.g., the revolt of Granada, problems of "heresy," and the subjugation of Moors and New Christians [*conversos*]) and the Catalonians, whose strong tradition of independence, with its own laws and privileges, accentuated by linguistic and cultural differences, made royal control difficult. Let us recall that the King was threatened in 1568–1570 with the second rebellion of the Alpujarras (Granada) and that the Catalonian problem turned into a revolution in 1640 (under Philip IV), matters that go well beyond the scope of this contextualization. It should be noted, however, that in the attempts to contemplate the origin of an imperial language, Herrera's commentaries, in contrast with those of other annotators, on the history of the sonnet in the Peninsula attribute to Boscán an important starting point, although they coherently accept that he was "a foreigner to the language" ("extranjero de la lengua"). Herrera's claim is motivated by an interest in constituting the theoretical grounds of a totalizing Spanish language as the legitimate language of the Empire, including the heterogeneity of historical existence, and in outlining how the languages of heteroglossia intersect each other and coexist in the present among different tendencies, schools, and circles. In his claim Herrera distinguishes the various strands (Andalusian, Castilian, Catalonian) that were excluded or included in the formation of the canon, thus conveying a potential polemic in light of the monological views on literary production.

Here I propose to reconsider the equation between the Spanish Crown and the greatness of the Roman Empire (regarding the colonies see Zavala, "Representing"), and Garcilaso's edition and annotation as a classic as being instrumental in establishing an economy of knowledge and truth based on a universal (read imperial) value. The newly awakened interests in poetry and the life of the mind achieve a kind of cultural hegemony that would overcome the forces of a dismembered Crown. From this viewpoint the science of language connects the subject with history and with the values of the centralized State. Both aspects of Castilian mythologies are constructs of a cultural imagination, one that articulates a whole dimension of humanism and literature by manipulating power through an apt control of scientific technology (grammar, rhetoric, the printing press). Such fields of knowledge were built into a hegemony of language, as a cohesive force aspiring to dominance over heterogeneous cultures and societies. At work in El Brocense's and Herrera's annotations—although from differing viewpoints—was the legitimation of a language and a culture *of* and *for* the Empire: Spanish ("lengua española" in Herrera) as a national language capable of strengthening the unity of the social and spiritual body of the Empire against a regional (and thus fragmentary) Castilian or Andalusian. The efficiency of the interpretive instruments of editing was a function of its transferential truth, reproduced as a set of assumptions of cultural evaluation and reproduction of value.

The metacommentary of El Brocense's interpretive system put forward a master code as he recreated the Augustan past through the surviving corpus of Latin literature. The specific axis was the work of Virgil, which had always been considered canonical, as it was part of a literary development in what seems, retrospectively, an attempt to create a Roman national literature to rival the literary monuments of classical and archaic Greece (Zetzel). Virgil's poem, which had become a school text after the poet's death in 19 B.C., was greeted as a Roman equivalent of the Homeric epics, while El Brocense, the humanist and Latin scholar, explicitly projected the poetry of Garcilaso as a new classic in a deliberate attempt to create a Castilian modern national literature, originating in the legitimating mytho-poetic classical antiquity. The historical conjuncture can now seem to coincide with that of the Roman Age, since in Augustan times this canonization coincided with the battle of Actium, in which Antony and Cleopatra were defeated by the forces of what was considered Eastern barbarism. The battle brought an end to a century of social upheaval and civil war in very much the same way that the reconquest of Granada had brought about the end of civil war and social strife in the Iberian Peninsula, in the view of sixteenth-century Spaniards. While establishing the Imperial Monarchy, there was, as I have suggested, a desire to recreate the past Roman Empire, as well as its cultural values.

For the commentators of Virgil, the choice of genre, as Zetzel reminds us, had important implications, and the goal of poetry was not to be original, but to follow a model so closely that the new might be taken for the old. El Brocense did not escape the idea of a prescriptive and overdetermined canon, which was framing a highly derivative literature, closely dependent on the normative system of the genres, although revealing changes in direction. This is his background as he projects as canon the new speech genres and establishes, based on Garcilaso, the discourse of cultural production (lyrical poetry) in Hispanic literary history. If *style* is not epiphenomenal, and therefore produces knowledge and is basic in the constitution of the subject, each genre is a social practice that implies multiple convergent planes, among them the semantic potential within the semiotic environment in which meaning is exchanged. The positive critical reaction we have learned from Jakobson/Lévi-Strauss is that a sonnet gives more than a grammar of a poem and that its effects are more than subliminal: those fourteen lines do not stand for a truism, or for a system of significations that does not signify anything. Therefore, the sonnet could well be the locus of the modern knowledge and power that made a monological imperial society possible. As such it cannot be isolated from the actual ways in which cultural texts contend for dominance. Now, according to Foucault, there tends to be a simple binary structuration of most genres, specifying a dominant (unmarked) position such as that of ruling class, adult, and male, and a repressed position appropriate to members of dominated classes, females, or children (95–98). Subject position means, then, the marginalization or excodification of certain classes of users whose status as nonsubjects is then concealed by the pseudouniversality of what is considered dominant.[5] The knowledge or *doxae* embedded in the sonnet, from its generic past, were the rejection of the public in favor of the private and the Alexandrian emphasis on slightness and elegance (on the classical, see L. E. Rossi).

El Brocense carefully followed the classical inheritance, recreating the legitimating Latin canon, while Herrera appropriated Garcilaso to project a unified Andalusian poetics not as an alternative, but as part of the whole. The question of "Spanish" as a totality here is an epistemological requirement for a comprehensive systematic theory of the State to break down the cultural barriers existing between different idiolects and traditions. These were the bases for editions by Tamayo de Vargas (1622) and Azara (1765). As a reminder, Tamayo y Vargas continually brings back the authority of the poet from Toledo as "Father of Poetry in our Language" and recurrently invokes the felicitous exemplarity of his poetry: "We must be grateful to the injuries of time that of the many works of Garcilaso enough survive to allow the admiration of his genius and to serve as examples for posterity" ("De las muchas obras de Garcilaso tenemos que agradecer a las injurias del tiempo las que bastan para admiración de su ingenio, y ejemplar para los de la posteridad" [Gallego Morell 643]). By 1765, Azara defines Garcilaso as a master instrumental code and a classic of national literary history. In all of the aforementioned editions, knowledge and power are categorized through language and the constitution of the subject through a fixed relation between signifiers and signified. Cultural referents (the classics) and codes were invoked as authorities to justify and legitimize territorial unity and the totalization or homogenization of literary discourse and genres through the borrowed language of mythology and the classics. The Hellenizing strain serves as a code of unification, in the desire to reconcile oppositions and differences through a single, comprehensive pseudouniversal vision.

In support of my hypothesis, I would like to readdress two other historical inscriptions of humanistic rhetoric (and grammar) as a mediating tool to legitimize centralized imperial power: the early work of Fernández Pérez de Oliva specifically addressing the discovery of America as "the invention of Indies" (Zavala, "Representing") and Antonio de Nebrija's (or Lebrija's) founding grammar (1492, studied by Rico in *Nebrija*), a metaphysical homogenization of a national language ("language is a companion of the Empire" ["la lengua es compañera del imperio"]). This grammar emerges as a concrete institutionalization of speech genres and literary history until the eighteenth century, although it was challenged as "regional" by the Erasmian Juan de Valdés in his *Diálogo de la lengua* (ca. 1535), a linguistic celebration of Castilian homogeneity against a dispersed, plural, decentered politics. Although not published until 1737 by the Valencian erudite Gregorio Mayáns y Siscar (anonymously and with self-censored cuts), it also became a master code of "proper" writing, including some paradigmatic names that became key authoritative figures of literary history. In these cases, historical awareness carried an absoluteness of a particular form as an ahistorical model of literary production. Finally, there is the "applied grammatology" of humanists such as Juan de Brocar and Juan Maldonado, among others, which demands that language be accorded a central role in defining and explaining civil society. According to Rico, the *litterae humaniores* is basically a means to acquire freedom through language, civil life, and contemplation (see *Nebrija*). This was the instrumental reason and the logic of social control, argued as a truth-telling enterprise.

These Renaissance humanists influenced others in at least three areas: (1) a conception of social totality; (2) a theoretical practice in which knowledge is inscribed in the structure as an essence of Castilian homogenization; (3) an epistemological break that marks the inscription of the rhetorical and of poetics in a scientific form of theorization. Grammar and linguistic science (what would later be called philology) were constituted in the order of discourse as hegemonic structures of power: one set of signifiers stands synecdochically for the whole and the other is repressed (Castilian/Catalonian, Castilian/Andalusian). The ideological component of this mediation (science of editing) is constituted as discourse in relation to unequal patterns of power and the specific appropriation of discourse by dominant social forces.

If the aforementioned is accepted, at the center of these historical forms of emerging legitimating institutions, El Brocense's and Herrera's annotations encoded a whole structure of language use and genre rules—both generic and sexual—into lyrical poetry, the sonnet, and other poetical genres connected with the question of how to project the subject of experience. Through the instrumentality of the science of language, meanings were fixed and the past (classical) was contemporized to authorize the present. This instrumental science involved two operations: dissection and rearticulation in order to engender certain rules of association for the purpose of assigning them to speakers conceived as the embodiment of universality. As a metalanguage, what it destabilized and set into play was the concept of culture and of subject, providing also a perspective on the reading subject since it presented the *doxae* of truth of history, human nature, and the social world. The emergence of editing as a science suggests the necessity that literary history be regarded at the same time from the viewpoints of the sciences of language and history.

In short, El Brocense, followed by other commentators, founded the metalinguistic rules governing the production of meaning for a particular semiotic environment: the structure of meaning presupposed in the structure of the genre of lyrical poetry, as a projection of the experience of the identity of a universal subject, thus excodifying other signifiers and signifieds. The history of the Petrarchan sonnet in Spain is dramatized by the exclusion of alternative discourses (the well-known opposition established by Cristóbal de Castillejo), which stand against the unifying rationalization of the universal modern genre instituted as classic master code. Herrera was justified, in this sense, in arguing about the contents and form of the sonnet (Gallego Morell) and privileging this speech genre in the constitution of knowledge: writing as a product of the foundations of the Empire and writing as a product of knowledge. The abandoning of military struggle within (the Reconquest) resulted in the "coming of good letters with the Empire" ("la entrada de buenas letras con el imperio"), and "ours have shaken off the yoke of ignorance" ("han sacudido los nuestros el yugo de la ignorancia" [88]).

By 1580 the *doxae* of knowledge was implicitly the whole enterprise of a poetics and science of language. The inscription of another alternative discourse (that of "popular" oral culture) into the literary production of the Renaissance is an invitation to a radical critique of hegemonic representations of subaltern groups. These should be framed between the two *doxae* of imperialism and humanism, subject-constitution and object-formation, as well as the neutralization of alternative discourses that refract cultural and social heterogeneity and heteroglossia.

To mark the moment when a civil society and the language of a particular culture and its new technologies are born, one could contrast the displacement brought about by the humanistic science of language. According to Francisco Rico, the original edition of Boscán-Garcilaso's poetry had performed a similar function to that of the *Cancionero general* (1511) ("El destierro"). If his assessment is correct, I would argue that such a function is quite different from the instrumentality of the classicism inscribed in the authoritative edition of the soldier-poet from Toledo that I have perused. This new articulation of the science of editing created a demand, and El Brocense published an annotated Juan de Mena (1582), exceeding the vulgata of *El laberinto de la fortuna* done by Hernán Nuñez (1499), which could be analyzed in lieu of the status of an emergent national literature. Mena (canonized by Nebrija, and admired by the humanists) since then has prompted affirmations as to his pre-Renaissance qualities, in particular his "national idea" (notably, Lida de Malkiel).

If my hypothesis is accepted, to the extent that the mediation of the newly articulated science of editing became a sort of identity-conferring metalanguage of the humanistic *doxae* that was constituted as a global culture, it is not difficult to see that the texts were canonized, and that they come to us thoroughly mediated, evaluated, and interpreted by the culture and cultural institutions through which they have been preserved (to borrow from Barbara Smith). In this historical conjuncture, editing—a mediating service known from the classical times of Rome and Greece—intensified the potential ideological truth-conferring function within the framework of the semiotic environment of the Empire and the canon formation of a national literature. The edition of Garcilaso's poetry initiates a new pattern of repetitions, internal to a literary series called lyrical poetry (the sonnet, the lyre), thus deflecting an existing pattern of lyric poetry (even the sonnet) into a new course and into the fixed identity of a pseudouniversal signifier. To date, this *doxa* is the parameter with which to value lyric poetry; Garcilaso's canonization designates the humanistic conception of a unified, centered, and centering self. This is the gendered subtext of this courtly love poetry, one that is articulated in the soldiering aspect of citizenship with its normative political implications, which thematizes the public and private spheres of classical capitalism.

It will be clear from the editorial history of Garcilaso that although there was a polemic about how to organize meaning, particularly between the organizing frame of El Brocense and that of Herrera, there was an overdetermination of genres and codes by a normative regulation and by the attempt to reappropriate literary discourse to the general structure of political hegemony. As a consequence of this mapping of models of organizing experience, the sonnet, and the lyre and love poetry, sanctioned by the institutions governing literary production (rhetoric, grammar, academics), became automatized and reproduced through the assigned institutional meaning, with fixed signifiers and signifieds and a doxical rule of topoi and ideologemes, in which human nature, social world, and truth convene, as well as a set rule on human and sexual relations.

As an expression of experience of the self, lyric poetry unfolded into the culturally given conception of love—the Neoplatonism of the repressed erotic impulse—addressed by a courtly defender of the polity to an audience of male men of letters. This cultural construct was socially and institutionally sanctioned, as much as the moral-political identity construct of the gallant soldier projected by Francisco de Aldana's sonnets. The lyrical love-poet was dramatizing to his sophisticated male audience universal questions on nature and the self through a register of subject positions within a game of language played by rules and a form of life. Within the community of courtly discourse, there were criteria for the "correct" uses of words, and the proper interpretation, as well as for the uses of the first person. Now, if Wittgenstein is correct, there is nothing that can be said in the first person that cannot be said in the third (22). Lyric poetry was the agency for an emergent science of the constitution of the subject, made coextensive with that of language; there was an interplay between the language of the Empire and the unified and centered self.[6] As a state of discourse, this courtly poetry was informed by power, and through Garcilaso's editions, political judgments were made in terms of a particular historically specific appropriation of discourse by dominant social forces.

Conceived along the lines of epistemological constructs, the Petrarchan sonnet "nationalized" by Garcilaso is not an epiphenomenal structure, or style, or versification, but should be understood within this history of mediations through which a speech genre is embedded with the *doxae* of a presumed truth of history, human nature, and the social world.[7] It is the location for codification and excodification of the users of the speech genre at the mytho-poetic level, and the empirical fieldwork of the patriarchal subject of experience established as a universal fact of human experience, designed to leave in the domain of the unthinkable the very thing that makes this conceptualization possible. As a discursive domain constituted by the mediation of the commentators with regard to the dominant ideology, the speech genre was formally open to contradictory uses, its *dialogy,* which Herrera tried to constitute. Within the framework of a plurality of uses of the Petrarchan sonnet, Garcilaso's performed a specific function of authority within the discursive economy as a whole. Since their inscription through El Brocense's edition, these utterances were automatized, from those of the "a lo divino" Garcilasists of the sixteenth and seventeenth centuries (including San Juan) to those of the Garcilasists of Franco's Spain. The continuous overdetermination of the genre and codes attests to the changing relations of dominance and social appropriation.

Examined as a form of interpretive politics, editing mediates as a mode of constructional principle that becomes a key factor for automatization as the dominant feature of the text. In the historical inscription I have proposed, it leads the reader to an institutional mode of organization and reconstruction of the symbolizing process, drawing attention to analogies and connections between properties immanent to the symbolizing element and properties characteristic of what is represented by it (I borrow from Renan). It mediates in the reconstruction of meaning and embeds the institutional meaning and the values of the specific social agreement. This techné depends for its effectiveness on the acceptance of a hierarchical social organization and on the moral values filtered through the organizing frame. It affects the reception of individual texts, inasmuch as philological science tended (and very often still does) to isolate utterances in order to relate them to a specific class (and sexual) ideology. This tendency to isolate the sign, to give it fixed meaning through its origin (authoritative master code), tends to limit the potential openness of genres and utterances, thereby perpetuating the illusion that there is nothing but authorities and static functions. In this respect, the interpellations of the social imaginary are hegemonized toward monological meanings produced in terms of appropriation by a ruling class. It could even be argued that, in its founding inception as a humanistic science, the practice of editing involves the fictive control of rhetorical and grammatical usage and a domestication of literary discourses, thus tending to establish literature as a positive science, with utilitarian ends: a segment of what the Frankfurt school called "instrumental reason," with its metaphysics of totalizing functionalism, which came to a peak in the eighteenth century.

I have offered this relatively detailed account of Garcilaso since it helps to pinpoint what is involved not only in the critical reading of the founding editions of canonical texts as integral parts of a national literature, but also in the criteria and interests that played an important role in the history of the silenced and marginalized utterances. I have suggested that Garcilaso's interpreters inscribed and framed his literary production as the imperial text of culture and as a model of substantial unity in the midst of a heteroglot and heterogeneous culture. The history of a text, however, involves readers, readings, and "reading formations" (to employ Tony

Bennet's valuable concept); it involves sedimented reading habits and the categories developed by inherited interpretive traditions as well as how "reading formations" represent ways of reading that are culturally determined and that mobilize texts in different ways. Such was El Brocense's reading formation, as a commentator and translator of classical texts, at a time when the borrowed language of mythology and classical antiquity was activated and mobilized to legitimate the unity of the Spanish-Christian-Catholic Empire. This doctrine was shaped at an early stage by its exposure to the philosophical influences of Greek and Latin as well as to Christian (Catholic) dogmas and tended to equate the Word of God with the Logos of revealed divine purpose, from the Conquest of Granada and the "discovery" of America (both in 1492) on.

This organicist ethos, with its mythology of nature (the courtly *locus amoenus*), was maintained as selective representation, precisely by access to writing and reading as means to encode and legitimize authority. The relation between that myth of origin and the present is bridged in the eighteenth century through the power of a more sophisticated science of language. The *Diccionario de autoridades* (1726–1734); Gregorio Mayáns y Siscar's pluridirected endeavor to revitalize the "classics" (Garcilaso, Hurtado de Mendoza, Fray Luis de Granada, Fray Luis de León, Góngora, Lope, the Argensolas, Cervantes, Saavedra Fajardo) in the concerted *Orígenes de la lengua española* (1737); the exiled Jesuit Francisco Javier Lampillas's *Saggio storico-apologetico della Letteratura Spagnola* (1778–1781); and Esteban de Arteaga's *La belleza ideal* (1789) were, with the multiple reeditions, part of a concerted indexing of the past through carefully annotated reeditions of the Hellenistic tradition, the Latin classics, and the "classics" of the Spanish Golden Age (Garcilaso, Cervantes, Quevedo, Fray Luis).[8] Hence the main question about this concerted project is essentially the epistemological question of legitimizing a discourse with a claim to theoretical consistency or truth. It should be noted, for our purpose, that Luzán's poetics develops a systematic structuring of the canons (in Spanish, the Greek etymology of *kanón* as norm, rule is preferred), unfolding a historical continuity and retracing the present as a patient and continuous development. In accordance with this, new disciplinary technology of a systematization of culture in the eighteenth century starts to flourish. The genealogy of the new scientific technology appears in the *Diccionario de autoridades* as the "knowledge and science of letters"; Lampillas stands among the first to give the term *literature* the degree of authority carried in our present use, instead of the classical "letters" (*las buenas letras* or *bellas artes*) or the fifteenth-century Catalonian acceptance of *literatura*, equivalent to the Castilian *letradura* or science of the *letrados*. Arteaga is familiar with the concept, however, which would seem to have been reenacted in Italy through the translation of Johann Bernhard Merian's memoirs on "literary history" to the Berlin Academy (1774, 1776, 1778). Arteaga prefers "imitative arts" and "representative arts," as he constructs his "modern" theoretical and philosophical systematization of literature (150).[9]

As the newly developed science of literary history is institutionalized, the concept of canon is established (in England it dates to David Ruhnken in 1768) and editions are intended to account for certain unlooked-for liabilities and blind spots to pursue a normative understanding. Incompatible projects of interpretation were often normalized (frequently through censorship) to introduce signifying practices into positive (instrumental) terms of self-identical meanings. Such projects, as well as alternative discourses, were referred back to some disorganizing center or thematic point of origin; to the early sixteenth-century list of blind spots—"apocryphal and superstitious" or "vane and without benefit"—were added the negative referents of "libertine," "heterodoxy," "heresy," "pornography."[10] Ignacio de Luzán's *Poética* (1737, 1789) offers a taxonomical catalog of the norms and canons (*reglas y preceptos*) established by the ancients (*antiguos*), based mainly on the authority of Herrera's evaluations. Embedded in Luzán's poetics is the normative, universal reason and the notion that "poetics is one . . . general and common to all nations for all times" ("Una es la poética . . . común y general para todas las naciones y para todos los tiempos" [147]).

The monopoly of instrumental reason over figurative language and fiction involved a sustained and rigorous attention to referential language, an insistence on the "real" (mimesis) against mere "writing" (fiction). This ontology remained largely captive to the same dominant motifs in the interpretive sciences: editing and literary history. By then, the institutional mode of organization had preserved the monologized dominant canons in the closed and structured selective list of literary works that already constituted literature. Luzán brings forth new encodements of the dominant registers, articulating the norms of writing, and the accepted intertextual networks, to stabilize discourse: "All arts need rules and precepts for the perfect construction of their artifacts" ("Todas las artes necesitan de reglas y preceptos para la perfecta construcción de sus artefactos"), writes the censor in the 1737 edition.

As my discussion suggests, to the claims of transcendent universal value instrumental reason adds new social and moral evaluations to its network of intertextuality to reconstitute and reinforce the "high culture" of the educated minority, against the menace of alternative (heterogeneous) discourse. As a further set of questions on "nation," history, and social issues takes on considerable importance, the canons of the mediated past are reenacted through a discourse that legislates a practice. The canon, so zealously guarded by the science of rhetoric and the institutional modes of organizing experience through the mediation of editing as a set of ethical and moral *doxae,* helped maintain the distance between those who govern and those who are governed. The decisive question in this new literary system (its production and its reception) is to differentiate the pattern of repetitions or the event that deflects them into a new course in the general structures of hegemony and the changing relations of dominance.

Notes

1. I particularly address the function and context of editing as an evaluative form of organizing experience. In this sense, there is a difference in the erudite apparatus of editors to establish the "correct" text previous to the episode of Garcilaso in the history of evaluations, mediations, and canon formation. We may also note that what is now privileged is a particular set of functions. In my view, prior to the edition of Garcilaso, the distinction between establishing the vulgata and annotating a text as an interpretive act to exercise a set of beliefs was not functionally raised.

"Power" and "politics" here are used in the sense of the strife to influence the distribution of power and impose a monolithic authority. It seems obvious that there is no one source of power, and there were competing forces in sixteenth-century Spain. It is worthwhile to reexamine Mena's exemplary reading from this perspective. Although it is well known that Nebrija considered him a classic together with Virgil and El Brocense, he argues that Mena was the first to have "represented" Castilian Spanish: "It is very fine for this poet to be held in great esteem, even if he were not as good as he is, because he is the first to have illustrated the Castilian language" ("Es muy bien que este poeta sea tenido en mucha estima, aunque no fuera tan bueno como es, por ser el primero que haya ilustrado la lengua castellana" [Mena]).

2. Frow has lucidly criticized Macherey, and Althusser and Balibar as well as Jameson in regard to the Lacanian imaginary (see specifically 33–40).

3. Todorov refers to the relationships between discursive practices and the structuring of discourse; see also Derrida. Regarding genres and canon formation, see the article by Fowler.

4. The main aporias or deadlocked reasoning came from those humanists, such as Las Casas, who centered on the ultimate paradox of a Christian-humanist empire, the so-called Black Legend. In this line of reasoning, I believe that the heterogeneous (regional) thinking of Cristóbal de Castillejo, for example, should be placed in terms of a resistance to the centralizing force of the humanist-universal *doxa,* especially since preeminent among the themes of that discourse is the nature/ culture opposition, which would theoretically impose such reductive binarism to the regional areas excluded through these value categories. What heterogeneous discourses challenged was the epistemological requirement that permits distinguishing between several qualities of discourse on social issues, and not types of versification, which were adjusted to the new contents. This point is worth developing to rewrite a Hispanic literary history.

5. I am extending Frow's interesting comments on genre. See also Zavala, "Representing."

6. Snell has offered conclusive information to show that the idea of the subject is a relatively late construction.

7. Christopher Caudwell studies the sonnet in relation to economy. See also Zavala, "Burlas," for a reading on the interplay between nature and economy in the seventeenth-century sonnets of Lope, Góngora, and Quevedo.

8. I have previously concerned myself with the reemergence of humanism and Golden Age writers during the eighteenth century as a constitutive part of the process of modernity and rationalization. See especially Zavala, *Clandestinidad,* where I bring forth a whole corpus of previously little-known material. I was unaware then of the intricate process of argumentation of instrumental logic and reasoning, which the present debate on modernism and postmodernism has brought forth.

9. See the letter from Arteaga to Antonio Ponz where he gives important information on Mateo Borsa's opuscule, *Del gusto presente in letteratura italiana* (1785), about which Arteaga himself wrote. In this same letter, he uses with ease the concept "literary history" ("historia literaria"). A detailed theoretical analysis of Arteaga and Lampillas would suggest a rethinking to the specific social and institutional structures of complex social formations.

10. I have dealt with discourse strategies as orientations to specific reading communities in the eighteenth century in *Lecturas* and "Textual Pluralities." Let me note here that within this frame, it would be possible to situate the alternative heterogeneity of Góngora's poetry, so polemical in his time, within my suggested problematization of legitimating a national literature. By the same token, the *doxae* inscribed in the sonnet and its appropriation by dominant (imperial) social forces, make the genre such a polemical tool for women. The seventeenth-century Mexican Sor Juana in particular brings forth the polemical dialogism of this speech genre. This point is worth pursuing.

Works Cited

Althusser, Louis, and Etienne Balibar. *Reading Capital.* Trans. Ben Brewster. London: New Left Books, 1970.

Angenot, Marc. *Glossaire pratique de la critique contemporaine.* Montreal: Hurtubise, 1979.

Arteaga, Esteban de. *Obra completa castellana. La belleza ideal. Escritos menores.* Ed. Miguel Batllori. Madrid: Espasa-Calpe, 1972.

Bakhtin, Mikhail Mikhailovich. *The Dialogic Imagination.* Ed. Michael Holquist. Trans. Michael Holquist and Caryl Emerson. Austin: Univ. of Texas Press, 1981.

Bennet, Tony. "Texts, Readers, Reading Formations." *Bulletin of the Midwest Modern Language Association* 16 (1983): 13–17.

Caudwell, Christopher. *Illusion and Reality: A Study in the Sources of Poetry.* New York: International Publishers, 1967.

Chaunu, Huguette, and Pierre Chaunu. *Seville et l'Atlantique.* Vol. VIII. *Les Structures.* Paris: A. Colin, 1959.

Derrida, Jacques. "The Law of Genre." *Critical Inquiry* 1 (1980): 55–81.

Elliott, John J. *Imperial Spain: 1469–1716.* [1963] London: Penguin, 1976.

Foucault, Michel. *The Archeology of Knowledge and the Discourse on Language.* Trans. A. M. Sheridan Smith. New York: Pantheon, 1972.

Fowler, Alistair. "Genre and the Literary Canon." *New Literary History* 11 (1979): 97–119.

Frow, John. *Marxism and Literary History.* London: Basil Blackwell, 1988.

Gallego Morell, Antonio. *Garcilaso de la Vega y sus comentaristas.* Granada: Univ. de Granada, 1966.

Gil Fernández, Luis. *Panorama social del humanismo español (1500–1800).* Madrid: Alhambra, 1981.

Lida de Malkiel, María Rosa. *Juan de Mena, poeta del Prerrenacimiento español.* Mexico: El Colegio de México, 1950.

Luzán, Ignacio de. *La poética. Reglas de la poesía en general y de sus principales especies.* Ed. Russell P. Sebold. Barcelona: Labor, 1977.

Macherey, Pierre. *Pour une théorie de la production littéraire.* Paris: Maspero, 1966.

Mena, Juan de. *El laberinto de fortuna o Las trescientas.* Ed. José Manuel Blecua. Madrid: Espasa-Calpe, 1968.

Renan, Yael. "Disautomatization and Comic Deviations from Models of Organizing Experience." *Style* 18, 2 (1984): 160–177.

Rico, Francisco. "*Laudes litterarum:* humanismo y dignidad del hombre en la España del Renacimiento." *Homenaje a Julio Caro Baroja.* Madrid: Centro de Investigaciones Sociológicas, 1978. 895–914.

———. *Nebrija frente a los bárbaros: el cánon de gramáticos nefastos en las polémicas del humanismo.* Salamanca: Univ. de Salamanca, 1978.

———. "El destierro del verso agudo. (Con una nota sobre rimas y razones en la poesía del Renacimiento.)" *Homenaje a José Manuel Blecua, ofrecido por sus discípulos, colegas y amigos.* Madrid: Gredos, 1983. 525–551.

Rivers, Elias, ed. *Garcilaso de la Vega: Obras completas.* Madrid: Castalia, 1974.

Rossi, L. E. "I generi letterari e loro leggi scritte nelle letterature classiche." *Bulletin of the Institute of Classical Studies* 18 (1971): 69–94.

Smith, Barbara Herrnstein. "Contingencies of Value." *Critical Inquiry* 10.1 (1983): 1–36.

Snell, B. *Las fuentes del pensamiento europeo*. Madrid: Razón y Fe, 1965.

Todorov, Tzvetan. *Les genres du discours*. Paris: Seuil, 1978.

Voloshinov, V. N. (M. Bakhtin). *Marxism and the Philosophy of Language*. [1929] Trans. Ladislav Matejka and I. R. Titunik. Cambridge: Harvard Univ. Press, 1986.

Wittgenstein, Ludwig. *Tractatus Logico-Philosophicus*. London: Routledge and Kegan Paul, 1922.

Zavala, Iris M. *Clandestinidad y libertinaje erudito en los albores del siglo XVIII*. Barcelona: Ariel, 1978.

——. "Burlas al amor: la poesía amorosa de Góngora, Lope y Quevedo." *Nueva Revista de Filología Hispánica* 29 (1980): 367-403.

——. *Lecturas y lectores del discurso narrativo dieciochesco*. Amsterdam: Rodopi, 1987.

——. "Textual Pluralities: Readings and Readers of Eighteenth-Century Discourse." In *The Institutionalization of Literature in Spain*. Ed. Wlad Godzich and Nicholas Spadaccini. Minneapolis: The Prisma Institute, 1987. 245-265.

——. "Representing the Colonial Subject." In *1492-1992: Re/Discovering Colonial Writing*. Ed. René Jara and Nicholas Spadaccini. Minneapolis: The Prisma Institute, 1989. 33-48.

Zetzel, James E. G. "Re-Creating the Canon: Augustan Poetry and the Alexandrian Past." *Critical Inquiry* 10.1 (1983): 83-106.

Chapter 5
The Politics of Editions
The Case of *Lazarillo de Tormes*

Joseph V. Ricapito

It is a sad destiny that some works of literature will end up in libraries covered by dust and fall into disuse for any variety of reasons: the end of a favorable period; new literary vogues that capture the imagination of the reading public; characters who no longer offer any tangibility with society.[1] This, however, cannot be said of *Lazarillo de Tormes,* which continues to engage the interest of the literary world some four and a half centuries after its initial appearance in 1554.

In the course of this time the work has been printed regularly and has elicited translations in many languages. The literary critic arrives at the conclusion that this book, like *La Celestina* and *Don Quijote,* continues to capture the imagination of scholars and readers. To what does this book owe the positive response of a public that will embrace the idea of yet another edition? The editions themselves appear and reappear; in some cases older editions are forgotten, replaced by newer ones. The question remains as to why *Lazarillo* universally maintains this hold on the public.

I

The future of *Lazarillo* is insured by its vitality and its nature as a literary work linked to an act of literary and social defiance by an author who was most probably a political, religious, and social dissident in his own time and place. The work therefore bears a polemic spark, becoming as it were an object of fear and censure, to such a degree that in 1559 it is placed on the Index, from which there emerges yet another edition, this time one in which the text suffers alterations that make it palatable and acceptable to the status quo. López de Velasco, speaking of *Lazarillo*, says, "It is such a live and proper representation of what it imitates, with such wit and grace, that it . . . deserves to be studied and so it was always agreeable to all" ("Es una representación tan viva y propia de aquello que imita, con tanto donaire y gracia, que en su tanto merece ser estudiado y así fue siempre a todos muy acepto").[2] How strange that this work, whose strength and piquancy are blunted by censorship, should continue in this altered manner and yet in time return to its original form. A further testimony of the work's vitality is seen in the fact that it generated numerous translations.

Focusing on an individual who is a symbol, the work and its intellectual and social ramifications irradiate outward in all directions. Few institutions will remain intact in its progressive march. The first personal involvements of the character reveal the social status of the family, and with it social marginality, a marginalization that will not change as Lazarillo stumbles from one "infamy" to another.[3] Still, Lazarillo and his family, as members of the *popolo minuto*, live in the shadow of a crumbling political and economic edifice, a matter worthy of concern for both the poor and the nobles. This keen focusing endows the work early with its social and political perspective, a detail that could not have been missed by anyone—regardless of social status—who read the work.

The question of marginalization is further reinforced when Lázaro's mother must survive in a situation not wholly accommodating to a widow who has no *rentas* from which to live. In fact, the author contrives to have the mother fall deeper into need by placing her in a *calle sin salida* when she takes up with the moorish Zaide. By any standards of society at that time her situation becomes more fixed in its infamy. The final denouement, the punishment of Zaide, "depresses" the wife even more into poverty and social ignominy.

With Lázaro's involvement with the blindman the author is projecting the status of society and politics by keeping the character fixed at a poverty level, and in this way allusion to the dominant elements of the society are studied indirectly by reflection. Lázaro's activity with the blindman deals with the lower elements of his society. The reflective or allusive powers are also present when we see the characters skirt the edges of their time and place, never rising to any point of prominence or even carrying out any meaningful and socially useful tasks. To readers sensitive to the social issues of the time and to those issues that are directly a product of some of the politics of the Emperor, the characters' wanderings are a thin and transparent cover for a background far more serious and socially implicating than a blind beggar might normally signify.

In the second chapter, religion as a social fact comes forth in the figure of the niggardly priest. Religion is a function of society, an entity for the expression of human sensitivity and spirituality. As a priest, the Cleric of Maqueda shares the stage in a social dialectic. The action is projected toward the reader on two levels: one level is largely symbolic and involves theological symbols, especially focused on the game involving the bread; on a second level the author projects his action on a purely prosaic and everyday communication. In the course of the chapter the reader becomes aware of the bare reality and the sterile lives of the characters. We can picture the avaricious priest in a threadbare cassock consumed by time; a house that is bare except for the rope of onions, the sure signs of the material/moral poverty of the abode. The reader's eyes become focused on the collection shell, rudimentary in its shape, passed from hand to hand, each coin recorded by the cleric's ever vigilant eyes. The Church itself is suggested in its plainness and simplicity as a social fact. Having established the avarice of the priest as the dominant focus of the chapter, an avarice that functions on the lowest level of human contact and intercourse, the author proposes life rather than theology on this level.[4] This precision of the most humble kind is the author's way of sharing with the readers what some of them know as a social datum—a priest whose human values are wretched. This is further intensified when the bread box is introduced. It is an object already broken down and decrepit, itself a metaphor of the disastrous state of the Church. Its rotting self is the most prosaic sign one could imagine. With the bread box the author brings together the prosaic and the divine by having this relic contain the bread.

The rest of the human elements are signs endowed with prosaic reality: the neighbors' imaginary mice and an equally imaginary serpent, the bloody bandages around Lázaro's head from the crushing blow he receives from the head-hunting cleric. All these objects are deliberately removed from any area of abstraction and project a sordid everyday reality; they can only be seen as props for a social polemic, the accoutrements of a Church gone wrong on the most basic level of discourse. Religion as a social fact is distorted in the process.

The process of the banalization of human objects beyond the divine is brought to its zenith in the experiences with the squire in the third chapter. The author constructs him as a collage that is displayed in multiple refractive lights; the treatment of the squire gives way to a consideration of *honra,* and this covers up his most terrible needs; his own words can scarcely conceal his frustrated opportunism to make a success at court, which he does not.

The squire's preoccupation with honor dominates the action. There is nothing religious, philosophical, or abstract about this concept. The concern is stuck to the squire like a Pasquinade. Having this character posture over his honor, an empty honor in this case, makes the squire move about more like a figure of the theater, prancing before a public in his spectacle. He is in effect a public *hazmerreír,* and, with Lazarillo, offers a contrapuntal scenario. Lazarillo indirectly reflects and contrasts the emptiness of his master, who passes in review with the hunger and the false honor showing through the squire's social posturing. The squire's clothing further reveals his threadbare existence as he contrives to pass as a man of parts. Only later will the true barrenness of his physical person be seen when Lazarillo emulates his model.

As intangible as the concept of *honra* is, it becomes alive when coupled with hunger. The hunger brings the theme down to earth where it ceases to be an abstraction. The socialization of honor is carried one step further when the author allusively associates the squire with Judaic life. He is after all from "La costanilla de Valladolid," a well-known Jewish ghetto (Rico 61, n. 89), and thus honor as a concept is reduced to ludicrous conclusions as an excess in the case of someone whose own social reality cannot sustain such a notion. In the final analysis honor is made to seem a joke in the social life of the author and his characters.

At the end of the third chapter, space (which has become a fundamental part of the scenario) is invoked once again as the squire disappears from sight, escaping from one place no doubt to take cover in another, traversing space again on an ever-moving treadmill.

The case of the Friar of Mercy returns to the earlier motif of religion and its representatives as a social fact. In an admittedly brief chapter the author skillfully magnifies the actions of the friar. Space is again used to portray the friar's own movement. His mobility through convents creates the perception of this character as a very busy individual, but a more subtle perception sees him as a pederast. Through the folkloric motif of the "broken-in shoes" the picture of a depraved churchman is created (Sieber 51–52). The brevity of the chapter is deliberate. What else can one say after revealing the friar's vice? In a sixteenth-century social and religious context the author daringly would associate the cloth with homosexuality. This is yet another example of the challenging content of this work.[5]

The fifth chapter returns to the motif of a coherent society already glimpsed in the first and third chapters. The action is concentrated in the heart of a microcosm: people sitting around a church, people playing cards, the town brought together in social contact and communication.[6]

In the first and second chapters, deceptions are predicated on a one-to-one level; in the third and fifth, deception arrives at a much wider audience. Nothing less than a whole society and a whole community is aimed at. In an effort to portray the skill of the pardoner and the bailiff the author of *Lazarillo de Tormes* resorts to the wiles of the institution of the sale of papal bulls. This practice, which attracted the censure of Erasmus and Luther alike, implies an indirect notion of public sales. The possible sale of bulls to an individual is foregone in favor of the selling of them to a collectivity. A series of episodes culminates in the final selling of bulls, described in the way that people rush to obtain them. The Renaissance ushers in the system of money over barter; the basis of medieval trade is lost to an economy of *geld*. The description of the people purchasing the bulls almost leaves the tactile impression of money pressed against the flesh. The successful swindle will allow the pardoner and his confederate to gloat over their skill. They do the extraordinary: they gull not only a whole community but also their own youthful assistant.

Money, *pecunia*, which was introduced in the first chapter when Lázaro exchanged in his cheek one type of coin for the other, reappears in the third chapter when the squire chances upon a *real*, appears again in the fifth chapter with the pardoner, and now reappears in the sixth chapter with the chaplain. We see here another churchman shaped in a social, not a religious, context. The chaplain has set aside his churchly duties and devotes his time to a business enterprise for which he employs Lazarillo. While there is only a brief description of Lázaro's happenings, the chapter rests on a double axis: the chaplain's devotion to money and business interests and Lazarillo's evolution into a social personality cognizant of the fact that society operates on a higher and more sophisticated level than begging or petty theft. The wish for lucre permeates all levels of society, and the clergy is not immune to its temptation. Clergyman and novice businessman, they embrace a goal far more fundamental than God or religion—the love of money and what it can obtain in a society in which gain supersedes spirituality. We can now see how the concern for "sales" in the fifth chapter serves as an introduction to the fuller and more commercialized theme of the sixth chapter.

As Lazarillo learns of the dangers and rigors of life with a bailiff, the fullest treatment of activity in a social and political framework is saved for the last chapter. His occupation as a town crier places Lazarillo perforce in the eye of society. He becomes its spokesman and carries its messages to all corners of Toledo, especially for the sale of wines. Lázaro's odyssey has shifted from the heart of the family to the heart of the city. Demonstrating the kind of parody and satire shown in the case of the squire whose posturing before others only elicits derision and laughter, Lazarillo too will be submitted to a similar treatment; his preening over his civil-service job only calls attention to the fact that he holds a position at the bottom of the social scale. His posturing about "things . . . never heard or seen" ("cosas . . . nunca oídas ni vistas") begins to sound hollow as we come close to the true ironic meaning of the phrase when we realize that the rogue's progress has entailed a passage from humility to social disgrace.[7] In this he echoes the squire's superficial attachment to an equally hollow concept of social honor.

Lazarillo's claims to social honor are belied by the fact that he shares his life and bed with the Archpriest. Lazarillo lives in a world so deceived and deceptive that *he* is now a social joke, a comic figure claiming an honor he does not have.

The final touch of irony is political. The author tells us in the final sentence(s) of the work that this voyage from humble beginnings to social degeneracy occurred during the reign of the Emperor Charles V. This final tag echoes the principal themes of the work: the dialectic of poverty, the corruption of the clergy, and the social consequences thereof. In a relatively short and highly compressed work the whole panorama of a crumbling and morally vacuous society and time is held up for exposure by the author.[8] This fundamental idea is precisely what will ensure the success of the work in centuries to come and in more than a dozen languages: the degeneration of an innocent individual by a society consumed with the wish for honor, survival, and social approval at any cost.

II

As an object of culture an edition is an act of communication: to make available a text to a reading public. It is an indispensable function of literary production in society.[9] The reader goes directly to the source of literature itself. But in this guise, the literary text is a compromised text, the product of an author without mediation, filled with authorial wishes and biases; an editor takes it upon him/herself to interpret the text for a potential reading public that is no less arbitrary than the compromised text of an author.

Editors come armed with predispositions toward particular literary theory, and offer multiple approaches toward literature generally and toward a work in particular. As exercises in literary communication these editions become important media for knowledge, thought, and philosophy. Editions can polemicize with competing literary theories and choose the introduction to carry out the war. I do not refer to personal motives in the preparation of a text, but certainly monetary ones play no small part, especially in the work of an author who may be in particular vogue. Editors themselves are often at the mercy of the whims and unaccountable gestures of series directors and editorial houses.[10] All of these considerations must be made when examining the role of editions in the republic of letters.

Some editions are of course more valuable and more significant than others. The normal progress of knowledge on a given subject causes satisfactory works to be left behind on library shelves. Newer editions purport to be more inclusive and subordinate the previous works to their own critical view. At the same time, the publication of an edition marks its own death at its appearance. My remarks of course take into consideration only the *serious* attempts at editing *Lazarillo*. The number of editions that do not add anything to the knowledge of the work is legion; the stacks of libraries are full of them. They are in the main useless repetitions of better works.

The editions to which I shall refer are more than popular ones. They are indicative of an intention that is communicative as well as polemic and displays an involvement in a politics of contention. Of these editions I shall review a feature that supports my thesis that the success of *Lazarillo* over the centuries lies in the ability of the work to involve a social and political dialectic at its core, and that its satire and criticism is what has prevented it from becoming a sclerotic work in the history of Spanish literature.

In the early modern edition by L. Viardot (1846), two basic characteristics of the work are noted: it is described as a satirical novel and a novel of manners. Luigi Sorrento (1912) believes that the sources of *Lazarillo* are life itself, and even Bonilla y San Martín (1915) displays a similar view when he suggests that the novel reveals a deep understanding of social types. Earlier, Caníbell (1906) suggested that the milieu produced the book.

In a particularly perceptive introduction C. P. Wagner (1917, to the Louis How translation) states that *Lazarillo* made use of the servant for social satire; in effect it was a satire of contemporary life. A similar satire of a religious nature occurs with the sellers of papal bulls (the insight here is more of a social criticism than a religious one). The author, according to Wagner, had a knowledge of the abuses within the Church.

H. J. Chaytor (1922) pointed to the satire of the work and attributes its success to the conditions existing in Spain at the time. The picaresque, according to Chaytor, offers a glimpse of the author's time and country. Chaytor's picture of the work coinvolves the social and historical aspects of the time. He also deals with a concept that is fairly indicative of the prevalent literary view, i.e., the work as a product of the Spanish national character.

Of a similar cast are the ideas of Crofts in his 1924 edition. He doubts whether Protestant readers would have any sympathy for the squire, and indeed believes that this character was a product of the economic problems of the time. According to him, other problems that caused the Spanish decadence were the corruption of the Church, administrative incompetence, and general chaos in industrial life. Crofts also thinks that it was the depiction of this decadence that ensured *Lazarillo* its success in France. Saugrain's 1561 edition, for example, focused on the picture of Spanish life and customs that the book presented.

The view that the picaresque genre (and with it *Lazarillo*) was a product of the social and historical life of Spain in the sixteenth century is voiced by Lorente (1924) and Berkowitz and Wofsy (1927). The dominant note of Berkowitz and Wofsy's perspective of *Lazarillo* highlights the satire of conditions of Spain and focuses precisely on the criticism of individuals, institutions, and society. Palumbo (1928) read *Lazarillo* as the author's satirical attack on a Spain wallowing in the decadence of the sixteenth century. Mazzei (1928) also assumes a marked social approach, viewing Spain and the fallen ideals of the imperial mission; the decadence was also a product of a negative economic situation. As a part of this attack the author, through his work, focuses on the three plagues of Spanish life: beggars, clergy, and nobility. The novel adopts a satirical purpose in its censure of these three orders.

In 1929, Giannini assumes a social historical view in which he believes that *Lazarillo* is a work in which social satire is basic and offers a good picture of sixteenth-century Spain. The reading public, according to him, relished these pictures of Spain. It is not surprising, then, given the various social and economic elements of discontent, that Soviet Russia should be interested in the Spanish classic. Several editions were produced in Russia, and it is reasonable to believe that the Soviets' view of Western decadence found an example in *Lazarillo*.

One of the most widely used editions of *Lazarillo* was the Clásicos Castellanos edition by Cejador y Frauca (1941). This edition, learned in its scope and thrust, may have molded the opinions of more readers than any other edition did. Just as others had done previously, Cejador reads *Lazarillo* as a lively satire of Spanish sixteenth-century life, the author being very much a social critic with shades of Erasmus's satire and criticism.

Luis Jaime Cisneros (1946) bridges the gap between society and literature by interpreting the observation of customs as a literary weapon. Characters in the book are treated with satirical purpose and their depiction was based on live models. This edition sees the novel as born out of the historical and social reality of Alcalá and Salamanca. This is in no way different from the belief of González Palencia (1947) who interprets *Lazarillo* as a satirical novel and novel of manners.

Américo Castro's view of the picaresque, expressed in several essays and in the introduction to the Hesse and Williams edition (1948), on the one hand attempts to qualify the limits of a positivistic, deterministic application of history and society to a literary work of art, and at the same time introduces a new idea that will fix various interpretations of *Lazarillo* and the picaresque for several decades to come: Castro's view that the author was probably a *converso* and the work eminently a literary and artistic expression that surpassed whatever social and historical materials of which it availed itself.

Six years later Allan Holaday (1954) would return to social interpretation by viewing the work as standing before a backdrop of social, economic, and political decadence, and the work records the moral damage caused by various disasters.

Claudio Guillén produced a landmark dissertation (1953) that has become, thanks to its wider availability in a special series, a fundamental piece of picaresque and *Lazarillo* criticism. In his edition (1966), following the steps of Castro, Guillén acknowledges the various incitements that cause the birth of *Lazarillo*, but at the same time he points to the artistic advances that *Lazarillo* had over its own literary and historical precedents.

The 1955 edition of the work by Alfredo Cavaliere is a brilliant philological study, as José Caso González's would be eleven years later. As Foulché-Delbosc had done in 1900, these works attempt to clarify basic questions of manuscripts, which Ricapito also does in 1988 by juxtaposing the three 1554 texts in a tri-interlinear edition. Cavaliere, like Castro before him and Guillén after, accents the passage from history to Art.

Bataillon (1958) sought to understand the work in terms of previous literary traditions, especially medieval *Schwankbuch* tales, and stresses the ironic vision of the work rather than the kind of virulent social criticism that previous and some contemporary editions highlight (although elsewhere he saw the success of the picaresque genre as due to the fact that Spain was *picarisée* from top to bottom). Marañón is another critic who sought strongly to bury the positivist canon of literature as a display of social and historical events. He reacts almost viscerally to depictions of Spain in terms of poverty and decadence; mysticism and the beauty of the ballad tradition are to be stressed over a Spain identified with *pícaros* and other dregs of society.

Harriet de Onís (1959) repeats the earlier view of the picaresque as a bitter social satire, but Martín de Riquer (1959), perhaps influenced by a general trend best articulated by Don Américo, emphasizes that history and reality in the work are not to be interpreted as factual and faithful to a historical situation in Spain in the sixteenth century.

In the following decade de Morelos (1960) and R. O. Jones (1963) repeat the social/historical argument.

Alberto Blecua (1972) acknowledges some social aspects of the time that the work describes, especially some of the problems relating to the clergy. The problem of *amancebamiento* of priests was well known to all, and therefore part of a recognizable social reality.

Ricapito (1976), very much in the tradition of Castro and Guillén, and strongly influenced by Gilman's and Silverman's work on the genre, poses *Lazarillo* as a literary reaction to an intellectual tradition in society and religion by offering the text as an Erasmian document in which the author expresses through the text his own dissatisfactions regarding the reign of Charles V, the presence of poverty, and the failure of a religious spirit to solve problems in Spain in the here-and-now. Castro's view that the work was written by a *converso* occupies an important place in Ricapito's discourse.

In the same decade, editions by Vaíllo (1976) and Piñero Ramírez (1977) include social and historical considerations. Vaíllo sees the *pícaros* as a small part of society; Piñero Ramírez repeats Castro's *converso*-author theory and joins to this Castro's view of the work as a criticism of *honra.*

Félix Carrasco (1982), in an introduction reflecting the concerns of contemporary criticism and literary theory, sees in *Lazarillo* a work that preserved things that clearly reflected features of real life. Carrasco also repeats the *converso*-author theory of Castro.

In 1987, an edition by Francisco Rico that originally appeared in 1967 is reprinted, with an expanded introduction. Rico's principal interest is variously studying, affirming, or denying literary sources. He does acknowledge some "ambiente" in the creation of the work, its realism, and the recognition of the social plague of *bulderos*, but his thrust is mainly literary.

Throughout the introductions of these editions the concern for the presence of history and facets of social life has been expressed in different ways. The blindman represented low-life and mendicancy; the squire, part of the impoverished nobility; the pardoner, a member of a religious order censured for its excesses; and Lazarillo, a representative of the impoverished lower classes. Several critics embrace in varying degrees the point of view that history/society alone does not necessarily explain the birth and development of the picaresque literary phenomena, especially *Lazarillo*. As we have seen, the New Criticism inasmuch as it is found in the work of someone of the authority of Dámaso Alonso shifts the focus of the criticism from the interpretations of history slavishly followed to a reading of the artistry that went into the work.

Another critical position that rejects the historical, deterministic position but cannot completely embrace the textual formalism of the New Criticism identifies *Lazarillo* only partially with a historical and social reality. Perhaps the best presentation of this view is seen in Alberto Del Monte's editions (1957, 1960, 1965). These same ideas are found in his excellent *Itinerario . . .* (1957). Without ignoring the artistic achievements of the work, Del Monte stresses social and historical concerns and links them with ethical concerns that the work expresses. Américo Castro's writing attempts to break the hold of a pure historicist reading, yet Castro refuses to ignore how a concept as important and rigid as that of *honra* molded and crafted literary realities in the *Lazarillo* and the theater of the seventeenth century. When he hypothesized that the author of such a work of "attack" must have been a *converso*, he was postulating the primacy of life over letters. Castro must be credited with two things: destroying the myth of the "España harapienta" as the *only* Spain, and opening up new vistas of historical interpretation that were legitimately founded yet did not obscure the meaning of *Lazarillo* as an important work of literary art. Marañón, who was offended by the effect that a nonqualified view of history had in creating a negative mind-set toward Spain, certainly shared Castro's sensitivities, as did Guillén who did not reject history and social life completely in favor of Art.

If I focus on the social and historical dimension of *Lazarillo* in its criticism it is because I think that this feature of the work is precisely what has piqued the curiosity of the public and ensured *Lazarillo* its durability as a text. In the many editions that I have consulted discussions of the validity and the pros and cons of the literary incitation are certainly present. In some cases, and the recent edition of F. Rico (1987) is an illustration, greater emphasis is placed on the literary than on the social. I do not wish to imply or state that there was not a tradition of literary intertextuality associated with *Lazarillo,* but the person who reads the work is less likely to be spiritually and emotionally involved with the fact that *Baldus* was an influence on *Lazarillo.* Of greater interest, I believe, is that in *Lazarillo* one reads about an individual who belongs to a metaeconomy of poverty, and as such touches upon a vast mass of humanity in every culture. This same individual must resort to numerous tricks in order to survive; his ingenuity therefore merely intensifies the source of hunger from which it derives—that the clergy, which occupies a notable position in Lazarillo's society, is really another antagonist in its blindness, corruption, and immorality. This work uncovers the polemic between the individual and the structures of power and authority (Charles V and the clergy), and in a manner in which language is arranged in a way that makes the process attractive as well as sympathetic. Were this not so in the case of *Lazarillo* the book would be languishing in libraries much as a work like *Baldus,* which is of literary historical interest only to specialists. *Lazarillo* boasts translations in more than a dozen languages and in editions aimed at authoritative specialists as well as children. This cannot be said of many other works, and this detail, which may seem trivial, is another indicator of the work's potential and realized appeal. Like *Don Quijote,* which possesses such a contagious inner world, *Lazarillo*'s relationship with a reader is entirely centripetal. The questioning of centralized authority is a basic part of world culture, both spiritually and politically, and this is one of the attractive features of the work.

A distinctive feature of *Lazarillo de Tormes* is the fact that the author, who obviously belonged to the educated class of his time, turns his back on the values of his own class by caricaturing such values as honor (as in the case of the squire), not to mention his rejection of the official Church in favor of ideas and values expressed and supported by a dissident faction at court and at the universities. This embrace with Erasmian thought, in the light of the ever vigilant enemies of Erasmus, can only be looked upon as subversive and even in a social way as revolutionary.

The author's framing of his story within the failure of Charles's imperial mission would also make him an enemy of the official politics of the governing regime. Louis Althusser defines the ideology of the ruling class as the "Ideological State Apparatuses" (*Essays* 17). The author of *Lazarillo* unquestionably has emerged from this dominant ruling class. Yet, one must acknowledge that, in its social and political contour, the Church was part and parcel of a statecraft. Althusser says:

> In the pre-capitalist historical period which I have examined broadly, it is absolutely clear that *there was one dominant Ideological State Apparatus, the church,* which concentrated within it not only religious functions but also educational ones and a large portion of the functions of communications and culture. It is no accident that all ideological struggle, from the sixteenth to the eighteenth century, starting with the first shocks of the Reformation, was *concentrated* in an anti-clerical and anti-religious struggle; rather this is the function precisely of the dominant position of the religious ideological state apparatus. (*Essays* 25; emphasis in the original)

For this reason the satire and attack on the clergy in *Lazarillo* does not belong to the order of medieval jestbooks and tales as Marcel Bataillon would have us believe, but to part of the author's critical focus on his government and its attendant values.[11] This is perfectly applicable to the world of *Lazarillo*. Within the eighteenth-century extension of his point, Althusser also focuses upon priests in a way that would be perfectly applicable to their role in *Lazarillo* and in sixteenth-century Spain, as I suspect the author intended.[12] If the reader keeps in mind the workings of the pardoner and his confederate, Althusser's further observation allows a better understanding of what the author of *Lazarillo* may have had in mind when he created the episode. Althusser states:

> There is therefore a cause for the imaginary transposition of the real conditions of existence: that cause is the existence of a small number of cynical men who base their domination and exploitation of the "people" on a falsified representation of the world which they have imagined in order to enslave other minds by dominating their imaginations. (*Essays* 37)

There is yet another important reason for the continued popularity of and interest in *Lazarillo*. The eighteenth and nineteenth centuries mark the rise of revolutions in Western Europe and North and South America. France, Italy, Spain, and Germany change the course of their political systems, and these political systems become populist republics and constitutional monarchies. In several of these countries the original poor and downtrodden rise up against the governments of aristocratic despots. Lazarillo cannot be cut away from his popular origins. He symbolizes the culture of poverty and the struggle to survive, often at the expense of one's dignity and honor. Althusser views this period as follows:

> Civil wars, the religious revolution of the Reformation, wars of religion, the transformation of the traditional structure of the State, *the rise of commoners*, the humbling of the great—these upheavals, whose echo can be heard in all the works of the period, gave the material of the scandalous tales brought back from across the seas the contagious dignity of facts real and full of meaning. What had previously been themes for compilation, extravaganzas to appease the passions of the erudite, became a kind of mirror for the contemporary unease and the fantastic echo of this world in crisis. . . . (*Politics*; 19 emphasis added)

Lazarillo crystalizes the conflict of the individual caught in a series of frustrated attempts to survive in a difficult and harsh world. He is systematically exploited by one master after another, and in spite of his attempts to raise himself above the difficulties of his life, in the end he does not succeed. Readers have always had a sympathy for Lazarillo, even if for the wrong reasons. This sympathy has attracted readers of all kinds and ages, for political as well as nonpolitical reasons, but basically the picture of Lazarillo that is retained is one of exploitation. The nineteenth century, with its industrial expansion and the exploitation of children in factories and sweatshops (which eventually called forth protective legislation in England, the United States, and other countries), could further understand and sympathize with a child or young person who is largely unprotected from the vanity, greed, and avarice of others, and whose innocence is distorted and perverted in the process, creating at the end an adult of dubious moral worth.

Even Third World movements, which bear the scars of exploitation on different levels, could also understand and sympathize with the satire and criticism of the author of *Lazarillo* as the work focused on the orphaned child being awakened to the cruel reality of his unprotected helplessness. In effect, the political and economic crises and situations from the sixteenth to the twentieth centuries have prepared the stage for a steady acceptance of a character who symbolized a personal as well as national crisis. Lazarillo is a character for all times and all places. The ready acceptance of such a character may explain the politics of editing *Lazarillo de Tormes.*

Notes

1. I assume Ferreras's point of view regarding the relations of literature and the society from which it emerges: "A literary work exists only if it finds itself in a relation of production or consumption of reading, of genesis or function; however, outside of these two moments, which are two processes, the text or the work, so disrelated, does not exactly exist" ("Una obra literaria, un texto, sólo existe o está, si se encuentra en relación de producción o de consumo, de lectura, de génesis o de función, pero fuera de estos dos momentos, que son dos procesos, el texto, o la obra, así desrelacionada, no existe exactamente" [9]). I accept the idea of the link between society, history, ambient, and the literary work. Jameson quotes Plekhanov on the subject who says: "'The characteristics of the artistic production of a given period stand in the closest causal relationship to the social mentality expressed in it. The social mentality of an age is however always conditioned by that age's social relations. This is nowhere quite as evident as in the history of art and literature . . .'" (Introduction to Arvon, x). Jameson also quotes Lucien Goldmann, who focuses on this problem in the following way: "'The writer of genius seems to us to be the one who realizes a synthesis, whose work is *at one and the same time* the most immediate and the most philosophically aware, for *his sensibility*

coincides with the ensemble of the process and of the historical evolution; the genius is he who, in order to speak about his own most concrete and immediate problems, implicitly raises the most general problems of his age and of his culture, and for whom, inversely, all the *essential problems* of his time are not mere intellectualizations or abstract convictions but realities which are manifested in living and immediate fashion in his very feelings and intuitions'" (xix; emphasis in the original). Jameson describes the problem as follows: "It is, however, the very essence of dialectical thinking that we do not have to do with some static logical system, in which abstract positions can be worked out in the void with some kind of finality, but rather with a doctrine of the concrete, for which each problem must be re-evaluated in the light of the unique historical situation in which it arises" (xiv-xv). Of particular importance to my approach are the observations of J. J. McGann. He says: "What is especially important for us to see about the critical edition is its aspiration to transcend the historical exigencies to which all texts are subject. A critical edition is a kind of text that does not seek to reproduce a particular past text, but rather to reconstitute for the reader, in a single text, the entire history of the work as it has emerged into the present. To the scholar's eye, the critical edition is the still point in the turning world of texts, a text which would arrest, and even reverse, the processes of textual change and corruption . . ." (93). Also in his conclusions he states: "Clearing ancient texts of their accumulated errors was an operation which required at once great technical skill and purpose, as well as a deep and humane sympathy for the work. Both the material form of the work and its aesthetic force and meaning developed as a function of its embedded *social and cultural nature.* To understand and appreciate Homer, or to edit his work, required a study of both with as full a sympathetic consciousness of the social context as it was possible to gain: because authors, their works, and their texts were not isolate phenomena. All were a part of a continuing process, a changing and sometimes even a developing history of human events and purposes" (118-119; emphasis added). The interested reader should also consult the following essay, which offers valuable insights of both a theoretical and practical nature on editing texts: "Observaciones provisionales sobre la edición y anotación de textos del siglo de oro," by J. Cañedo and I. Arellano, in the work that they jointly edit, *Edición y anotación de textos del siglo de oro.*

2. The *Lazarillo* is so referred to in the *Lazarillo castigado* (1573) and is cited in the edition of Félix Carrasco (18).

3. Lazarillo's difficulties, and those of his mother, are basically economic in nature. Arvon notes: "We know that from the Marxist point of view the basic structures of his life, which is regarded as the totality of human relations, depend upon economics, a term that embraces all man's efforts to master and exploit nature. There is a fundamental parallelism between this underlying economic structure and the various ideologies, be they political, religious, artistic, or philosophical; in principle, any given infrastructure will have a corresponding superstructure with the same characteristics. Hence the dominant ideas of each historical period must always be interpreted as the ideas of a class that a certain economic system has made the predominant power" (24-25).

4. In support of the "intentionality" of an author, Macherey quotes Baudelaire: "'Throughout the entire composition there should not be allowed a single phrase which is not also an intention, nothing which does not contribute, directly or

indirectly, to the premeditated design.' The poet displays his method of work, emphasizing their intermediary and subordinate function, their role in the real purpose of the narrative. As merely the product of a technical secret, the work is by no means what it appears; it lurks, deceptively, *behind* its real meaning" (22; emphasis in the original). Elsewhere on this same subject Macherey says: "In reply to the first we might say that the power of the narrative is the product of an intention, a decision, a will. It was the author who issued his decree: he allowed the protagonist, and subsequently the reader, to climb over the wall. The unexpected is the very token of the creative authorial presence. The finished text is the product of a series of choices to which the reader submits, as a spectator rather than a participant, receiving from on high" (47–48). I wish to underscore that the narrative presentation is eminently a product of a severe intentionality, whose purpose is to study critically the predominant ideology of the era of Charles V through the adventures of Lazarillo.

    5. Macherey brings up the topic of "silences" in a text. He states: "The speech of the book comes from a certain silence, a matter which it endows with form, a ground on which it traces a figure. Thus, the book is not self-sufficient; it is necessarily accompanied by a *certain absence*, without which it would not exist. A knowledge of the book must include a consideration of this absence" (85; emphasis in the original) and "can we make this silence speak? What is the unspoken saying? What does it mean? To what extent is dissimulation a way of speaking? Can something that had hidden *itself* be recalled to our presence? Silence as the source of expression. Is what I am really saying what I am not saying? Hence the main risk run by those who would say everything. After all, perhaps the work is not hiding what it does not say; this is simply *missing*" (86; emphasis in the original). I believe that Lazarillo's silence on the subject is far more damning than any further narrative, and I find Macherey's idea here very perceptive.

    6. Although Althusser is speaking about an eighteenth-century situation, he focuses on a facet of priests and the Church that is particularly applicable to the *Lazarillo*: "The first answer (that of the eighteenth century) proposes a simple solution: Priests or Despots are responsible. They 'forged' the Beautiful Lies so that, in the belief that they were obeying God, men would in fact obey the Priests and Despots, who are usually in alliance in their imposture, the Priests acting in the interests of the Despots or *vice versa,* according to the political positions of the 'theoreticians' concerned. There is therefore a cause for the imaginary transposition of the real conditions of existence: that cause is the existence of a small number of cynical men who base their domination and exploitation of the 'people' on a falsified representation of the world which they have imagined in order to enslave other minds by dominating their imaginations" (*Essays* 37).

    7. Macherey perceptively studies the play between beginnings and endings, and how they act upon each other. These ideas are very applicable to the *Lazarillo,* which has a structure that begins, so to speak, with the end (see his *A Theory of Literary Production*).

    8. Arvon points to the complex relationship between an author and his or her class and time, especially if the author belongs to a class that is politically and economically responsible for the problems that he or she is highlighting. Arvon says: "Literature, however, escapes the limitations of this false consciousness. Great works are never cast in the partisan mold of a single class; they express the rela-

tionships of various classes within society as a whole, enabling their authors to rise above their class biases, in a manner of speaking. Thus a writer may very well prove to be a political conservative as an individual, and the author of a progressive work as an artist. As a man, he belongs entirely to his class, whose ideology he shares completely, *whereas as an artist or a writer who has become aware of the dialectic of history, he brings to light the objective elements, the real dynamic forces underlying social evolution*" (32–33; emphasis added). Speaking of editing the works of Keats, McGann makes an astute observation: "... since the authority for the value of literary productions does not rest in the author's hands alone. Authority is a social nexus, not a personal possession; and if the authority for specific literary works is initiated anew for each new work by some specific artist, its initiation takes place in a necessary and integral historical environment of great complexity. Most immediately—and this is what concerns us here—it takes place within the conventions and enabling limits that are accepted by the prevailing institutions of literary production—conventions and limits which exist for the purpose of generating and supporting literary production. In all of these periods those institutions adapt to the special needs of individuals, including the needs of authors (some of whom are more comfortable with the institutions than others). But whatever special arrangements are made, the essential fact remains: literary works are not produced without arrangements of some sort" (48).

9. On the question of this phase of literary production see Ferreras. See also McGann, 42–43.

10. A good example of this is unfortunately a personal one and deals with Ediciones Cátedra. My edition of *Lazarillo de Tormes* went through more than twelve editions, which attested to its commercial and intellectual success. Yet Cátedra replaced it with Francisco Rico's reedited *Lazarillo*. This strange policy was also applied to the very fine and successful editions of *Guzmán de Alfarache* by Benito Brancaforte and *La Celestina* by Bruno Damiani.

11. Althusser further states: "The foremost objective and achievement of the French Revolution was not just to transfer State power from the feudal aristocracy to the merchant-capitalist bourgeoisie—to break part of the former repressive State apparatus and replace it with a new one (e.g., the national popular Army), but also to attack the number-one Ideological State Apparatus: the church" (*Essays* 25–26).

12. See also this chapter's note 6 concerning priests.

Works Cited

Althusser, L. *Politics and History: Montesquieu, Rousseau, Marx*. London: Verso, 1982.

———. *Essays in Ideology*. London: Verso, 1984.

Anonymous. *La vida de Lazarillo de Tormes.* . . . Ed. R. Foulché-Delbosc. Barcelona: L'Avenç, 1900.

———. *Vida del Lazarillo de Tormes*. Ed. Eudaldo Canibel. "Joyas Literarias" de la Bibliografiá Española, I. N. p., 1906.

———. *La vida de Lazarillo de Tormes.* . . . Ed. L. Sorrento. Strasbourg: Heitz/ New York: Stechert, 1912.

———. *La vida de Lazarillo de Tormes.* . . . Ed. A. Bonilla y San Martín. Madrid: Ruiz, 1915.

————. *The Life of Lazarillo de Tormes.*... Intro. C. P. Wagner. Trans. L. How. New York: Kennedy, 1917.

————. *La vida de Lazarillo de Tormes.*... Ed. H. J. Chaytor. Manchester: Manchester Univ. Press, 1922.

————. *The Pleasant Historie of Lazarillo de Tormes.* Ed. J. E. V. Crofts. Oxford: Blackwell, 1924.

————. *Lazarillo de Tormes.*... Ed. M. J. Lorente. Boston: Luce, 1924.

————. *La vida de Lazarillo de Tormes.*... Ed. A. de Olea. Munich: Hueber, 1925.

————. *La vida de Lazarillo de Tormes.*... Ed. H. C. Berkowitz and S. A. Wofsy. Richmond, Va.: Johnson, 1927.

————. *Lazarillo de Tormes.* Ed. P. Mazzei. Milan: Signorelli, 1928.

————. *Lazarillo de Tormes.*... Ed. C. Palumbo. Palermo: Trimarchi, 1928.

————. *La Storia di Lazzarino di Tormes.* Ed. A. Giannini. Rome: Formaggini, 1929.

————. *La vida de Lazarillo de Tormes.*... Ed. J. Cejador y Frauca. Madrid: Espasa-Calpe, 1941. [Clásicos Castellanos.]

————. *La vida de Lazarillo de Tormes.*... Ed. L. J. Cisneros. Buenos Aires: Kier, 1946.

————. *Vida de Lazarillo de Tormes.* Ed. A. González Palencia. Zaragoza: Ebro, 1947.

————. *La vida de Lazarillo de Tormes.*... Ed. A. Castro. Intro. E. Hesse and H. Williams. Madison: Univ. of Wisconsin Press, 1948.

————. *The Life of Lazarillo de Tormes.*... Intro. A. G. Holaday. Trans. J. G. Markley. New York: Liberal Arts, 1954.

————. *La vida de Lazarillo de Tormes.*... Ed. A. Cavaliere. Naples: Giannini, 1955.

————. *La vie de Lazarillo de Tormes (La vida de Lazarillo de Tormes).* Trans. and Intro. by M. Bataillon. Ed. A. Morel-Fatio. Paris: Aubier, 1958.

————. *Lazarillo de Tormes.* Ed. G. Marañón. Madrid: Espasa-Calpe, 1958.

————. *The Life of Lazarillo de Tormes.*... Ed. H. de Onís. Great Neck, N.Y.: Barron's, 1959.

————. *Lazarillo de Tormes.* Ed. A. Del Monte. Naples: Pironti, 1960.

————. *The Life of Lazarillo de Tormes.*... Intro. L. de Morelos. Trans. W. S. Merwin. New York: Doubleday, 1960.

————. *La vida de Lazarillo de Tormes.*... Ed. R. O. Jones. Manchester: Univ. Press, 1963.

————. *Lazarillo de Tormes.*... Ed. C. Guillén. New York: Dell, 1966.

————. *La vida de Lazarillo de Tormes.*... Ed. J. Caso González. Madrid: Anejos del *Boletín de la Real Academia Española,* anejo XVII, 1967.

————. *La vida de Lazarillo de Tormes.*... Ed. Alberto Blecua. Madrid: Castalia, 1972.

————. *La vida de Lazarillo de Tormes.*... Ed. J. V. Ricapito. Madrid: Cátedra, 1976.

————. *La vida de Lazarillo de Tormes.*... Ed. C. Vaíllo. Tarragona: Arbolí, 1976.

————. *Lazarillo de Tormes.*... Ed. P. M. Piñero Ramírez. Madrid: Nacional, 1977.

————. *La vida de Lazarillo de Tormes.*... Ed. F. Carrasco. Madrid: Sociedad General Española de Librería, 1982.

————. *La vida de Lazarillo de Tormes.*... Ed. F. Rico. Madrid: Cátedra, 1987.

————. *Tri-Interlinear Edition of Lazarillo de Tormes*. . . . Ed. J. V. Ricapito. Madison, Wis.: Hispanic Seminary of Medieval Studies, 1988.

Arvon, H. *Marxist Esthetics*. Trans. Helen R. Lane, with an introduction by Frederic Jameson. Ithaca: Cornell Univ. Press, 1973.

Cañedo, J., and I. Arellano, eds. "Observaciones provisionales sobre la edición y anotación de textos del Siglo de Oro." *Edición y anotación de textos del Siglo de Oro*. (Anejos de Rilce, num. 4, Univ. de Navarra, Institución Príncipe de Viana.) Pamplona: Univ. de Navarra, 1986. 10-13.

Del Monte, A. *Il romanzo picaresco*. Naples: E.S.I., 1957.

————. *Narratori Picareschi Spagnuoli del Cinque e Seicento (Prima Parte)*. 2 vols. Milan: Vallardi, 1965.

————. *Itinerario del romanzo picaresco spagnuolo*. Florence: Sansoni, 1957. [Spanish trans. *Itinerario de la novela picaresca española*. Barcelona: Lumen, 1971]

Ferreras, Juan Ignacio. *Fundamentos de sociología de la literatura*. Madrid: Cátedra, 1980.

Gilman, Stephen. "The Death of *Lazarillo de Tormes*." *PMLA* 81(1966): 149-166.

Guillén, C. *The Anatomies of Roguery*. Diss., Harvard Univ. 1953. Rpt.

Macherey, P. *A Theory of Literary Production*. Trans. G. Wall. London: Routledge and Kegan Paul, 1978.

McGann, J. J. *A Critique of Modern Textual Criticism*. Chicago: Univ. of Chicago Press, 1983.

Rico, F. *La novela picaresca española, I*. Barcelona: Planeta, 1967.

Riquer, M. de. *La Celestina y Lazarillos*. Barcelona: Vergara, 1959.

Sieber, Harry. *Language and Society in* La vida de Lazarillo de Tormes. Baltimore: Johns Hopkins Univ. Press, 1978.

Silverman, Joseph H. Review of *La vie de Lazarillo de Tormes*, ed. Marcel Bataillon. *Romance Philology* 15(1961): 88-94.

Viardot, L. *Histoire de Gil Blas*. . . . Paris: Dubochet le Chevalier, 1846.

Chapter 6
Editing Theater
A Strategy for Reading, an Essay about Dramaturgy

Evangelina Rodríguez

(*translated by Laura Giefer*)

Within the concept of writing as a creative process, in the beginning was the *text*. The text, or creation, is offered as the object of another *text* (gloss, commentary, or exegesis), and both develop a series of operations that constitute the noble tradition of textual criticism. As defined by Alfonso de Palencia in 1491, "poesia est poetarum ars et *textus omnis* eorum": art and science meet at the point of origin for the production of meaning.[1] Now that I am asked to reflect upon my experience in editing the theater of Calderón, I find it inspiring to take as a referent an author who, as his most prestigious critics have commented, wrote without preliminary drafts and had the sagacity to define (in the comedia *No hay cosa como callar* [*There's Nothing Like Keeping Quiet*]) feminine beauty as "an impression without errata and a transference without emendation" (Ed. Valbuena Briones 115, lines 69–70).[2] Surely Calderón understood that the only possibility of adapting literature to the scientific method was through a philological operation. By philology is meant a search for a method that permits us to eliminate, as far as possible, what is subjective in the study of the text (Blecua 9), in the processes used for restoring it to its original state, in dating and deciphering it, and in formulating variations and creating a referential and critical apparatus that guarantees its reading and its authenticity (Greimas and Courtes 1786). Moreover, philology must begin to look outside the text, evaluating it within its complex cultural, historical, pedagogical, and formal reality, a process that is necessarily interdisciplinary and inescapably linked to literary theory.[3]

Philological work would thus guarantee an objective approach to an author, to his/her way of knowing, to his/her tradition, and to the certain utility of his/her text. Such are the exigencies of the humanist Alonso de Madrigal, preceding the unilateral and dogmatic orthodoxy later applied by the most celebrated schools of textual criticism. We cite as examples the school of thought of Karl Lachmann and Henri Quentin, which focused on the classification of materials according to the rule of *recensione sine interpretacione et possumus et debemus*, or that of Joseph Bédier who applied an almost totally subjective model. In some way, the (simplistic and erroneous) adscription of the problem of the editing of texts to a positivist method is justified in this aberrant dichotomy. Furthermore, one must recognize that until very recently the point of departure for the treatment of texts in Spanish criticism has been these two reverential fears which, in their time, brought about the methodological syncretism of the Center for Historical Studies. The Spanish philological tradition, in a perpetual reaction against the erudition of Marcelino Menéndez Pelayo, was to adopt as law two key stages in research: restoring texts to their pristine state and understanding them within the cultural environment in which they were produced (Portoles 107–108). The *historical* reading presupposed by this attitude was to advance a wager on the future as it has nourished, consciously or unconsciously, the method by which present-day researchers have approached classical texts.[4] Immersion in meaning and history, however, has not resolved the theoretical contradictions that are often formulated by editors of classical texts (or, even worse, that sometimes are not formulated), contradictions between the so-called *ecdotica* (a method that attempts a scrupulous depuration of original texts) and the *hermeneutic* (the interpretive apparatus and consequent ideological positioning of the editor in and around the text).

Personally, I have always resorted to the etymological sense of a web whose knots and interwoven threads are an interpretation.

As Jan Frappier points out, in the interpreter's adventure, philology is the discipline and/or method that puts limits on imagination and fantasy but also supports the right to conjecture and deduction (373–441). Achieving the equivalence of a philological and hermeneutic *tejne* is, therefore, the first contradiction left unresolved by the editing of Golden Age classics (and clearly, I am now speaking from concrete experience), regardless of the fact that V. Branca and Jean Starobinski were, in 1977, already betting on it in their work *La filologia e la critica letteraria.*[5] The second contradiction emerges when the apparent security of method and rules crumbles in the face of a text's unique, individual, unrepeatable condition, which is studied in each of its diverse copies or printings, almost like eternally new epiphanic manifestations of a single work. As Alberto Blecua has said, textual criticism is exercised on a concrete text that has been composed and transmitted during specific historical circumstances which are, as such, never identical (12). So then, if scientific certainty is affirmed by the repetition or frequency of a fact, what is to be done when it is observed that classical texts as objects are seldom identical, even when dealing with the genealogy of the same work?

When theatrical texts are discussed, the application of ecdotic norm (the search for a prudently stable original) is revealed as another contradiction (and this time especially significant) for the investigator. A few years ago, while studying *El fuego de la riqueza o destrucción de Sagunto* (*The Fire of Wealth or the Destruction of Sagunto*) by Manuel Vidal y Salvador, I explicitly expressed my distrust of the concrete and finite classification of this dramatic work ("Pertinencia" 321+). This text of limited aesthetic importance, by a secondary author from the late Baroque period, revealed itself as an interesting symptom of the principal problems of editing manuscripts and theatrical works in the seventeenth century: the work is known because of a manuscript copy preserved in the Municipal Archives of Madrid (thanks to Pedro Antonio Espinosa),[6] dated June 13, 1690, and contains obvious modifications, suppressions, and observations (annotations and erasures in the text, for example, in order to reduce the number of lines or the distribution of characters) of another editor (Antonio Eusebio Laplana),[7] for a different scenic presentation, possibly dated June, 1692, in Valencia. The tangible observation of a text clearly manipulated for successive performance persuaded me to think that the result of a search for a specific characteristic of the theatrical text would have to be its permanent status as provisional. One might consider, therefore, the arrogance of taking on the challenge of producing a critical annotated edition with its pertinent variants, when perhaps the most truthful process (to satisfy the punctilious heirs of Quentin) would involve authenticating those unique and provisory phases of theatrical texts through a paleographic edition, if not simply a facsimile.

Yet, the experience of editing Calderón has convinced me that the very process of textual depuration is an interpretation and that the undervaluing of an editor's alleged neutrality in this process is the best guarantee of a suture between history and meaning in this erudite operation.[8] To use a more theoretical language, one might say that if textual criticism and the labor of critical editing cannot escape the cold objectivity of a semiotic analysis, neither can they avoid suicide in the particular and sensible history of the text, of the editor, and of the reader.

Studying Calderón de la Barca within this context cannot fail to be a challenge for the scholar. Because we lack a complete critical revision of his works, a statistical and quantitative systematization has been attempted, based upon a collection of *Obras Completas* (Complete works), of doubtful reliability. I am referring to Hans Flasche's *Concordances,* based on Antonio Valbuena Prat's edition.[9] Taking rigorous steps for the purpose of reconstructing the playwright's originals can be disappointing for various reasons. To begin with, there was a virtual absence of signed manuscripts, a common feature among the most important authors since, according to the experts, the special interest awakened by the new comedy *(comedia nueva)* among readers consolidated its circulation through print, to the detriment of the manuscript form, which was reserved for the actors' copies.[10] Second, it was impossible to ensure the absolute identity of the eventual variations of any one edition; once detected, certain errata could be corrected, while for economic reasons they were preserved in already published folios.[11] A third reason is the frequency of falsified editions or *contrafacta* which, exploiting the success of the plays, were reproduced with publishers' imprints and different dates (see Moll). Finally, one should remember the extreme difficulty that playwrights faced in controlling printed editions, since commercial procedures (i.e., the collections of *Partes* were usually sold separately) facilitated alterations or editions by authors and actors. A case in point would be the editions produced after Calderón's death by friends such as Don Juan de Vera Tassis. With exceptional critical sensibility, Miguel de Toro y Gisbert, and, more recently, Angel Valbuena Briones point to the editorial line going through Vera Tassis—Apontes—Hartzenbusch as decidedly incorrect in many cases. All of this invites an exhaustive study, beginning with a healthy skepticism, of printed versions and manuscripts, including the apparently innocuous ones, in order to produce a scrupulous compendium of variations.

Naturally, an encyclopedic method of classifying them is insufficient: choice will be inevitable. Hence, the assumption that the function of the editor of classical theatrical texts becomes a type of protodramaturgy, as if it were the first moment in which the text (a sketch for live theater) gathers interpretive energy that will transform it into action.

When, along with Antonio Tordera, I undertook the task of editing the short Calderonian plays (*Entremeses . . .*), some of these problems became evident. In the first place, editing the texts of the interludes (in the demanding tradition of popular practical theater, which is very close to the methods of improvisation and the free script techniques of the *lazzi* in the *commedia dell'arte*) reveals the concept of the original text as a dynamic, unstable, and enormously frail nucleus. As Elisa Ruiz has suggested:

> The original is not a perfectly complete and static work, but an essentially dynamic product. In reality, we are dealing with a complex process which is initiated by an internal discourse or a manifestation of an endophasic language. It is later exteriorized by means of an initial redaction . . . and eventually undergoes a fairly long series of revisions. . . . Frequently, only copies of copies are preserved, and furthermore, the texts are usually authentic works of marquetry. (72–73)

Since, in principle, the historical redefinition of the genre was more urgent for us than the neopositivist and late philological task of indisputably affirming authorship, Antonio Tordera and I decided to establish a corpus of twenty-four dramatic works whose uncertain state was quickly highlighted by other researchers (see articles by Rull, Granja, and Lobato). The corpus of Calderón's *opera minora* has shown itself to be as difficult to determine as that minor genre in general. Unlike other Baroque dramatic works, it is defined through manuscripts both before and after 1640, when printed collections of these short plays began to proliferate, which is in itself a highly interesting phenomenon of the sociology of literature. The need for companies to possess an ample and interchangeable repertoire of works belonging to this genre promoted the existence of manuscripts that, on occasion, differed from the editions because they were probably handled by actors. The most notorious case might be that of manuscript 15197 of the National Library of Madrid, handwritten by the author Matías de Castro,[12] *Entremés del sacristán mujer, nuebo de don Pedro Calderón, escribiose para María López (The Interlude of the Sacristan Woman, a new [play] by don Pedro Calderón, written for María López.)*[13] The interlude appears to have been produced before 1651, the date of actress María López's death. In contrast to the printed version in the collection *Laurel de entremeses (Laurel of Interludes)* (Zaragoza, 1660), the manuscript offers greater accuracy in the choreographic stage directions and certain burlesque additions, to which we will return later. Other works, such as the masquerades *La garapiña (The Sugar Coating)* and *Los guisados (The Stews)*, were circulated in the seventeenth century in purely written form, while manuscripts like that of the interlude *La rabia* (manuscript 15196 of the National Library of Madrid) offer not only already customary characteristics such as deletions indicated by a bracketing of the last twenty-five lines (let us keep in mind that the closing music extended the interlude substantially and made necessary a considerable expansion of the cast of actors), but also indications that the manuscript was handled by the lawyer Jerónimo de Peñarroja, and was his own copy, or at least the one he used in his role as intermediary between the company's actors and the producer from whom they sought contracts. On the back of page six of the manuscript, in different handwriting, appears: "Licentiate Don Jerónimo de Peñarroja: I have seen the interlude and it does not seem bad to me; those gentlemen are the ones who must be happy with it, for I have nothing to say on the matter" ("Señor Licenciado D. Jerónimo de peñarroja; e bisto este entremes y no me parece mal, esos señores son los que han de contentarse que yo en eso no supongo"). This fact once again points out the multifaceted character of the manuscripts of plays and demonstrates to what degree it is urgent to review them in order to deal with the concept of theatrical document.

Such a corpus offered not only the difficult task of attribution, but also that of the depuration and correction of the *variorum*, since, in a genre so highly codified in its style and mechanisms of strophic construction, the *usus scribendi* of the author (possibly of Calderonian stature) appears notably veiled. For this reason, we believe that editing minor theatrical genres must rely more upon aspects of *interpungere* (punctuation suitable for modern usage) and *mutare* (restitution of alterations) than on *delere* (deletion of words) or *supplere* (conjectural inclusions in apparently depurated passages), the latter aspects being the inclinations of nineteenth-century editors like Juan Eugenio Hartzenbusch. Hartzenbusch is a prime example of an editor's intervention in the text of works whose parodic character frequently makes them objects of obvious censorship. E. M. Wilson studied the changes made by the censor in *El José de las mujeres* (*The Women's Joe*). The edition of the aforementioned interlude, *El sacristán mujer*, demonstrates that what in manuscript 15197 was proof of the company's or playwright's freedom to improvise roguishly, has now become a reading tempered by caution. For example, in the section corresponding to lines 138–145 of the interlude there is an alternative text in the margin which reads: "I fired up your corral / thinking of marrying you / and when your father learned of it / he beat me with a hot bread stick" ("eché leña en tu corral / pensando casar contigo / y tu padre que lo supo / me dio con un pan caliente").[14] This may be a variant of a popular song or composition but, at the same time, the undoubtedly erotic character of words like "corral," "firewood," or "bread" is undeniable. Of course, even Hartzenbusch, as he edits the interlude *Las Carnestolendas* (*Shrovetide*), eliminates unashamedly the scatological and carnivalesque vein of Calderón.[15] In 1850 Hartzenbusch deems irreverent what Calderonian good humor had written around 1660 and deletes the lines with this insubstantial comment: "For my part I don't want / such shitty fruits" ("Yo por mi parte no quiero / frutas tan cacareadas") (see note 15).

To conclude with the problem of editing Calderón's short dramatic work, I would have to refer to the abundance of *suelta* editions, separated from seventeenth-century collections or from eighteenth-century printings of the same—and which interfere in textual transmission—as well as to manuscripts (the source of appreciable variations). In Calderón's case, we have at least eleven *sueltas* of the interludes *El dragoncillo* (*The Little Dragon*), *El desafío de Juan Rana* (*The Challenge of John Frog*), and *El Toreador* (*The Bullfighter*), printed in Seville, Valencia, Barcelona, or Salamanca, which demonstrate in my opinion the commercial interest and circulation enjoyed by the genre well into the eighteenth century.

Experience in handling numerous *suelta* editions was essential for the critical edition of the Calderonian tragedy *Los cabellos de Absalón*, a text with a complex plot and debatable authorship. As is known, Calderón begins with an obvious revision of Act III of Tirso de Molina's *La venganza de Tamar* (*The Vengeance of Tamar*), although its tragic project later is reoriented toward the passionate and political plot of Absalom's personality. Yet, even if we were to admit that Calderón transcribed the third act of Tirso's work in its entirety (using a type of excessive intertextuality), this fact cannot be assumed when dealing with the problem of textual depuration. For this reason, in my edition I assumed a different point of view from that of Gwynne Edwards who, when editing *Los cabellos de Absalón*, adopts as her base text the *suelta* c.108.bbb.20 from the British Library, only because of its closer proximity to Act III of Tirso. Edwards follows an obsolete practice of textual criticism in which superior authority is conferred upon the most widely circulated text (*textus receptus*) without considering its testimonial quality. This methodology (which has its origin in the biblical tradition, in which dissemination was of essential value) is a very controversial method when used to reconstruct the dramatic text of a specific author. In this concrete case I had to opt for (and so have defined the process as dramaturgical method or strategy) the most complete critical revision possible of the texts (*testes* in its classical denomination), relying not only upon the hypothetically oldest version but also upon the one that would contribute the greatest amount of clues and/or information about the performed text (stage directions, for example). Faced with the lack of original manuscripts, I even had to infer the existence of a *suelta* or an intermediary text between the aforementioned copy from the British Library (dated around 1650) and the Toledo edition of 1677, the source of substantial corrections and improvements, giving rise to the Vera Tassis edition in *Octava Parte* (1684). The loss of a textually important edition implies a thorough collation of editions preserved vis-à-vis the somewhat simple *stemma* proposed by Edwards or Helmy Fuad Giacoman (who adopts as base text for his edition the *suelta* copy D.173.2.V.I. from the Boston Library). *Los cabellos de Absalón* offers a vertically developed textual history with two fundamental lineages. The first is derived from the *suelta* of the British Library dated around 1650, from which came the Boston Library copy (chronologically later, however, than the Toledo edition and the Amsterdam edition of 1726). The other comes from the lost intermediary text which, in correcting numerous anomalies in the British copy, gives rise to the valued edition contained in the *Libro nuebo extravagante de comedias escogidas* (A New Extravagant Book of Selected Comedies) (Toledo, 1677), to the Vera Tassis edition (1684), the Apontes edition (1760), and the numerous eighteenth-century *sueltas*, which in turn form the basis of modern editions, beginning with those of Juan José Keil (1830) and Hartzenbusch (1849).

In the process of detecting variations, whether stylistic or not, significant or immaterial, particular mentions should be made of the function that certain concrete interpolations can assume in the global dramaturgical treatment of the work. As a result, textual criticism applied to theater can consider additions from outside the limited range of the lineages of the texts studied. In fact, the philological tradition has always integrated among its variants elements that were foreign to the original, authentic text, for purposes that were probably didactic, political, or rhetorical. In no other way could an editor of *Los cabellos de Absalón* view the interpolations that Sanchis Sinisterra's textual dramaturgy imposed upon the staging of the work directed by José Luis Gómez in 1983, above all in the scene in which David's great tragic contradiction (as Father; and also King) is resolved, a scene in which he is forced to assume reasons of State and harangue the troops in battle. This long fragment, which was nonexistent in Calderón's original, clearly directs the work's meaning toward passion for power and political intrigue.

This last case is an obvious example of the rapprochement that we have been enunciating between the function of the editor (who, while reconstructing a text, concomitantly constructs the semantic plot that sustains it) and that of the dramatist. To edit a classical text is to assume the role of an interested intermediary; the role of a messenger of its reading who, from a contemporary vantage point, attempts to have history impose a coherence on the ravages of time upon a worn-out text, which sometimes has been desemanticized. In some way, the editor must convert the reader into a parallel interpreter and the text itself from a space of infinite meanings into one of concrete meanings that are circumscribed by the coherence of the double historical moment (his or her own and that of the work). The editor does it, creating a new complex and polyhedral text (text-gloss-notes, of personal interpretation and of authorities [*jurare in verba magistrum*]), and together the two texts confer verisimilitude (in the Aristotelian sense of the term) on the personal exegesis, or on extratextuality in general.

In order to break the bonds of sterile positivism, the critical editing of texts must perforate from the work (understood as a structure or system) toward the ensemble of surrounding series or systems that go from the literary to the historic-cultural world, all of them manifested in the text through a framework of allusions and decipherable references. The result of this labor can never be a cento of quotations or tracings of other texts, but rather an essay or an attempt at the production of *semiosis.* The edition must be, then, a comprehensive and intelligent dynamic for reading, in which the reading superimposes itself upon that inert object that is the text, situating it within the action. As Ezio Raimondi said when studying the linguistics of Humboldt, "the concept of structure concerns the producer more than the product, the activity of intelligence more than the ensemble of the text and its abjective physiognomy, its internal compagination" ("il concetto di struttura riguarda piú il productore che il prodotto piú l'attività dell'intelligenza che l'insieme del testo e la sua fisonomia oggetiva la sua compaginazione interna" [220]). By ensuring the complicity of editor and reader, the critical edition also manifests itself as an act of communication. Furthermore, by affirming itself in the meaning that results from the faithful depuration of a text, it perhaps shows itself to be the most stable methodological approach, in contrast to growing deconstructionist skepticism (see Culler) with the aim of acquiring a certainty "which seems to have disappeared from the gnoseological horizons of new criticism" (Mainer 34).

My experience in editing classical texts[16] makes me understand it as the acquisition of a *tejne* that could be explained with the modern concepts of I. A. Richards's *close reading* and with the traditional phases of reading that the Greeks called *clinamen* (to sit down at the work table); *tessera* (to approach the text); *kenosis* (to empty, to exhaust it); *demonizacion* (to build, to construct it); *askesis* (to give it shape, to put it into practice); and *apophrades* (to declare, to reveal it) (see Bloom). The philological conduct, understood as a means and not as an end, is what, to my way of thinking, must sustain the research of literary history.[17] For by being history and, consequently, a transmission mediated by the course of time, literary history finds in the critical editing of its texts the action that conspires against the errors of time, and the coherent instrument connecting with the moment from which one speaks.

Notes

1. *De sinonymis elegantibus liber primus incipit,* fol. 7.

2. A few lines earlier he had written: "for as soon as a talented character / with watchful vigilance / to public censorship / plans to give some study / having become a self-prosecutor / rips one document, and burns another / and unhappy with everything / erases this one, and amends that other / until finally satisfied / with the care that it has cost him / transfers the first draft to copy / and gives the copy to the printer" ("porque así como un ingenio / cuidadoso se desvela / cuando a públicas censuras / dar algún estudio piensa / que hecho fiscal de sí mismo / un pliego rasga otro quema / y mal contento de todo / esto borra aquello enmienda / hasta que ya satisfecho / del cuidado que le cuesta / da el borrador al traslado / y da el traslado a la imprenta" [lines 47–58]).

3. The association of philology with more than merely textual study has been highlighted since antiquity. Marouzeau observed that "textual studies cannot be done without people, ideas, customs, history, art, civilization (45)." Bloomfield recalled his search for cultural meaning and background. Finally, Ferdinand de Saussure extended the philological object to customs and institutions.

4. I speak of *historical* reading in accordance with the formulation of Ramón Menéndez Pidal *(Antología de prosistas españoles):* "It is essential that the grammatical, rhetorical, and literary observations that consistently must arise when reading the classics not be misdirected through the field of abstract considerations and take on a primarily historical orientation" ("Es preciso que las observaciones gramaticales, retóricas y literarias que continuamente han de surgir en la lectura de los clásicos no se descarrien por el terreno de las consideraciones abstractas y

tomen un aspecto principalmente histórico" [19]). Similarly, Américo Castro *(Lengua, enseñanza y literatura)* has said: "Editing a text means understanding and interpreting it. Therefore, it is not sufficient to know paleography, or to copy attentively; on the contrary, one must proceed slowly, deciphering at each step the manuscript or the printed text's possible lesson . . . Philology is an essentially historical science; its problem consists of lending the greatest possible meaning to the written manuscripts, reconstructing the states of civilization that lie inert in the pages of the texts" ("Editar un texto significa comprenderlo e interpretarlo, por eso no basta saber paleografía ni copiar atentamente sino que hay que ir viendo a cada paso si es posible la lección del manuscrito o del impreso . . . La filología es una ciencia esencialmente histórica, su problema consiste en prestar el mayor sentido que sea dable a los monumentos escritos, reconstruyendo los estados de civilización que yacen inertes en las páginas de los textos"[54]).

5. "Philology, by means of its historical, linguistic, and exegetic tools, points not only to the reconstruction but also to the interpretation and hermeneutics of written texts from the past . . . Thoroughly understanding and reasonably evaluating a literary work means to philologically and historically realize the message by way of the framework, the reality of the text itself, the message—simultaneously personal and social—that was entrusted to that work, as well as through the significance it had in the spiritual and practical life of its time and the meaning that it still and forever retains" ("La filología mediante sus útiles históricos, lingüísticos, exegéticos apunta por consiguiente no sólo a la reconstrucción sino también a la interpretación, a la hermeneutica, de los textos escritos del pasado . . . Comprender a fondo y evaluar razonadamente una obra literaria quiere decir darse cuenta filológica e históricamente, a través del entramado y de la realidad del texto en sí mismo, del mensaje— a la vez personal y social—que se encomendó a aquella obra y del significado que aquélla tuvo para la vida espiritual y para la vida práctica de su tiempo, y del significado que mantiene aun y siempre"[91]).

6. Pedro de Espinosa, a prompter in Juan Antonio Mathias's company in Lisbon in 1701, is cited in *Genealogía, origen y noticias de los comediantes de España*. Given the manuscript's date, it is possible to identify both men. See Shergold and Varey 244 (I.864).

7. It is probable that Antonio Eusebio Laplana is the harpist, actor, and author of comedies cited in *Genealogía* as Antonio de la Plana, who was in Valencia in Joseph Antonio Guerrero's company, beginning in 1677 (see Shergold and Varey 153 [I.429]).

8. For a summary of themes in Golden Age theater, see Casa and McGaha.

9. For a reflection on the utility of these indices, see the discussion concerning the study by Veronique Huynh-Armanet and Isabelle Santi.

10. See Alberto Blecua 214: "The principal problems of theatrical transmission lie in printing done without authorial permission, editions that may come from the comedic actors' copies, with additions, suppressions, and changes that are not always possible to distinguish from the author's variants" ("Los principales problemas de la trasmisión teatral radican en las impresiones llevadas a cabo sin permiso del autor, ediciones que pueden proceder de copias de comediantes, con adiciones, supresiones y cambios que no siempre resulta posible distinguir de las variantes del autor").

11. So it happens in the *Primera Parte* of Calderón's comedies, as D. W. Cruickshank points out (79–94).

12. This is the actor Matías de Castro y Salazar, called *el Alcaparrilla*, who died about 1692, according to information from *Genealogía*.

13. The actors and actresses who interpreted the roles are more often mentioned in the interludes than in the copies and publications of major theatrical works. The resulting data are of exceptional interest because they help estimate with great accuracy the date of composition (or at least the date of performance) of the minor work in accordance with the time when the actors cited in the *dramatis personae* were part of the same company. In this way, for example, we were able to put forth a hypothesis for dating this minor Calderonian work. See the diagram on pages 215–218 of *Calderón y la obra corta dramática del siglo XVII*.

14. In fact, Gonzalo Correas included this variation in his *Arte de la lengua española castellana* (manuscript 18969 of the National Library of Madrid, dated 1625): "I tossed kindling in your yard / thinking about marrying you / give me my firewood I tell you / that I don't want to get married" ("Eché leña en tu corral / pensando casar contigo / dame mi leña te digo / que no me quiero casar"). Cf. Margit Frenk, *Corpus de la antigua lírica popular hispánica (siglos XV al XVII)*, 941. Another variant of manuscript 3915 from the National Library: "Passing by your window / I placed a log at your door / your skittish father found out / out of envy he bought a cap" ("Pasando por tu bentana / heché un leño en tu portal / tu padre denque lo supo / de imbidía compro un bonete").

15. For an example of the use of ingenious puns based on vulgar terms for excrement, see lines 156–164:

> Gracioso. ¿Mucha de la cagancaña
> cagalón e cochelate
> calamerdos, merdaelada
> turo para vuensace?
>
> Rufina. ¿A quién digo, camarada?
> Yo le perdono mi parte.
> Que tan espesas viandas
> entre once y doce seran
> mejores para vaciadas . . .

16. I should add that editing and annotating the manuscript from *Actas de la Academia de los Nocturnos* has been as enriching as editing Calderón. Given the text's mixture of verse and prose and the solid rhetorical construction of its discourses—which are virtual encyclopedias woven with quotations, some authentic and others apocryphal—it has been a valuable exercise for testing the philological method of making a text legible and manifesting its polyphony of meanings. See the volume corresponding to the first sixteen sessions of 1591.

17. See Picchio: "It is necessary to admit that philological behavior is a critical activity in every sense of the word, an attitude having a constant that can be characterized as a continual process of adaptation (with a rigorous verification of all the data and all that is presumed to be data) to a determined historical situation that it endeavors to reconstruct . . .; philological work is always inclined to redefine itself in relation to the renewed interpretive techniques that are offered to it, by a generous . . . critical methodology" ("Il faut bien admettre que le 'comportement' philologique est une activité critique au plein sens du terme: une attitude dont la

constante est le processus d'adequation [en vérifiant rigoureusement toutes les données, ou tout ce qui peu être considéré comme tel] a une situacion historique determinée, que l'on veut 'reconstituer.'" [II, 319]; "... le travail du philologue, toujours enclin à se redéfinir par rapport aux techniques d'interpretation renouvelées grâce à une méthodologie critique généreuse...." [II, 320]).

Works Cited

Blecua, Alberto. *Manual de crítica textual.* Madrid: Castalia, 1983.

Bédier, Joseph. *Les Légends épiques.* 4 vols. Paris, 1908-1913.

Bloom, Harold. *The Anxiety of Influence: A Theory of Poetry.* New York: Oxford Univ. Press, 1973.

Bloomfield, Leonard. "Why a Linguistic Society?" *Language* 1 (1925): 1-5.

Branca, Vittore, and Jean Starobinski. *La filologia e la critica letteraria.* Milan: Rizzoli, 1977.

Calderón de la Barca, Pedro. *Los cabellos de Absalón.* Ed. Helmy Fuad Giacoman. Chapel Hill, N.C.: Hispanófila, 1968.

———. *Los cabellos de Absalón.* Ed. Gwynne Edwards. New York: Pergamon, 1973.

———. *No hay cosa como callar.* Ed. Angel Valbuena Briones. Madrid: Espasa-Calpe, 1973.

———. *Los cabellos de Absalón.* Ed. Evangelina Rodríguez. Madrid: Espasa-Calpe (forthcoming).

Casa, Frank P., and Michael McGaha. *Editing the Comedia.* Ann Arbor: Univ. of Michigan, Michigan Romance Studies, Vol. 5, 1985.

Castro, Américo. *Lengua, enseñanza y literatura.* Madrid: V. Suárez, 1924.

Cruickshank, D. W. "The Text of *La vida es sueño.*" *The Textual Criticism of Calderón's Comedies.* London: Tamesis, 1973. 79-94.

Culler, Jonathan. *On Deconstruction: Theory and Criticism after Structuralism.* Ithaca: Cornell Univ. Press, 1982.

Frappier, Jan. "Le Graal et ses feux divergentes." *Romance Philology* 24 (1971): 373-441.

Frenk, Margit. *Corpus de la antigua lírica popular hispánica (siglos XV al XVII).* Madrid: Castalia, 1987.

Granja, Agustín de la. "Calderón de la Barca y el entremés de *La melancólica.*" *Ascua de veras. Estudios sobre la obra de Calderón.* Granada: Univ. of Granada, 1981. 57-58.

———. *Entremeses y mojigangas de Calderón para sus autos sacramentales.* Granada: Univ. of Granada, 1981.

———. "Cinco obras cortas atribuibles a Calderón." *Bulletin Hispanique* 86, 3-4 (1984): 355-378.

———. "Los entremeses de *La premática* de Calderón." *Estudios Románicos dedicados al Profesor Andrés Soria Ortega.* Vol. 2. Granada: Univ. of Granada, 1985. 257-274.

Greimas, A. J., and J. Courtes. *Semiótica: Diccionario razonado de la teoría del lenguaje.* Madrid: Gredos, 1982.

Hartzenbusch, Juan Eugenio, ed. *Las Carnestolendas. Comedias de don Pedro Calderón de la Barca.* Vol. 4. Madrid: Biblioteca de Autores Españoles, 1850. 632-635.

Huynh-Armanet, Veronique, and Isabelle Santi. "Propuestas para un estudio informatizado del teatro menor español." In *El teatro menor en España a partir del siglo XVI.* Madrid: Consejo Superior de Investigaciones Científicas, 1983. 307–315.

Lobato, María Luisa. "Segunda parte inédita del entremés *La jácaras* atribuido a Calderón." *Rilce* 2.1 (1986): 119–140.

Madrigal, Alonso de. *Quarta pars abulensis super Mattheum.* Venetiis, 1529.

Mainer, José Carlos. *Historia, literatura y sociedad.* Madrid: Espasa-Calpe, 1988.

Marouzeau, Jules. *La linguistique ou science du langage.* Paris: Librairie Orientaliste Paul Genthner, 1944.

Menéndez Pidal, Ramón. *Antología de prosistas españoles.* 2nd ed. Madrid: Centro de Estudio Históricos, 1917.

Moll, Jaume. "Sobre la edición atribuida a Barcelona de la *Quinta Parte de Comedias de Calderón.*" *Boletín de la Real Academia Española* 53 (1973): 207–213.

Palencia, Alfonso de. *De sinonymis elegantibus liber primus incipit.* Hispali, 1491.

Picchio, Stegnano. *La méthode philologique.* Vols. 1–2. Paris: Gulbenkian, 1982.

Portoles, José. *Medio siglo de filología española (1896–1952): Positivismo e idealismo.* Madrid: Cátedra, 1986.

Quentin, Henri. *Essais de critique textuelle.* Paris: Librairie Auguste Picard, 1926.

Raimondi, Ezio. *Scienza e Letteratura.* Turin: Einaudi, 1978.

Rodríguez, Evangelina. "Pertinencia, pertenencia, ambigüedad del texto teatral: *La destrucción de Sagunto* por Manuel Vidal y Salvador." *Cuadernos de Filología de la Universidad de Valencia* 3, 1–2 (1981): 321 + .

―――, and Antonio Tordera. *Calderón y la obra corta dramática del siglo XVII.* London: Tamesis, 1983.

―――, and Antonio Tordera, eds. *Entremeses, jácaras y mojigangas de Pedro A. Calderón de la Barca.* Madrid: Castalia, 1983.

―――, Josep Lluis Canet, and Josep Lluis Sirera, eds. *Actas de la Academia de los Nocturnos.* Valencia: Institut Valencià d'Estudis, Investigació, 1988.

Ruiz, Elisa. "Crítica textual. Edición de textos." In *Métodos de estudio de la obra literaria.* Ed. Jose María Diez-Borque. Madrid: Taurus, 1985. 72–73.

Rull, Enrique. "El entremés *Los degollados* y su posible atribución a Calderón." In *El teatro menor en España a partir del siglo XVI.* Madrid: Consejo Superior de Investigaciones Científicas, 1983. 203–210.

Saussure, Ferdinand de. *Curso de lingüística general.* Buenos Aires: Losada, 1945.

Shergold, N. D., and J. E. Varey, eds. *Genealogía, origen y noticias de los comediantes de España.* London: Tamesis, 1985.

Toro y Gisbert, Miguel de. "¿Conocemos el texto verdadero de las comedias de Calderón?" *Boletín de la Real Academia Española* 1–5 (1918): 401–421, 531–549.

Wilson, E. M. "Inquisition and Censorship in Seventeenth-Century Spain." *Entre las jarchas y Cernuda.* Barcelona: Ariel, 1977. 261–277.

―――. "Una metodología para precisar los textos de la *Segunda Parte de Comedias* de Calderón." *Homenaje a Kurt y Roswitha Reichenberger. Estudios sobre Calderón y el teatro de la Edad de Oro.* Barcelona: PPU, 1989. 39–46.

Chapter 7
Editing Problems of the *Romancero*
The Romantic Tradition

Pere Ferré

The *romancero*: Memory and Writing

Since the *romancero* is one of the genres belonging to the so-called oral literature, it may seem, at first, inappropriate as a subject in a volume entitled *The Politics of Editing*. One should remember, however, that the *romancero*, born as many other medieval genres, to be preserved by memory, found another way of life after the fifteenth century, when it started to become available in writing as well.

This new form of transmission is documented for the first time by a modest notebook belonging to a student of the Balearic Islands,[1] and throughout the fifteenth century several songbooks in manuscript form (the *cancioneros*) contain ballads or *romances* among their texts.[2] In the sixteenth century, *romances* fill large portions of printed volumes that were meant as compilations of whatever was considered to be a literary work, and also circulated in the very popular form of leaflets or chapbooks (*pliegos*), which were printed more or less everywhere and provided considerable profits to the typographers who found in them some of that century's best-sellers.

The *romancero,* then, has lived a double life from 1420 until now, preserved under two different forms that often crossed each other: manuscript or printed writing and human memory.

Establishing the Text of a *Romance:* An Act of Editing Politics

The problems faced when one tries to establish texts whose natural form of preservation is memory, may now seem clearer. To begin with, the act of writing down a *romance* using graphemes is already a matter of editing politics, not only because the form of preservation changes, but especially because it implies a kind of choice, giving to one version of the poem the solemn importance of the document. Frequently, the chosen version is not exactly a transcription of what was *heard* but much more the final result of a reelaboration, often built through the depuration of a group of versions; in other words, it is the result of an editor's choice between several lessons obtained of that text, plus the actual creation of his/her own lessons.

This is most likely the typical behavior of sixteenth-century editors. Let us consider, for example, Antonio Rodríguez-Moñino's statement about the *Cancionero de romances* of Antwerp (1550) and its editor's position:

> A very brief prologue precedes the text and it makes clear that the work is the personal task of the printer. Says Martín Nucio: "I have undertaken the task of putting together in this *cancionero* all of the ballads known to me."...
>
> Regarding exclusions, Nucio assures us that a few old ballads are missing which he omitted either because they were unknown to him "or because I did not find them to be as perfect and as polished (*cumplidos*) as I had wished." Other ballads printed by him have some errors, but these must be "attributed to the copies from which I gathered them for they were very unreliable, and to the softness of memory of some of those who dictated them to me for they could not remember them perfectly."
>
> One can see clearly the two ways in which the *cancioneros* were formed: on the one hand there was the written tradition, on the other the oral. It is easy to imagine Nucio—or whoever charged him with the task—taking

notes dictated by some soldier from Extremadura, Castile, Andalucía, or la Mancha, ably stimulating his memory the same way in which, more than three centuries later, the forerunners of the resurrection of the *romancero* were to do, with Amador de los Ríos and Aguiló at the head of them.

Nucio also points out that he has done a bit of textual criticism: "I was careful to see that there were as few mistakes as possible, and it took more than a little work to bring them together and to amend and add to some imperfect ones." One must keep these words in mind in establishing variants among Nucio's texts, if these are chapbook versions that correspond to them exactly: we could be facing personal corrections. (12–13)[3]

These considerations could be made about many other sixteenth-century editors, not to mention, of course, those who did nothing but use in their editions texts already printed by their predecessors.

We should still consider, in order to underscore briefly the main points about the ancient printed tradition, the remakes of *romances* at the hands of poets and playwrights during Spain's Golden Age or *Siglo de Oro*. One thinks of Lope de Vega or Vélez de Guevara, for instance, who used the *romancero* in their plays, sometimes even developing the subject of one specific *romance* but more often including versions or fragments in order to conform to the public's wishes and tastes, or to correspond to the interests and reasons of State politics.[4] Another point to remember is the favor granted during this period to certain themes as opposed to others, a matter excellently treated by Giuseppe Di Stefano but still deserving new approaches in order to clarify some of the ideological reasons behind the choice of those themes (see "Marginalia").

In none of the cases, however, was the concern of all these editors and users of the *romancero* to rigorously establish a text. The search for a scientific approach to this problem will come centuries later, precisely when positivistic criticism begins to face it. Even so, there is a discernible difference between positivistic thought and the actual politics of editing in this field, as one could easily verify by putting together, for instance, the opinions of Carolina Michaëlis de Vasconcelos and Diego Catalán. Their differences are certainly not superficial; on the contrary, they reflect a profound ideological antagonism.

To Michaëlis, a fair representative of positivistic thought, the modern traditional versions are convincing proof of the corruption inflicted to literature by the "common people" (see "Estudos"). To Catalán, however,

> the ancient versions ordinarily suppose an act of appropriation of the poem-song on the part of the "learned" minorities, a conscious integration of that alien artistic object in the official artistic sphere. Consequently, as it is fixed through writing with a new intentionality, the song loses for us its primogenial poetic properties; the "document" masks the "being" of the poem that we seek to study. (452)[5]

Romanticism and the Editing of Ballads

The Romantic generation played a role of particular importance for the knowledge and revelation of a genre that survives since the Middle Ages: the Romantics were indeed the first modern editors of the *romancero*. I am not thinking now about those who followed in the Iberian Peninsula the steps of the northern and central European Romantics, by taking from the old *romanceros* and leaflets or chapbooks (*pliegos*) the ancient versions printed in the sixteenth century. I am instead referring to those who, corresponding to a new spirit, tried to listen to the living oral tradition of their own time. They understood the importance of ancient popular knowledge to the renewal of the idea of nation. In that knowledge the deepest sense of "genuine nationality" lay and from the popular community they learned their own expression. From the 1820s on, then, we find in the Iberian Peninsula a steady work of collecting and editing *romances*. The editions resulting from that work followed very specific criteria.

Garrett, the Pioneer

The pioneer in this type of activity in the Peninsula was the Portuguese Almeida Garrett (1799–1854), who published the first *romances* collected from the modern oral tradition in 1828,[6] although he had initiated his research sooner, in 1824.[7] In this way, Portugal was the first of the Iberian nationalities to reveal the *romancero*.

After *Adozinda*, Garrett included some separate versions in several publications until he eventually gathered and edited his *Romanceiro* in three volumes, between 1843 and 1851.[8] The criteria he uses in this edition are the most diversified, and they are a good example of the Romantic conception of the politics of editing in this field.

In his first volume, we find side-by-side remakes of traditional *romances* and texts created by Garrett himself, which places the collection under the domain of poetic invention. The procedure is the same one Garrett used in 1828: he takes the Iberian ballads as inspiring themes and develops those themes as any other kind of Romantic poetry.

The second and the third volumes raise different problems, since the editor's retouching follows another kind of criteria. His words show clearly these new concerns:

> Through the work that gave birth to this collection, it is my intention to fill in a significant gap in our literature. I do not wish to write a scholastic piece of work, and so be placed among philologists and collectors of antiques, adding one more volume to the shelves in their libraries. I wish to accomplish something useful, a popular book; and in order that it may be so, I must make it as pleasant as my knowledge and ability allow me. Let the academies produce the critical and chronological dissertations for the learned. Mine is a different task: to popularize the study of our primitive literature, of its oldest and most original documents, so that the literary revolution that has broken out in the country may have a guide, pointing out to the young minds among its ranks the real types of nationality they are looking for, and which should be searched for among ourselves, not among foreign patterns.[9]

The *romancero* becomes then a weapon at the service of the literary revolution proposed by the leader of the Romantic movement in Portugal. It is indeed a revolution submitted to poetics, to a specific poetics, as Garrett states:

> For conscience's sake, those who raise the cry for freedom amongst a people should find out the rules, point out aims, provide the means for that freedom so that it does not turn out into anarchy. It is not enough to warm the hearts against usurpation and despotism; once destroyed, law must take its place. And the law should not come

from abroad: it must rise from one country's beliefs, memories, and needs, so that it becomes its natural law and does not replace usurpation by another.[10]

Traditional poetry has then the highest role to play in the formation of this new order, and that is why its transmission and knowledge become a priority for Garrett. The way in which this accomplishment should be achieved is also pointed out in his foreword. First, as we have seen, the national sources should be carefully studied and put to use:

> What has to be done is to study our primitive poetic sources, the *romances* and the legends in prose, the fables and old beliefs, and old superstitions; to read them in bad Mozarabic Latin, half *Suevo* and half Gothic in obsolete documents; in the bad Portuguese of charters and ancient laws; and in the coeval Castilian—since Hispanic literatures were one till late in time. As for the tone and true Portuguese spirit, that has to be studied in the great national book, which is to say the people and its traditions, its virtues and vices, its beliefs and mistakes. And through these alone shall the truthful and legitimate national poetry be reborn, once it has been ripped, through classic influence, off the Shroud of barbarity where it was wrapped when it died and which it wore while still living.
>
> Facing this aim, to gather and restore the folk songs, *romances*, ballads, or whatever one chooses to call them, is one of the first tasks we lacked. That's what I've done, or, at least, what I had in mind to do.[11]

These paragraphs are the key to the volumes published in 1851: Garrett intended to compile a solid and comprehensive poetic catalog of what he considered to be national poetry for use by the young poets. The last two volumes provided the materials that would inspire the new poetry, according to specific rules; these rules were already applied in the first volume in 1843, by Garrett himself. In this way, the younger generation of poets in charge of building a new national consciousness out of the legitimate models of the past (and all this through poetry), would find in Garrett's *Romanceiro* a set of materials along with the recipes to use these materials as models in their own creations.

"Gathering and Restoring . . . Folk Songs"

The Romantic poets, as well as Martín Nucio back in the sixteenth century, could not conceive of editing a ballad without retouching it. The principles followed by the editors in the nineteenth century, however, were to be different.

The literary revolution proposed and led by Garrett is clearly in accordance with the Romantic conception of social changes obtained by means of popular education. Artists were social catalysts assuring the function of a complex relationship; they learned from the people and at the same time they taught them. So, on the one hand, Garrett, liberal politician that he was, speaks firmly of the impossibility of making a revolution without the people, but, on the other hand, he places the learned classes in charge of the ethical and aesthetic education of the lower classes. Within the people, or the "good savages," these artists would find genuine purity and habits and customs not yet corrupted by foreign contact, as had happened to the aristocracy. The people preserved the national culture, as well as a natural law that emerged in several forms of expression, most of all in artistic manifestations. This idealized entity called "the people," however, lacked the aesthetic preparation that the poets, according to Shelley, were supposed to transmit.

The project was, in a word, for the poets to drink from the clear source of popular culture in order to learn again the forgotten knowledge and then provide the source itself with the purified stream of their Romantic revolutionary products. This was the work Garrett tried to perform, or at least start, in his poetic catalog of 1851. The texts he presented were the result of his own work based upon several versions he had collected, when necessary, using lessons that had nothing to do with the true oral tradition.

An Example of Garrett's Remaking

In the second volume of Garrett's *Romanceiro* we find, on pages 21–24 and 32–35, two *romances* under the titles of "The Hunter" ("O Caçador") and "The Bewitched" ("A Enfeitiçada"), respectively. Those texts correspond to the themes of "The Enchanted Princess" ("Infantina'") (*A caçar va el cauallero a caçar como solia*) and "The Baffled Knight" ("Caballero burlado") (*De Francia partio la niña de Francia la bien guarnida).* Garrett knew both *romances* through the modern oral Portuguese tradition and through Agustín Durán's and Eugenio Ochoa's divulgence of those *romances.* Garrett even edits the Castilian versions in order to allow the confrontation with his own.

To a reader who may not be familiar with the traditional *romancero,* Garrett's texts would be just two more *romances* preserved by collective memory in the nineteenth century. A more specialized reader, however, will notice immediately how close the Portuguese versions are to the Spanish ones, and will remember that those two *romances* do not exist in pure forms in Portuguese oral tradition; they only survive today contaminated by each other. All of these reasons lead one to put in serious doubt the legitimacy of Garrett's versions. Let us compare, for instance, the following verses:

> Oh, fear not, gentle knight!
> There is no cause for fear.

> Não te assustes, cavaleiro,
> Não tenhas tamanha frima.
> (Garrett)

> Gentleman, do not look so surprised,
> I bid you, be not so frightened.

> -No te espantes, caballero,
> ni tengas tamaña grima.
> (Ochoa)

or the following:

> -Oh, whoever lost what I'm losing
> deep suffering should endure!
> I take the law into my own hands.
> Thence, here my life comes to an end.

-Oh, quem perdeu o que eu perco
grande penar merecia!
Justiça faço em mim mesmo
e aqui me acabo co'a vida.
(Garrett)

A knight that loses so much
deep suffering should endure:
I will be my own judge
and take the law into my own hands.
Let my hands and feet be chopped off,
my body dragged along the village streets.

Caballero que tal pierde,
muy gran pena merescia:
Yo mesmo seré el alcalde
yo me seré la justicia.
Que me corten piés y manos
y me arrastren por la villa.
(Ochoa)

The influence of Ochoa's version upon Garrett's is clear, especially when the last verses are missing in more than two hundred versions I know of this *romance* found in Portugal.

On the other hand, if we look now at Garrett's manuscript, we find the following version:

Hunting was the huntsman, in some shadowy woods,
When a maiden he saw seated on a cold crag.
- What are you doing, here, maiden, what are you doing,
[fair maiden?
- While in my godmother's arms, by seven fairies I was
[charmed

Here to linger for seven years, seven years and one
[more day.
Those years are over today, tomorrow the day shall be,
Will you, gentle knight, wish me to bear you company?
A long way had gone by, and the maiden smiling was.
- What are you laughing at, sweet maiden, what are you
[laughing at, fair maiden?
- I am not laughing at your horse, or at its garments
[either,
I am laughing at the knight and at his own cowardice;
For when having a maiden riding along, he did treasure
[her virtue.
- Back, back we ride, dear maiden, back we ride, fair maiden,
For my spur was lost behind at the fountain we drank from.
- Ahead, gentle knight, ahead, for back I would not ride;
If your spur is made of silver, a golden one my father would
[give you,
For at my father's dooryard gold is weighed every day.
- Fair maiden, do not take leave, tell me whose daughter
[are you, then?
- I am the daughter of the King of France and of Queen
[Constantine.
- To the Devil with all women and with those who trust
[them may!
I thought I was carrying a mistress, and a sister of mine
[I found.[12]

Without affirming that this manuscript version has not been subject to any retouching, I believe that it provides sufficient proof to show that the traditional version that Garrett knew presented both themes contaminating each other. Later they were separated in two different texts by Garrett, when he was preparing his edition, according to the Castilian versions he knew.

Contamination as Textual Corruption

In a study published in 1954, the French specialist Paul Bénichou wrote: "The mixture of texts in the oral tradition does not constitute a contamination or something irregular or disturbing as the word suggests. Rather, it is a type of invention and normal recreation" ("le mélange des textes, dans la tradition orale, n'est pas une contamination, avec ce que ce mot suggère d'irrégulier ou de choquant: c'est un mode d'invention et de recréation normale" [280]). Bénichou's observation focuses on the crucial point of the problem we are dealing with because for Garrett, as well as years later for the positivist Carolina Michaëlis,[13] contamination is nothing but a corruption that needs to be corrected. That is what Garrett himself admits in a way when he declares, regarding his version of "A Enfeitiçada": "In some of our provinces it has, in its oral version, appeared combined with the previous *romance* 'Caçador' (The Hunter), and it is difficult to disentangle them" ("Em algumas das nossas provincias anda confundido, na versão oral, com o romance precedente do 'Caçador' e custa a desenvencilhá-los" [*Romanceiro*, II, 30]).

It is obviously false to say that "in some of our provinces" that ballad is mixed with the other. The "confusion," as Garrett calls it, is on the contrary totally systematic in modern oral Portuguese tradition. Daniel Devoto has already spoken to that same fact: "The ballad of 'la hija del rey de Francia y el Caballero burlado,' known since the fifteenth century, still lives in the oral tradition (generally contaminated, since much earlier, with two others: 'La Infantina' and 'Don Bueso')" ("El romance de La hija del rey de Francia y el Caballero burlado, conocido desde el siglo XV, vive todavía en la tradición oral [contaminado por lo general, y desde antiguo, con otros dos: La Infantina y Don Bueso]" [383]).

When he tried to *desenvencilhar*—to separate—the two themes, Garrett did not try to establish rigorously, in the philological sense, two different texts. This would be an absurd demand to make on the Romantic poet. On the contrary, what he did was just to respect a politics of editing conceived to present texts as close as possible to the primitive poetry, the "poetry of the stuttering age of people," as he puts it. Garrett has built, then, two poetic documents, purified of rough popular corruption, so they could be read by "readers of all classes," and "enjoyed by the young people" (*Romanceiro*, II, viii).

This is, in fact, a political strategy visibly acting through editing criteria, and these criteria were constantly applied to the *romancero*. At a time when, in the name of the people, the liberal bourgeoisie tried to impose its ideology, replacing the absolutist aristocracy in the leading role, these details were certainly not to be neglected, as Garrett himself understood, and as his example documents.

Notes

1. This is the first *romance* to be documented in writing, copied by Jaume de Olesa around 1420. The original manuscript is now at the National Library in Florence, and has been published for the first time by E. Levi, "El romance florentino de Jaume de Olesa."

2. For knowledge of the manuscript versions of *romances* in the fifteenth century, see S. G. Morley, "Chronological List of Early Spanish Ballads," and the information given by Giuseppe Di Stefano in his "Estudio crítico," especially 54–56.

3. "Un brevísimo prólogo precede al texto y en él consta que la obra es tarea personal del impresor. 'He querido—dice Martín Nucio—tomar el trabajo de juntar en este cancionero todos los romances que han venido a mi noticia'. . . .

Con respecto a las exclusiones, asegura Nucio que faltan algunos romances viejos aunque muy pocos, que no puso porque no llegaron a su noticia 'o porque no los hallé tan cumplidos y perfectos como quisiera.' Otros de los que imprime tienen algunas faltas, pero éstas se deben 'imputar a los exemplares de adonde los saqué que estauan muy corruptos y a la flaqueza de la memoria de algunos que me los dictaron que no se podían acordar dellos perfectamente.'

He ahí bien claras las dos vías de formación del *Cancionero*: de una parte la tradición escrita, de otra la oral. Poco trabajo cuesta imaginar a Nucio—y a quien encargase la tarea—tomando nota de los textos dictados por algún soldado extremeño, castellano, andaluz o manchego, excitando su memoria hábilmente, tal como tres siglos y pico después habían de hacer los adelantados de la resurrección del romancero con Amador de los Ríos y Aguiló a la cabeza.

Señala también que ha hecho su poquito de crítica textual: 'yo hice toda diligencia porque vuiesse las menos faltas que fuesse possible, y no me ha sido poco trabajo juntarlos y enmendar y añadir algunos que estauan imperfectos'. Hay que tener en cuenta estas palabras siempre que vayan a establecerse variantes de textos de Nucio no conocidos por pliegos sueltos que se correspondan *exactamente* con ellos: podemos estar en presencia de correcciones personales."

4. It is interesting to observe how Lope de Vega transforms the *romance* dedicated to the death of Don Jaime's (the Duke of Braganza) wife, changing it completely in order to provide a happy ending. Vélez de Guevara, in turn, transforms a savage mountain girl, the protagonist of the *romance* "La serrana de la Vera," into a woman full of reasons to commit her cruel assassinations, and also

manages a tranquilizing reestablishment of order within the story. Guevara also creates a most interesting confusion when he uses the only two verses known before the nineteenth century of the *romance* dedicated to the death of Prince Don Juan, the son of the Catholic King and Queen: the causes given for the Prince's death are the ones that were traditionally given for the death of Prince Don Afonso, the only male child of King Don João II of Portugal.

Regarding Lope de Vega, in the play *El más galán portugués* (where the *romance* recalling the murder of Don Leonor appears), the changes imposed on its source go well beyond the fact that, being a comedy, the public's taste would not allow the playwright to deal with the truculent death of the Duchess of Braganza. Those changes have a political reason: the Iberian union made it difficult to write about a theme that pitted one against the other—the most important Portuguese noble house and the powerful Spanish house of Medina Sidonia.

Vélez de Guevara's confusion of the causes of the death of the two princes is obviously not innocent, for he attributes the death of the heir of the Spanish Crown to a fall when the prince was riding on horseback. This is precisely what had caused the death of the heir to the Portuguese throne, near Santarem. Critics have held that the playwright's confusion was probably due to a series of resemblances: they were both royal heirs, both their deaths were chronologically close and provoked deep dynastic conflicts, which were developed in *romance* form.

In my opinion, there are deeper reasons for the replacement of Prince Don Juan's causes of death, and the legend developed around the Spanish heir's death supports my suspicions. The young prince's fragility is largely referred to in the documents of that period, which frequently mention the attempts made by the royal physicians to have Queen Isabel interfere and keep her son away from his wife. The references made by the Emperor Charles V, in letters addressed to his son, to the unfortunate end of his great-uncle, Philip II, and advising him to temper his instincts are also known. It is then very likely that Vélez de Guevara would have tried to avoid or even oppose that legend, attributing Don Juan's death to a more "dignifying" cause.

5. "Las versiones antiguas suponen, de ordinario, un acto de apropiación del poema-canción por parte de las minorías 'cultivadas', una consciente integración de ese objeto artístico ajeno en el ámbito artístico oficial. En consecuencia, al quedar fijado por la escritura con una intencionalidad nueva, el canto pierde, para nosotros, sus propiedades poéticas primigenias; el 'documento' nos enmascara el 'ser' del poema que tratamos de estudiar."

6. On this date João Baptista de Almeida Garrett published in London his volume called *Adozinda*, where he includes the two first versions from the modern oral Portuguese tradition. They are a version of "Silvana" contaminated by "Delgadinha" and a version of "Bernal Francés" contaminated by "Aparição da amada defunta." The poem "Adozinda" was composed by Garrett himself, based upon the version of "Silvana" and "Delgadinha."

7. A manuscript called *Cancioneiro de Romances, Xacaras, Solãos e outros vestigios da antiga poesia nacional pela maior parte conservados na tradição oral do povo e agora primeiramente colligidos por J.-B. de Almeida-Garrett* indicates the date of the beginning of his recollection: "começado em 1824." This manuscript is now at the University of Coimbra (Sala Ferreira Lima da Faculdade de Letras da Universidade de Coimbra), under number 14657.

8. The first volume appeared under the title *Romanceiro e Cancioneiro Geral. I. Adozinda e Outros.*; the second and the third have only *Romanceiro* as title.

9. "Pretendo supprir uma grande falta na nossa litteratura com o trabalho que intentei n'esta collecção. Não quero compor uma obra erudita para me collocar entre os philologos e antiquarios, e pôr mais um volume na estante dos seus gabinetes. Desejo fazer uma coisa util, um livro popular; e para que o seja, torná-lo agradavel quanto eu saiba e possa. As academias que elaborem dissertações chronologicas e críticas para uso dos sabios. O meu officio é outro: é popularizar o estudo da nossa litteratura primitiva, dos seus documentos mais antigos e mais originaes, para dirigir a revolução litteraria que se declarou no paiz, mostrando aos novos ingenhos que estão em suas fileiras os typos verdadeiros da nacionalidade que procuram, e que em nós mesmos, não entre os modelos extrangeiros, se devem incontrar" (*Romanceiro*, II, v–vi).

10. "E obrigação de consciencia para quem levanta o grito de liberdade n'um povo, achar as regras, indicar os fins, apparelhar os meios d'essa liberdade, para que ella se não precipite na anarchia. Não basta concitar os animos contra a usurpação e o despotismo; destruido elle, é preciso pôr a lei no seu logar. E a lei não hade vir de fóra: das crenças, das recordacoes e das necessidades do paiz deve sahir para ser a sua lei natural, e não substituir uma usurpação a outra (*Romanceiro*, II, vi).

11. "O que é preciso é estudar as nossas primitivas fontes poeticas, os romances em verso e as legendas em prosa, as fábulas e crenças velhas, as costumeiras e as superstições antigas: le-las no mau latim musárabe meio suevo ou meio godo dos documentos absoletos, no mau portuguez dos foraes, das leis antigas, e no castelhano do mesmo tempo—que até bem tarde a litteratura das Hespanhas foi quasi toda uma. O tom e o espirito verdadeiro portuguez esse é forçoso estudá-lo no grande livro nacional, que é o povo e as suas tradições e as suas virtudes e os seus vicios, e as suas crenças e os seus erros. E por tudo isso é que a poesia nacional hade resuscitar verdadeira e legítima, despido, no contacto classico, o sudario da barbaridade, em que foi amortalhada quando morreu, e com que se vestia quando era viva.

Reunir e restaurar, com este intuito, as canções populares, xácaras, romances ou rimances, solãos, ou como lhe queiram chamar, é um dos primeiros trabalhos, que precisavamos. E o que eu fiz—é o que eu quiz fazer, ao menos" (*Romanceiro*, II, xii–xiii).

12. Indo o caçador à caça por uma mata sombria,
viu estar uma donzela sentada na penha fria.
- Que fazeis aqui, donzela, que fazeis, ó donzelinha?
- Sete fadas me fadaram nos braços de mi' madrinha
que aqui andasse sete anos, sete anos e mais um dia.
Hoje se acabam nos anos, amanhã se acaba o dia,
quereis vós, ó cavaleiro, que eu vá em vossa companhia?
Passado largo caminho a donzela que sorria.
- De que vos rides, donzela, de que rides donzelinha?
- Não me rio do cavalo nem da sua fitaria, rio-me do
cavaleiro mais da sua covardia; c'uma donzela à garupa
e catou-lhe cortezia. - Atrás, atrás, ó donzela, atrás, atrás,
donzelinha, que na fonte onde bebemos deixei a espora perdida.
- Adiante, cavaleiro, que eu atrás não tornaria;
se a sua espora é de prata, meu pai de ouro lha daria,

que às portas de meu pai se mede ouro cada dia.
- Vinde cá, ó donzelinha; dizei-me, de quem sois filha?
- Sou filha d'El-rei de França e da rainha Constantina.
- Leve o diabo mulheres e mais quem nelas se fia!
cuidei que levava amante e levo uma irmã minha.

I have modernized the spelling and I have used the long verse in the transcription of pages 142 and 147 of the manuscript.

13. See, for instance, the words of Michaëlis de Vasconcelos: "o triste mas grande, merecimento de publicações diplomaticas de taes recitações degeneradas consiste em patentearem aos olhos dos eruditos documentos fidedignos e vivos do grau de fragmentação, obliteração, fusão e confusão a que vae chegando a poesia epico-lyrica do povo português e dos seus limitrophes, na Galliza e nas Asturias" (162).

Works Cited

Bénichou, Paul. "La belle qui ne saurait chanter: Notes sur un motif de poésie populaire." *Revue de Littérature Comparée* 28 (1954): 257–281.

Catalán, Diego. "El romancero medieval." *Comentario de textos, IV. La poesía medieval.* Madrid: Castalia, 1983.

Devoto, Daniel. "Un ejemplo de la labor tradicional en el romancero viejo." *Nueva Revista de Filología Hispánica* 7 (1953): 383–394.

Di Stefano, Giuseppe. "Marginalia sul Romanzero." *Miscellanea di Studi Hispanici* (1969–1970): 139–178.

———. "Estudio crítico." *El Romancero.* Madrid: Narcea, 1983.

Garrett, João Baptista de Almeida. *Cancioneiro de Romances, Xacaras, Solãos e outros vestigios de antiga poesia nacional pela maior parte conservados na tradição oral do povo e agora primeiramente colligidos por João Baptista de Almeida-Garrett.* Univ. of Coimbra, MS 14657.

———. *Adozinda.* London: Em Casa de Boosey and Son e de V. Salva, 1828.

———. *Romanceiro e Cancioneiro Geral. I. Adozinda e Outros.* Lisbon: Typographia da Sociedade Propagadora dos Conhecimentos Uteis, 1843.

———. *Romanceiro.* Vols. II, III. Lisbon: Impresa Nacional, 1851.

Levi, E. "El romance florentino de Jaume de Olesa." *Revista de Filología Española* 14 (1927): 134–160.

Michaëlis de Vasconcelos, Carolina. "Estudos sobre o Romanceiro peninsular." *Revista Lusitana* II (1890–1892): 156–179.

Morley, S. G. "Chronological List of Early Spanish Ballads." *Hispanic Review* 13 (1945): 273–287.

Rodríguez-Moñino, Antonio. *Cancionero de romances (Anvers 1550).* Madrid: Castalia, 1967.

◆ Chapter 8

Toward a Feminist Textual Criticism
Thoughts on Editing the Work of
Coronado and Avellaneda

Susan Kirkpatrick

Feminist critics who challenge the established canon find themselves of necessity engaged in tasks of textual criticism and editing. Whether recuperating works of women writers that have lain forgotten in archives or reinterpreting writing that has been transmitted along the margins of the canon, the feminist critic faces the most difficult labors of textual criticism, from the basic spadework involved in tracing the bibliographic history of a work to the subtle decisions of editorial choice. In these endeavors, however, we must not simply reproduce the assumptions of a practice—textual criticism—that helped to produce the very canon we challenge.[1]

The dominant line of textual scholarship, descending from W. W. Greg through Fredson Bowers and G. Thomas Tanselle, is based on a Romantic notion of the autonomy of the author and the sacredness of *his* intention. Such a notion, alien in the first place to the literary persona of many women writers, denies a fact that inevitably becomes apparent to the feminist critic who reconstructs the story of writings that were passed over in the process of canon formation—the profoundly historical and social nature of literary production. In *A Critique of Modern Textual Criticism*, Jerome McGann argues against the idea of a single authoritative text that can embody the pure intention—original or final—of the author:

> Authority is a social nexus, not a personal possession; and if the authority for specific literary works is initiated anew for each new work by some specific artist, its initiation takes place in a necessary and integral historical environ- ment of great complexity. Most immediately . . . it takes place within the conventions and enabling limits that are accepted by the prevailing institutions of literary produc- tion—conventions and limits which exist for the purpose of generating and supporting literary production. (48)

An author's work is scarcely autonomous, McGann continues, for "as soon as it begins its passage to publication it undergoes a series of interventions which some textual critics see as a process of contamination but which may equally well be seen as a process of training the poem for its appearances in the world" (51).[2] Insofar as McGann's critique conceptualizes the constitution of authority and the production and transmission of texts as a social process, I believe it can be very useful to feminist scholars, who must work against the grain, reconstituting from their own social vantage point previously excluded objects of study.

In this essay I want to address provisionally the problematics of feminist textual criticism by suggesting some of the issues and possibilities raised by the project of recuperating and reediting women's texts from nineteenth-century Spain. As illustrations, I will briefly consider two examples of challenging editing tasks that await Hispanic scholars: the long overdue editions of the works of Carolina Coronado and Gertrudis Gómez de Avellaneda, leading figures among the Romantic women poets.[3]

The fact that these two poets, far from having been forgotten or unrecognized, were accorded distinctive places in the Spanish literary canon in itself presents an initial problem, for the canon transmits an image of each of them as "author" that conditions the contemporary reader's experience of their work. The definitive paradigm of these images can be found in Juan Valera's influential anthology, *Florilegio de poesías castellanas del siglo XIX*. Published at the end of the nineteenth century (1902), this anthology by a renowned man of letters and literary critic hands down from his own century to the next a list that purports to provide a repre-

sentative sample of its best lyrical production. The anthology includes both Coronado and Avellaneda—and gives them more space
than it does many male poets. In Coronado's case, however, this
attention in effect marginalizes her as an avatar of the "eternal
feminine."

The selection of poems and the comments justifying that selection enshrine an image of Carolina Coronado that corresponds to
the cultural ideal of Spanish womanhood, an ideal reduced to the
dual elements of maternity and piety. From a poetic corpus that
includes powerful expressions of women's claustrophobia, sarcastic
denunciations of masculine "tyranny," and moving calls for women's
solidarity, Valera chooses three poems for his anthology. The first,
"Love of Loves" ("Amor de los amores"), sublimates a feminine
quest for something more as a desire for union with God. The
second, "To My Daughter, María Carolina" ("A mi hija María
Carolina"), written after Coronado's marriage when she had more
or less given up writing poetry, celebrates her experience of mother-
hood and laments the time wasted in writing poetry:

> Would that I could recover my
> fertile youth, spent on useless
> echoes of poetry, and give you
> all my years one by one.
>
> La juventud fecunda que he gastado
> En inútiles ecos de poesía
> Quisiera recobrar, y uno por uno
> Darte mis años sin guardar ninguno. (119)

The third poem, "To a Poet of the Future" ("A un poeta del
porvenir"), written late in Coronado's life, at the turn of the century, reflects anxiety about passing on the torch of poetic inspi-
ration to generations born under what she regarded as the
mechanistic and materialistic sign of the twentieth century. Valera's
selection thus portrays Coronado as resistant to change, as well
as devout and maternal, fitting her into the mold of a stereotype
of Spanish women that lasted well into the twentieth century.

Valera's characterization of Coronado in his afterword explicitly draws out the implications of his selection. In comparison with Avellaneda, he asserts, she is "more sincere, more spontaneous, more original at times, and always more womanly, or at least less like men poets in what she writes, representing in short more distinctly and exclusively the *eternal feminine*" ("más sincera, más espontánea, más original a veces y siempre más mujer, o sea menos parecida en cuanto escribe a los hombres poetas, representando en suma más distinta y exclusivamente el *eterno femenino*" [370; emphasis added]). Few critics have indicated so succinctly the disadvantageous terms on which women were admitted to the nineteenth-century canon: they were valued either for their dissimilarity to the male standard or for their dissimilarity to their sex. Either way they were in some sense positioned outside the norm.

Transmitted in this way, the image of Carolina Coronado and her work virtually assured that she would receive no major critical attention in the twentieth century. As Noël Valis has observed, "as the *poetisa* of romantic longings, [she] seemed fatally locked into the fortunes of literary fashion" (Review 134). To break through this deadly glass coffin, feminist scholars must return to the earliest documents of her writing, to her first collections of poetry, to her periodical publications, to her manuscripts when possible. These provide the sources for a story very different from that of a *poetisa* embalmed in the eternal feminine; they tell the dynamic and still meaningful story of her work as an unfolding social process.

The example of Coronado's relationship with Juan Eugenio Hartzenbusch, the established and influential writer who acted as her mentor, will serve to illustrate the possibilities of a feminist recuperation of the textual history of Coronado's work. If, as McGann suggests in the passage cited earlier, the history of a poem reveals the training that transforms the writer's intentions into a communicative form, understanding the effects of this "training" is crucial to the interpretation of the meanings embedded in the work of a pioneering woman writer who, like Coronado, steered her productions into a distinctly male-gendered set of institutions. It would appear that Hartzenbusch, who edited and supervised the publication of Coronado's first book of poetry, played an active role in shaping the poems of this collection for their appearance before a public steeped in a strongly masculinist tradition. Here we come upon one of the most basic of the difficulties facing the feminist textual critic: the lack of a sustained body of archival scholarship that could tell us whether the manuscript copy revised by Hartzenbusch survives. If it does, the analysis of the effect of Hartzenbusch's editing would need to introduce an element—gender difference—new to the operations of textual criticism, for the crucial question to be asked would be how Hartzenbusch's perspective as a member of an almost exclusively male critical and literary establishment interacted with the feminine standpoint from which the works were written. Even if the manuscript does not survive, however, dashing definitively any hope of reconstructing the process by which a woman's first poetry was fitted out for reception in a male-dominated literary world, the surviving manuscripts of Coronado's letters to Hartzenbusch do permit us to consider the impact of his mentoring.

Among that correspondence, which is preserved in the manuscript collection of Spain's National Library (Madrid), is found the handwritten copy of a poem that Coronado sent to Hartzenbusch in a letter dated December 31, 1842 (carta 196). She notes that she had mistakenly left it out of the package of manuscript poems she had sent him for publication in the collection that came out in 1843. With a directness that contrasts sharply with the tone of the poems that were eventually published in the 1843 collection, this poem protests the constraints that society forces upon women. The first stanza announces the main theme: the female poet cannot express her inner pain for fear of being ridiculed in a society that devalues and disparages female experience. As she states a few stanzas later, "If a young girl weeps, it's foolish childishness" ("Si llora joven doncella / es necia puerilidad" [Fonseca Ruiz 179]), but emotions and griefs concerning money, power, and related male enterprises are taken seriously. The poet then turns the tables by questioning the values produced by male domination of society:

> Imprudent little gods who in
> erecting great cities, strong walls,
> arches, bridges, leave poverty
> and calamities to their
> descendants.

> Diosecillos imprudentes

> que alzando grandes ciudades,
> fuertes muros, arcos, puentes
> legan a sus descendientes
> miseria y calamidades. (180)

Playing with avian metaphors for gender in which men are figured as "free falcons" (*libres azores*), the poem further accuses them of egotistical blindness to the "narrow cage" (*la estrecha jaula*) that encloses the sighing doves. This poem, at once a protest against male power and an account of the difficult situation of the woman poet who expresses the supposedly puerile concerns of her sex, explicitly links male domination of society to cultural and psychological controls that inhibit women's self-expression. The fact that Hartzenbusch did not comply with Coronado's request to add this poem to the collection whose publication he was supervising dramatically exemplifies the suppression protested in the poem itself.

The contrast between this unpublished poem and the general characteristics of the poems published in the 1843 collection, which received Hartzenbusch's editorial shaping, tells us much about the effects of that "training process." Less graceful, less unified and balanced than the poems that passed through the mentor's hands, this unpublished poem reveals conflicts and dissonances that may have been edited out of the others. Its two main themes—the silencing of women's pain and the disastrous consequences of masculine values and power—remain rather unintegrated. The mode of lyrical lament associated with the first theme contrasts sharply with the satirical, almost scornful tone of the critique of male values. The unedited poem conveys formally as well as thematically the woman poet's difficulty in finding a communicative form in which to express women's experience of subordination; the speaking subject moves jerkily between three modes—a self-deprecating confession of her fear of scorn, a protestation at the pain produced by repressing emotion, and a self-justifying anger that ridicules masculine power—as if trying and abandoning a series of never entirely suitable poetic forms and modes.

Clearly, this unedited poem adds a whole new dimension to the reading of Coronado's early collection. For one thing, it shows that the feminist concerns that appear explicitly in the poems she published in periodicals between 1844 and 1850 were already present when she was writing the poems collected in 1843. Its note of protest reverberates with certain half-tones in some of the poems in that collection—"The Executioner Husband" ("El marido verdugo"), "Rosa Bianca," "The Songs of Sappho" ("Los cantos de Safo")—to suggest a counterpoint to the resigned, ladylike melody heard and praised by canon-shapers such as Juan Valera (Kirkpatrick 222–231). Furthermore, the unedited poem reveals to us how contradictory and conflictive that process was through which an expressive impulse originating with an early-nineteenth-century Spanish woman became a socially communicative form, a poem. The whole set of meanings that we can find in the early poems is made evident to us neither in the uneasy protests of the unedited poem nor in the smooth, conventionally feminine surfaces of the published collection; rather, it is in the conjunction of the two that we can see how the poem is produced in the push and pull between the subordinated and the dominant.

A textual history of Coronado's subsequent work would show the dynamism of these social processes of poetic production. In the years following the publication of the collection, Coronado continued to correspond with Hartzenbusch about her writing, but cast off his tutelage by publishing in literary journals poems similar to the one he had suppressed, poems whose themes and styles were echoed by numbers of other women poets publishing in the same journals. In reconstructing this story, we can only surmise that in the response to her first book, the poet discovered a public different from the one Hartzenbusch had in mind, a public that in receiving the suppressed messages of female resistance and protest encouraged their explicit expression in the poems she then designed for appearance in a literary world that increasingly included her own gender. Such is roughly the process Coronado described a decade later when, carried in a contrary direction by the dialectic of cultural process, she disparagingly recalled the sense of mission she shared with other women poets in the mid–1840s:

> I lamented in childish verses women's slavery, their loneliness and sorrows. . . . Josefa Massanés, born and raised in circumstances that were also unusual, complained as I did of the narrowness of our lives; and some innocent girls,

following our example, filled the pages of literary journals with anguished tears for our shared misfortune. These tears, many of which were nothing but echoes of mine, broke my heart and inflamed my mind with indignation at the tyranny of men. . . .

[Y]o me lamentaba en infantiles versos de la esclavitud de la mujer, de su soledad y su tristeza. . . . Josefa Massanés, nacida y educada en circunstancias también particulares, se quejaba como yo de la estrechez de nuestra vida; y algunas inocentes niñas, siguiendo nuestro ejemplo, llenaban las páginas de los periódicos literarios de lágrimas dolorosas por el común infortunio. Estos gemidos, muchos de los cuales no eran sino ecos de los míos, desgarraban mi alma y encendían mi mente de indignación contra la tiranía del hombre. . . . ("Galería" 3)

A detailed textual history of Coronado's works—particularly that of *La Sigea*, the novel whose first part was originally published in *El Semanario Pintoresco Español* in 1850 and whose second part came out in book form in 1854, as well as that of "Galería de poetisas españolas," a work planned as a book but published in parts as periodical articles between 1850 and 1857—would tell too the story of this final turn against the feminist positions she had taken earlier. For if in the interests of constructing a countermyth of Coronado as heroic feminist, we were to ignore her return to the fold of domestic ideology after 1852, we would miss the dramatic struggles among competing discourses that play themselves out in her work. What I have hoped to suggest in these brief examples is the complex social significance that a feminist reconstruction of the full history of Coronado's texts can make legible in a corpus that for Valera embodied the changeless essence of the feminine.

The work of Gertrudis Gómez de Avellaneda poses a set of quite different problems for the feminist textual critic. Anxiety about gender difference was so extensive in nineteenth-century European society that even the field of the feminine was divided into male and female: Valera's comparison characterizing Gómez de Avellaneda as the masculine woman poet and Carolina Coronado as the feminine woman poet follows a long line of nineteenth-century critical commentary that presented the two women poets as polar contraries. The two poets to some extent internalized the distinction. Whereas Coronado, who cultivated spontaneity as a Romantic virtue easily assimilable to the cultural idea of femininity, rarely if ever revised, Avellaneda was an inveterate reviser. Unwilling to trust her works to the hazards of literary fashion, Avellaneda attempted to control the transmission of her work and of her image as author by editing her definitive *Obras* at the end of her life, and the versions that were ultimately "authorized" in her final edition were often very different from the first printed versions. The two subsequent editions of her complete works—the centenary *Works* (*Obras*) published in Havana in 1914 (hereafter O1914, following the system of Deyermond and Miller) and the recent edition of the *Obras* by J. M. Castro y Calvo in Spain's Biblioteca de Autores Españoles (O1974)—accept in regard to the poetic texts the authority of the author's final wishes as they were embodied in the 1869 edition that she supervised (O1869). We have here, it would appear, a case in which the apparatuses of the literary institution have respected the self-definition of a woman writer instead of redefining her in terms of the male bias of that institution, as they did Carolina Coronado.

This seemingly clear-cut case also requires radical feminist re-editing and revisionist textual criticism, however. The uncritical, even sloppy editing Avellaneda's work has received reveals, in the first place, a sexist bias. Deyermond and Miller point out that in simply reproducing the texts of the 1869 edition with a few additions, the Cuban centenary edition (O1914) was perhaps justified, since it was intended to be a "patriotic tribute" rather than a "scholarly edition" (41); but no such justification excuses the Biblioteca de Autores Españoles edition (O1974), which in simply following the text of O1914 is, as Deyermond and Miller tartly remark, "a reprint of a reprint" (42). It is difficult not to see in Castro y Calvo's "abdicat[ion of] his function" as editor (Deyermond and Miller 42), the assumption that the work of this woman author does not merit a careful critical editing.

It could be argued on behalf of O1914 and O1974, however, that these standard editions have operated on the conventional assumption of textual criticism since the nineteenth century—that the last printed version authorized by the writer generally represents the "author's final intentions." But, as McGann has shown, this assumption is dubious for a number of reasons, especially because of the highly social and collective nature of the processes of publishing a poem (*Critique*, Chapter 3). As we have seen in the case of Carolina Coronado, the impact of audience expectations and response on whatever could be considered an autonomous authorial aesthetic impulse is particularly significant for a nineteenth-century woman writer just beginning to claim a legitimate place for her sex in the production of print culture. Awareness of the pressures and constraints on women who became "public" through writing inevitably raises the question of whether Avellaneda's final version of her work represented a conclusive self-definition or whether it might be more accurately described as self-censorship.

Her exclusion of her first two novels brings this issue clearly into focus. Avellaneda's decision to omit these two works from her definitive *Obras* may reflect an aesthetic judgment of her earliest fictional production, but this seems unlikely, given her tendency—in poetry, at least—to revise extensively rather than to discard work that did not satisfy her. The content of these two early works of fiction makes it more probable that Avellaneda's decision was political. *Sab* (1841) was the first published abolitionist novel in Spanish, and still in 1869 could not be published in Cuba. Indeed, a Cuban journal that did publish the novel in 1883 stated that it had been excluded from the 1869 *Obras* in order to permit the distribution of the latter on the island.[4] Her second novel, *Two Women* (*Dos mujeres*) (1842–1843), did not touch on the controversial issue of slavery, but did question—as *Sab* did too—whether women could find happiness and fulfillment in marriage. This novel's exclusion cannot be explained as the result of a change in Avellaneda's views, for in Cuba in 1860 she wrote a polemical series of feminist articles titled "Woman" ("La mujer") (see Miller, and Santos). It is, then, difficult to avoid the conclusion that *Sab* and *Dos mujeres* were omitted from the 1869 *Obras* as a matter of expediency. That is, the selection of works for the definitive edition was a form of self-censorship, aimed at making the *Obras* palatable to the largest possible public.

The case is so clear in regard to these two novels that the editors of O1914 restored them to the centennial edition. Yet the example shows that there are good reasons to ask to what extent the versions of poetic texts published in 1869 can be considered the most authentic. The feminist textual critic, in particular, must be concerned with the subtle pressures exerted by Avellaneda's perception of her readers' gender biases and political attitudes as she revised her poetry for the edition through which she hoped to reach her widest audience.

To say this is to point to the most formidable obstacle to a new edition of Avellaneda's poetical works: the lack of a scholarly critical edition that would bring together and order the numerous and widely scattered versions of her poetry. Deyermond and Miller have outlined with convincingly detailed examples the tasks and difficulties that await the editor of a critical edition of Avellaneda's poetry: collecting from archives, private albums, and nineteenth-century periodicals the poems—some in manuscript—that have never been collected, as well as accounting for the often overwhelming number of variants. Yet a scholarly instrument of this sort, while facilitating the feminist editor's project, will not take its place. For if we see our goal as that of recuperating women's writing from the past and transmitting it to our contemporaries in such a way as to make possible a liberating reconstruction of our history, we must find and relay to readers what remains meaningful today in the mass of documents organized by the scholarly edition.

In imagining what a feminist edition would be like, I would argue that while it would not be like a critical edition in including all variants, neither would it seek the "definitive" text as a standard edition would. Beth Miller, writing about Avellaneda's feminism, offers a clue about how the feminist editor might approach the textual variants. She discusses at some length the poet's habit of revising her own work because this rewriting not only reveals Avellaneda's ideological development but attests to her "literary ambition and professionalism" ("Gertrude" 204). This point suggests the particular interests at work in a twentieth-century feminist critic's attention to a nineteenth-century woman writer. From our perspective, the meaning of Avellaneda's writing will have more to do with her relation to the institutions of power and knowledge of her time than with the aesthetic form of a putative "final" text. Thus, the ambitions revealed by her ceaseless rewriting, the standards of professionalism that she strove to match, the degree to which she was involved in the public politics of the day or alternatively focused on the domestic politics of everyday life—these will be the concerns of a feminist construction of Avellaneda as an author, the questions through which the feminist will find meaning in a transmitted work. Miller, for example, commenting on the radical changes undergone by Avellaneda's sonnet to Washington, concludes: "These changes may be traced to the historical events of the years between 1841 and 1869 and to the changing political and intellectual climate in both Europe and America" ("Gertrude" 205). Miller is not interested so much in the aesthetic effects of the changes—though she mentions them as related to the "intellectual climate"—as in what they tell us about the poet's immersion in history.

The relation of writer and writing to history is of signal importance to the feminist reader and critic—though not only to her—precisely because of the inherited set of cultural distinctions between the genders that has defined women as outside or beneath history. While writers like Coronado and Avellaneda have not been entirely excluded from Spanish literary history, they have, as we have seen, been marginalized within it. In the process of remedying this situation, feminists must reclaim for these writers their historicity as well as their engagement in the whole range of discourses of history. To insist on transmitting a single variant of Avellaneda's work as the standard one—whether on the grounds that it is the author's final intention, or that it is more aesthetically pleasing, or that it represents the author's freshest and thus most autonomous impulse—is to deny this historicity. Feminists have increasingly found it in their interests to challenge all forms of essentialism; like the fixing of an identity based on social position, the fixing of the text in some standard version freezes the historical dynamics that give it a fluid and never-finished existence. It is precisely in this fluidity of changing variants, the process through which she shaped and reshaped her works and her self as author in relation to her public over time, that Avellaneda's work is most meaningful to us.

These reflections make the feminist textual critic's task no easier, I suspect. The problem of how concretely to configure an edition that would highlight textual fluidity over textual fixity remains daunting: a critical edition using footnotes to record every variant runs the risk of becoming unreadable, but fully printing each variant in succession becomes bulky and tedious. Perhaps we must give up the idea of a perfect edition as an essentialist one. If a feminist edition can register the complex interaction between the idea of a work and its multiple material realizations, it will have done more than enough: not only will it have recuperated a woman writer in all her historicity for equally historical contemporary readers, but it will have reminded the scholarly world that the task of editing is itself historical and therefore—thank goodness—never done.

Notes

1. I have been able to find only scattered scholarly work on the problems of feminist textual editing. Katherine King's dissertation discusses editing practices as a factor determining the place of women-authored poems in the mechanics of canon formation. Mary Ann Caws's article plays suggestively with the effects of a husband's editing on voice in texts by Sylvia Plath and Virginia Woolf. Jerome McGann offers the example of gender-sensitive review of a new edition of a woman poet's work in his discussion of Rebecca Crump's edition of Christina Rossetti (*Beauty* 207–220).

2. Because the particular concerns of textual criticism require distinctions that cannot be conveyed by the indiscriminate use of the term "text," I shall endeavor in this essay to follow the terminological distinctions established by McGann (*Beauty* 114, note 3).

3. Since this essay was written, feminist editions of both writers' poetry have been published in Castalia's Biblioteca de Escritoras series (1990, 1991); see Works Cited. The publication of Coronado's complete works, edited with an introduction and notes by Noël Valis, reproduces the 1852 edition, but modernizes spelling and punctuation and corrects obvious typographical errors. Although the Castalia edition thus makes the major part of Coronado's poetic opus available to contemporary readers, it does not pretend to be either the complete poetical works or a critical edition.

4. Miller ("Gertrude the Great") reprints the text of the statement from *El Museo* (209); her source is Figarola-Caneda and Boxhorn (77).

Works Cited

Bowers, Fredson. *Textual and Literary Criticism*. Cambridge: Cambridge Univ. Press, 1959.

Caws, Mary Ann. "The Conception of Engendering; The Erotics of Editing." In *The Poetics of Gender*. Ed. Nancy K. Miller. New York: Columbia Univ. Press, 1986. 42–62.

Coronado, Carolina. Cartas a Juan Eugenio Hartzenbusch. Ms. 20.806, cartas 195–230. National Library, Madrid.

———. *Poesías*. Prologue by Juan Eugencio Hartzenbusch. Madrid: Imprenta de Alegría y Charlain, 1843.

———. *La Sigea*. 2 vols. Madrid, 1854.

————. "Galería de poetisas españolas contemporáneas: Introducción." *La Discusión* (1 May 1857): 3.

————. *Poesías.* Ed. Noël Valis. Madrid: Castalia, 1991.

Crump, Rebecca, ed. *The Complete Poems of Christina Rossetti.* Vol. 1. Baton Rouge: Louisiana State Univ. Press, 1979.

Deyermond, Alan, and Beth Miller. "On Editing the Poetry of Avellaneda." *Studia Hispánica* 1 (1981): 41–55.

Figarola-Caneda, Domingo, and Emilia Boxhorn. *Gertrudis Gómez de Avellaneda: Biografía bibliografía e iconografía, incluyendo muchas cartas inéditas o publicadas, escritas por la gran poetisa o dirigidas a ella, y sus memorias.* Madrid: Sociedad General Española de Librería, 1929.

Fonseca Ruiz, Isabel. "Cartas de Carolina Coronado a Juan Eugenio Hartzenbusch." *Homenaje a Guillermo Gustavino.* Madrid: Asociación Nacional de Bibliotecarios, 1974. 171–199.

Gómez de Avellaneda, Gertrudis. *Sab.* Madrid: Imprenta Calle del Barco, 1841.

————. *Dos Mujeres.* 4 vols. Madrid: Gabinete Literario, 1842–1843.

————. *Obras literarias de la señora doña Gertrudis Gómez de Avellaneda. Colección completa.* 5 vols. Madrid: Rivadeneyra, 1869–1871.

————. *Obras de la Avellaneda.* Edición Nacional de Centenario. 6 vols. Havana: Imprenta de Aurelio Miranda, 1914 [-1920].

————. *Obras de doña Gertrudis Gómez de Avellaneda.* Ed. José María Castro y Calvo. Vol. 1. Biblioteca de Autores Españoles. Madrid: Atlas, 1974.

————. *Poesía y epistolario de amor de amistad.* Ed. Elena Catena. Madrid: Castalia, 1990.

Greg, W. W. "The Rationale of Copy-text." *Studies in Bibliography* 3 (1950–1951): 19–36.

King, Katherine Ruth. "Canons without Innocence: Academic Practices and Feminist Practices Making the Poem in the Work of Emily Dickinson and Audre Lorde." Diss., Univ. of California, Santa Cruz, 1987.

Kirkpatrick, Susan. *Las Románticas: Women Writers and Subjectivity in Spain, 1835–1850.* Berkeley: Univ. of California Press, 1989.

McGann, Jerome J. *A Critique of Modern Textual Criticism.* Chicago: Univ. of Chicago Press, 1983.

————. *The Beauty of Inflections: Literary Investigations in Historical Method and Theory.* Oxford: Clarendon Press, 1985.

Miller, Beth. "Avellaneda, Nineteenth-Century Feminist." *Revista Interamericana* 4 (1974): 177–183.

————. "Gertrude the Great." In *Women in Hispanic Literature: Icons and Fallen Idols.* Ed. Beth Miller. Berkeley: Univ. of California Press, 1983. 201–214.

Santos, Nelly A. "Las ideas feministas de Gertrudis Gómez de Avellaneda." *Revista Interamericana* 5 (1975): 276–281.

Tanselle, G. Thomas. "The Editorial Problem of Final Authorial Intentions." *Studies in Bibliography* 29 (1976): 167–211.

Valera, Juan. *Florilegio de poesías castellanas del siglo XIX.* Vol. 3. Madrid: Fernando Fé, 1902.

Valis, Noël. Review of *Carolina Coronado de Perry* by Alberto Castilla. *España Contemporánea* 2, 4 (1989): 134–136.

◆ Chapter 9

Framing Contexts, Gendered Evaluations, and the Anthological Subject

Myriam Díaz-Diocaretz

> *The problem of the second subject who is reproducing (for one purpose or another, including for research purposes) a text (another's) and creating a framing text (one that comments, evaluates, objects, and so forth).*
>
> —Bakhtin, *Speech Genres* 104

Preliminary Remarks

The politics of editing an anthology of Latin American poetry by women cannot be reduced to the single issue of an intervention of feminist ideology, for it concerns the conjuncture where ethics and aesthetics, the individual and collective frames of the editor, interact with the dominant norms and values that ground literary history and tradition. This essay is based on the analysis of some thirty anthologies of Latin American poetry published in Spanish from 1957 to 1989; it does not consider the anthologies produced within a single, specific national context. My current research is intended as a prelude to editing an anthology of Latin American poetry by women. The comments presented are observations in the process of construction of my own framing contexts.

I. The Anthology as a Responsive Mode of Understanding

As a *"material* bearer of meaning" (see Bakhtin, *Speech Genres* 105), an anthology is a cultural object, mechanically, technologically reproduced, and reprinted; a commodity in the market through bookstores and book fairs, an item borrowed and lent. These aspects of anthologies have been the object of analysis in sociologically oriented approaches to literature. My view, however, will take the factors of textuality and textual practice as they operate and converge dynamically on the anthology understood as the editor's text mediating discursive production.

While it is a material object of culture, as bearer of texts by different selected authors, an anthology is also what I call a *trans-material* bearer of meaning;[1] just as language has a transmaterial nature, an anthology, being a conveyor of texts generating verbal interaction, communicates *a mode of understanding*, a particular development of a literary tradition, a cultural phenomenon, or an epoch (Díaz-Diocaretz, *The Transforming Power* 61). It incorporates a field of tradition, and it is an instrument of power. In its cultural context, the anthology reaffirms, reproduces, and legitimizes a form of collective knowledge. An exchange of recognition occurs between the anthology, tradition, and their receptors. Mikhail Bakhtin's concept of "text" as the "primary given" in the human sciences is quite useful for drawing a working outline for the analysis of the anthological subject I propose (*Speech Genres* 103–104). It consists of a framing subject that creates the anthology as a product of the "model" or "implied text," in its still unrealized but potential form, composed of the set of "exemplary texts"; it refers to the editor's plan (intention); it concerns the realization of the plan through the assembled texts. My focus is on the initial givens inducing the editor to exclude women or to position the work of women poets in specific, marginal fields.

It is well known that in the editing process the compiler seeks to combine personal taste with the taste of a community of readers; hence, issues of ethics interact with aesthetics. Both the editor's ethical act in selecting poems or poets to contribute to their greater public accessibility and the aesthetic act by which the selection is sorted have political effects. Furthermore, each anthology is a selection that as a whole will be unique in its specific *situation*, in its "who," "what," "where," and "when." The framing context, the gendered evaluations, and the anthological subject define the space-time—the *chronotope*—of an anthology (Bakhtin, *The Dialogic Imagination*). Whereas most editors affirm that the process of selectivity follows configurations of their personal taste, this particular ethical and aesthetic conjuncture is predetermined by the cultural conventions of collective probabilities and restrictions, which are revealed in different culturally and historically defined variants.

There are many sides to the anthology's role as an event of culture. One of its most significant features is its interrelatedness to literary history and to canon formation. In my analysis, and keeping in mind this interrelatedness, the framing texts are: the introductions, the formal divisions (thematic, critical, chronological, geographic, and so forth), the bibliographical references of support, and the critical commentaries. These framing texts form, of course, the margins of the editor's overall text constituted by the selection of poems. Through these frames the editor's viewpoint is constructed. Such frames express a new context which in turn channels the editor's attempt to convey a mode of objectivation. The anthology, in this way, emerges as a social territory defined between the borders of tradition, innovation, and the tradition of "rupture." Therefore, the anthology's *framing contexts—uttered* and *unuttered—*communicate the editor's knowledge and specific modes of understanding relevant to evaluations, hierarchies, and exclusions. They affect the anthology as the editor's site of *responsive* understanding. Following Bakhtin's analogy of the text as utterance, we can advance the idea that the anthology "always *responds* to a greater or lesser degree, that is, it expresses the speaker's [the editor's] attitudes towards others' utterances and not just his attitude toward the object of his utterance" (Bakhtin, *Speech Genres* 92; emphasis in the original). While the question of the editor's "choice" and the corresponding framing contexts are not "individually" produced, it is important not to dismiss the editor's own ideological frames, for these are reflected not only in the introduction or in the particular arrangement and distribution of texts with particular emphases. The editor's ideological frames structure the anthology as a whole in the same way that the observer and the observed in collective and individual scientific and humanistic thinking mutually interact. In other words, "The experimenter constitutes part of the experimental system . . . *The person who participates in understanding constitutes part of the understood utterance*" (Bakhtin, *Speech Genres* 123; emphasis added).

Bakhtin explains the relationship between the observer and the observed world in a way that applies also to the field of the literary text as imaginary object:

> The person who understands (including the researcher himself) becomes a participant in the dialogue, although on a special level. . . . The observer has no position *outside* the observed world, and his observation enters as a constituent part to the observed object. . . . Understanding itself enters as a dialogic element in the dialogic system and somehow its total sense. (*Speech Genres* 125–126; emphasis in the original)

If we apply this analogy to the field of Latin American poetry in Spanish we see how this body of anthologies—both early and contemporary—constructs a world that concurs with tradition and contributes to reaffirm it. In contrast, the anthologies of feminist orientation or the selections including "women only" are aimed at a counterresponse. This counterresponse, however, can still be carried out within patriarchal parameters. Yet, they follow the plan of "refuting" as an answer to, and therefore, as a form of evaluation of, what already exists: understanding and evaluation. Understanding is impossible without evaluation. Understanding cannot be separated from evaluation: they are simultaneous and constitute a unified integral act (*Speech Genres* 142).

Evaluation is part of the observed world constructed by the anthological subject, and a significant part of it is conveyed through the editor's selection of texts.

II. The Anthological Subject

In the previous section I explained that as a form of "understanding," the anthology—this "transmaterial" form and at the same time "material bearer of meaning"—is, to a great extent, an "implied text" created by the editor's participating in the dialogue within tradition through the "choice" of authors and texts (Bakhtin, *Speech Genres* 103). The editor is more than an individual "social being," for it is not simply the individual whose personal taste is reflected in the selection. The logics of tradition predetermines his or her choice, since the choice itself enters the dialogues in culture.

Consequently, in the present framework, editing an anthology is not simply the process of individual choice or subjectivity—as most editors affirm in their introductions—but it is a dialogic relationship not limited to an act isolated from the dynamics of culture; it is a dynamic set of discursive positions predetermined by the cultural contexts, a product of conjuncture of conventions, and especially of *discursive formations* (Foucault, *L'archéologie*). Hence, the editor is part of *the anthological subject.*

While being highly individually ideological, the role of editing not only is collectively defined by the market and publishing conditions of material forces, but is also constructed at a crossroads of several discursive and cultural fields. Regardless of the function of individuality involved in the problem of choice, the source from which the editor selects the authors is a network of discursive formations circulating in the forms of literary criticism, reviews, judgmental opinions, biographical dictionaries, literary histories, studies of specific literary movements, the concept of "generations" (so widely used in literature in Spanish), prefaces, prologues, predominant selections in other anthologies, key figures considered innovators in each epoch, or standard definitions of genres. The anthology is in fact constituted by literary and extraliterary heterogenous subjects, existing in dispersion rather than as a single subject; it creates an imaginary space, converging points as "fields of concomitance" (see Foucault, *L'archéologie* 71, 77) to produce various discursive formations such as a specific nationalist project, themes of specific political engagement, or, as in the case of *modernismo*, of a political and aesthetic character. The editor gathers descriptive, critical, and biographical material from different forms of discourse-defining artistic phenomena, establishing "norms," which in turn will help to substantiate whether or not an author fits the relevant parameters.

All these criteria antedate the anthology and offer the forms of social discourse that pave the way for inclusion and exclusion. The editor relies on *what has already been expressed* in order to develop the fields of coexistence concerning a poet's recognition or exclusion; s/he seeks a direction toward a *comprehensive understanding of culture* on the basis of the already accepted truths, of what is already justified and presupposed by the tradition and its recognized "authorities" through critical commentaries, or written testimonies of the "masters." Implicit in this multiplicity of discursive fields are also the underlying exclusions produced through the selection itself (Foucault, *L'archéologie* 77). While the anthology acts as a sign—a guarantee, in mass culture—of permanence, as a recognition of a poet's singularity, the artistic value given to the authors is also the result of various discourses that circulate and affect one another. In the editor's eyes, the function of criticism is one of source in order to justify choice, basing the evaluating criteria on the words of the "authorities"; evaluations emerge from those discourses rather than from what the editor believes are the result of personal choice. Tradition and its milestones are also an important part of the anthology's *framing context.*

Yet the boundaries are not clear between the editor's individual choice and the collective assumption that states, for instance, that the selected texts or poets are worthy of "representing" a given culture, period, or movement. This set of choices as evaluation— by definition intersubjective and exclusionary—comprises, as a whole, a construction that adjusts to a set of worldviews given in the social discourses and in the editor's own worldview and evaluation. These choices are a conjuncture of texts proposed implicitly by the collective subjects of a specific historical time and social space. They contain the common spatial purview of the readers while their evaluation is being anticipated. Equally significant is the function of the "rules of formation," as conditions of coexistence, support, transformation in which concepts, themes (e.g., "nationalism," "the city") emerge and disappear (Foucault, *L'archéologie* 53).

My approach takes the anthology as the meeting place not of single authors, but of *author-functions* and discursive phenomena, constituted as social formations, *out of which the very important construction of gender originates* unfolding potential social influence. The poet's work results from the mediation of several discursive fields that are preforming the cultural position it will occupy; an author, a poet, rather than an individual, becomes an *author-function*, as I have shown elsewhere (Foucault, "What Is an Author?" 159; see also Díaz-Diocaretz, *The Transforming Power*). Developing in the domain of discourses in circulation, a given individual's poetic discourse is the ensemble of its different modes of existence, of the contexts in which it has been used, of the forms in which it is reproduced, of the critical evaluations it receives, and of the readers' appropriations (Díaz-Diocaretz, *The Transforming Power*).

As editor, my obvious intention is to produce a collection that will be "representative," a value intrinsic in any anthology by definition. But as a critic I ask myself, "representative" of whom and of what? As a poet, I am aware of the absence of twentieth-century women poets—*poetisas* and *poetas*—in the histories of literature in Spanish, the literary histories of the Spanish American tradition and the Hispanic world at large. As a woman with a feminist consciousness and from my subject rolés of editor, critic, poet, I question the gendered self-centeredness of that tradition.

III. Gendered Evaluations

In the domain of anthologies of Latin American poetry, the movement of Modernism *(modernismo)*, now considered canonical, is considered the highest point of development of Latin American poetry; the movement has served as a mode of identification for a poetry emerging as a distinct transnational literature that is—by historical necessity—correlated with the development of poetry in the Spanish tradition. The anthologies that claim to be of "Latin American poetry" or of "Spanish America" are essentially selections of poetry by men. Both these pseudouniversal collections and the feminist anthologies that begin to appear in Spanish in the 1960s coexist as competing culturally constructed fields. Not surprisingly, the common denominator that stands out in the anthologies—covering from *modernismo* to the present—is a predominating absence of women in most collections, as a gendered factor.

In the 1980s, and now the 1990s, when there is *some* public knowledge of women poets' existence in Latin America, some public knowledge that we women participate in different areas of society, when evidence about the oppressive function of patriarchy has reached most Latin American countries, and when more and more women are speaking up against a male-centered cultural, social, and economic domination, one might ask, why is this structural exclusion of women not diminishing? The norms of Hispanic "Evephobia"—a counterpart to Marianism and a Latin American form of sexism—are also still rampant within the literary world. Furthermore, when some women poets or critics have had the opportunity to edit an anthology, the internalization of the patriarchal paradigms still lingers on in their selection, in their evaluative viewpoint, and in their discourses.

I will now consider the hypothesis that the positive segregation of women's poetry, as a separate section in an anthology on the one hand, and an anthology of poetry "by women only" on the other, might be an adequate solution. Feminist anthologies or anthologies of women poets have been fruitful and constructive as part of consciousness-raising in the United States within English and literary studies from the 1970s on. Women poets have been more visible, better appreciated, and more widely read thanks to the cultural act of being anthologized. In the context of these questions, my interest as editor is drawn to the *axioms of thinking* that construct anthologies, axioms that function as special features to orient these cultural forms toward tradition; for example, toward the established movements of *modernismo, postmodernismo, vanguardia*, which in their inception are already excluding women. These axioms of thinking predetermine the decisions of inclusion and of exclusion of poets or poems.

Quite evidently, the *criteria to select*—as "exclusionary principles" in Foucauldian terms—are peculiar to each historical period, to the specific "question of emergence" of anthologies (Foucault, *L'archéologie* 40); both editor and anthology belong concretely in the evolution of Latin American or Hispanic American poetry.

The discursive formations articulating literary criticism and literary history that legitimize primarily poetry by men institute and strengthen the field of Latin American poetry by *propagating the absence of poetry written by women*. It is a poetry constrained by a patriarchal dominance, imposed through the masculinist orientation of the anthologies. The customary justification for the exclusion of women is precisely the axiom of absence, because supposedly "there are almost no women poets." The problem of exclusion does not lie in the exclusion or marginality reflected in the anthologies, for poetry by women is systematically dismissed in all the other coexisting and preexisting forms of social discourse relating to Latin American poetry. Women's poetry has a repressed existence, a muted circulation in its process of emergence, in its developments within the continuities of Latin American literature. If an editor is constrained by the framing contexts of social discourse, of literary history and tradition, unfortunately in turn s/he reproduces those constraints which function as a system ruling the dissemination, the mutual coexistence and support of the ways in which particular groups include or exclude texts and authors (Foucault, *L'archéologie* 48). The occasional inclusion of a few women poets is hardly noticed in the multitude of male authors. Masculinist editors even exclude not only "new" poets—those writing after the 1950s—but also, in some cases, even Gabriela Mistral, who, after all, has been recognized by the traditional world for her poetry. The editors' presuppositions relating to artistic quality and literary value, applied to women poets, seem irrelevant, for the latter are ignored to such a degree that "theoretically"—from the editors' points of view—their writing is "not poetry" and consequently, as poets, "they do not exist."

It is generally accepted in literary history that the presence of women poets in Latin American literature begins to emerge with *modernismo*. Since then, however, women's poetry as such has proven to be unclassifiable for traditionalists and masculinist editors and critics; the displacement of poetry by women to a sphere of its own is not clear to editors and critics; and, most important, the literary establishment still resists the integration of work by women within the norms and canons of Latin American poetry. In other words, women poets do not actually seem to belong within what is understood as Latin American poetry per se, nor do they seem to hold a position of merit "parallel" to tradition. The label of "nontraditional" or "antitraditional" assigned to the themes of poetry by women is the most salient example of this situation.

IV. The Third

In a *feminist* or woman-oriented selection of texts by women there is, first of all, a consciousness of the ideologically male-oriented anthologies. Second, the inclusion of women is a transmaterial sign of "responsive understanding" as an effect of that consciousness.

Although the predominantly traditional anthology's addressees, as an implied text, are or can also be of both sexes, the dominance of the *gendered axiom as an unuttered masculinist structure of address* produces the social marginality of women poets as social group (Díaz-Diocaretz, "Sieving"). It further indicates that, quite simply, the anthology is not only intended, addressed, and designed, but also clearly oriented to a gendered subject, a collectivity of masculinist interlocutors forging a congenial audience. This feature is not usually made explicit in the Hispanic world, and therefore it constitutes an unuttered evaluation, an enthymeme (Díaz-Diocaretz, "Sieving"). As such, the most common *enthymeme of the anthological subject* in Latin American poetry is a male-oriented, male-identified selection and audience. By "male" I do not mean "constituted by men," for this is not a biologically defined aspect, but masculinist as a socially constructed feature. It is male-oriented because even women editors may practice the masculinist axioms by generating a male mode of thinking as the "model text" and a male-identified framing context that ignores the unsolved problem of women's poetry existing in nobody's land, or as a realm "of their own" called "feminine poetry" (*"poesía femenina"*). Obviously, reader-oriented aspects structure the anthology's projected reception in an ideologically gendered form. Such is the anthology's *gendered sociality.*

In a selection of only women poets, awareness of the existence of ideologically biased male-centered anthologies is a determining reason for its emergence; the inclusion of "women only" is a strategy considered as a *remedial* event (e.g., a "corrective alternative," in feminist terms of the 1970s, as Florence Howe once put it). This type of anthology is also a product of "responsive understanding," which, like its motivating text, is also gendered. We should ask ourselves about the nature of this "feminist" responsive understanding. Clearly the assumption perpetuating the idea that there are no women poets is a polemic "common horizon" for the anthologies' projected addressees. A common knowledge and understanding of the gendered "nature" of poetry considered worthy of being anthologized is instrumental in producing the viewpoint of "the other" in the selection, and in constructing a model text in which the authors are no longer individuals, but *gendered* "collective bearers of speech" (Bakhtin, *Speech Genres* 126).

There is a collective evaluation—saturated by a biological determinism—that is shared by the anthological subjects and its patriarchal addressees: on an extraverbal level, women's absence reinforces the presupposition that poetry by women is hierarchically inferior and that only male poets are worthy of being highly valued. The editor seeks a *responsive understanding of agreement* that projects a collectivity's viewpoint that will not polemicize the anthology's framing context, that will implicitly accept it, that will share its modes of understanding. Significantly, this particular collective addressee does not participate overtly in the anthology, nor is it represented. It functions as *a structure of understanding*, in the sense given by Bakhtin in his concept of *the third* (Bakhtin, *Speech Genres* 14).

Who is the third in the anthological subject of Latin American poetry? The third in the masculinist anthologies is a structure that ignores the contributions of women poets, which effaces them, and contains a selection designed for those who will be "reading as a man," following a socially constructed, patriarchally determined, unuttered structure of address (see Culler 43–64).

I have shown that the collective evaluations are gendered precisely because the collectivity that is being presupposed is homosocial: male authors oriented to the "gendered third." A masculinist anthology shares this gender preference with feminist anthologies, but they have crucially diverging orientations and their "third" in each case is quite distinct. The difference lies in the fact that the monologism of criticism and tradition is reflected in the "models" composed of the "exemplary texts" of tradition that the editors of these anthologies do not question. In a masculinist anthology, the framing context is not only gendered but biased.

Given that the common feature of "the observed world" in the anthological subject of Latin American poetry is gender biased, the idea of creating an anthology of feminist orientation is a "reactive" attitude, in the sense of "refuting" the masculinist axioms, as an answer with the implications I have suggested in the previous pages (Bakhtin, *Speech Genres* 13). Consequently, a feminist anthology in its cultural emergence contains an *implicitly polemical framing context* that is lacking in the masculinist anthology. In this implied polemics a different receiving collective consciousness constructs the anthology; at the same time, it is *being formulated* by the anthology. The patriarchal texts (of the exclusionary anthologies) are challenged by the "reactive text" that responds. Most important, the polemic framing context modifies the "imagined text" of the unuttered audience, composing in this way a *different third* in which the responsive understanding converts the male authors into the absent other, and introduces a different *receiving collective consciousness.*

Consequently, the complexity of the discursive formations of the anthological subject is far from biologically determined. We only need to be reminded of the few examples of feminist orientation. The collection *The Defiant Muse* edited by Flores and Flores unfolds a doubly gendered viewpoint in its editing subject given that it contains poems by women only (a factor in the sphere of authorship) and what are defined as *feminist* poems (in the sphere of perspective) in which the gendered evaluation is an a priori condition to construct a "model text" based on an implied notion of what constitutes a "feminist" poem.

In addition to the immediate reader-responding addressee, the editing subject presupposes a "higher superaddressee," Bakhtin's proposed agency of the third whose absolutely just responsive understanding is presumed. Quite significantly, drawing from the characteristics of the monologism of the male-dominated anthological subject predominating in Hispanic culture, I wish to stress that monologism has a third that excludes all other modes of understanding and knowledge but its own. This monologism does not succeed in suppressing the absent other, however. The monologism of criticism in literary history and the history of culture attempts to suppress forms of knowledge, but it is itself a product of "relationships to meaning," which are always dialogized (Bakhtin, *Speech Genres* 121).

The third in the anthologies of Latin American poetry has been essentially homosocial. A "feminist anthology" is the site of *gendered resistance* to the given, to tradition, and of course, to the canon, as a *response* to those exclusionary practices. The gendered nature of resistance is crucial in the context of Latin American poetry because several anthologies exist that are also constructed with a third imbued in political contexts, particularly as expression of rebellion and revolution. Revolutionary poetry resisting an oppressive reality exemplifies the anthology as a site of resistance in general (not gender specific).

I will briefly refer to two anthologies of Hispanic American poetry in which women poets are legitimized through inclusion.

The first is *Antología comentada de la poesía hispanoamericana,* edited by Hellen Ferro. Ferro's anthological subject features an illustration of its interrelatedness with literary history and also reveals some aspects of the editor's gendered evaluations.

This anthology's major overt framing texts are: (1) a *reproduction* of a "synopsis" of the chronological evolution of poetry in Spanish America previously included by the editor in one of her own books, *Historia de la poesía hispanoamericana* (5); (2) the editor's forthcoming work as contributor to a "Diccionario biográfico de poetas hispanoamericanos" which has also informed and influenced her present selection; and (3) the following major thematic divisions: Modernism; Modernist Preciosity; Colors and Antagonistic Words; The Intimacy of Impressionism; Eros; Confession and Messianism; The End of the Modernist Swan; Nationality; Landscape of the City; Landscapes in Recent Years; From Nationalism to Communism (including Gabriela Mistral's "Sun of the Incas" ["Sol de los Incas"]); The Vanguard (including Alfonsina Storni's "Boat-school" ["Buque-escuela"] and "Antipoem of Happiness" ["Antipoema de la felicidad"]); Negroid Poetry; Love Poetry; *Feminine Poetry* (including seventeen women poets); and Culteranism (which included Mistral's "Nocturne of Descent" ["Nocturno del descendimiento"])" (emphasis added).[2]

Ferro's awareness that she has separated poetry by women in a different section under the heading of "Feminine Poetry" ("Poesía Femenina") is acknowledged as she warns the reader that "we do not make an exception." Using the position of this editorial "we," however, she admits that nearly all the women poets included in that special section could be included in several (not all) of the other thematic and artistic divisions of the book (289). Whereas Ferro seems ambivalent about this mode of legitimizing women poets and of keeping them in their space of marginality in her introductory framing text, she shows no resistance to the patriarchally oriented superaddressee in the anthology itself. Thus, she is fully aware of the framing contexts of previous anthologies and the contexts of tradition and has no intention of deviating from them. The fact that "men continue assembling women poets under the title of 'Feminine Poetry'" helps her to justify her own repetition of this event and to show her intention of giving poetry by women more legitimation and representation (289). The editor's anthological framing text (e.g., her introduction to the section: "Las mujeres poetas" ["The Women Poets"]) is indeed in agreement with her own consciousness as a woman in a world of men, but the anthological realization of her intention contradicts this consciousness, for she does not transgress.

Evidently, within traditional bounds, the women poets in this anthology are excluded from topics such as "Landscape of the City," "Eros," and "Love Poetry." The few women poets included in some of the sections—as I indicated above—give a first impression of being odd inclusions, if one is not familiar with anthologies of Latin American poetry, but in fact they represent the "norm," the habitual treatment of poetry written by women. Ferro is fully aware that the world of poetry is a masculinist one and that if women are admitted into it, it is not without reluctance (289). In her prologue, among other ideas from her "Historia de la poesía hispanoamericana," she reiterates that "our poets were men of action rather than of contemplation" (5). The internalization of the patriarchal axioms I have described are further revealed in the implicitly gendered evaluations of Ferro's observation that: " . . . *if the anthology were devoted solely to 'feminine poetry,' we would have to resort to a number of more 'generic' themes:* love, death, rebellion, frustration, religion, landscape, ontological poetry" (289; emphasis added).[3] The underlying statement here is a biological and gender deterministic view—so widely criticized by some Anglo-American critics of poetry by women in the past two decades— that presupposes that the themes explored by women are inherently different from those developed by men.

I single out two other statements mainly to show the patriarchal axioms in this editor's framing context, significantly represented also in the language of logistics, a common code in the Hispanic world at large to refer to the "battle of the sexes": " . . . women have reached equal standards as men, but *men put them aside out of lack of trust,* as if to isolate them, just in case the Amazons decide to attack" (290; emphasis added). This assumption leads to the next: " . . . women do attack but in a different way and a few times they manifest to men that they are no longer the masters of the world as they think they are" (290).

The second anthology I refer to contains only women poets of Hispanic America, edited by the Spanish poet and now member of the Spanish Academy of the Language, Carmen Conde. In her framing texts, she proposes her selection as an exemplary text (*libro-ejemplo*) for others to follow in order to present more generously the creative work of "americohispanas," especially the work of contemporary poets not included in her selection (11). Conde's third as superaddressee is clearly the cultural context of Spain. Her editorial worldview and the position from which she "reads" the women poets are bound by *Castilian ideology,* for it is evident that a contemporary version of the Spanish expansion overseas is revealed in her language. She writes: "The great Spanish poetry, a conqueror of the highest prestige, leaped and reached the new continent" (12). She goes on to praise Latin American literary works as a "happy and extended replica" of Spanish poetry. In addition to her framing context of Europe as the center and origin of all that is to be praised, Conde introduces each of the women poets in the traditional mode of the male-oriented, male-dominated methods: by quoting the words of a patronizing (male) poet; by referring to a poet's husband and the commentaries he has written; using criticism, anecdotes, and reports by a well-known (male) admirer of a given poet; excerpts from a (male) poet's praise; praise from a poet's recognized and famous *master*; recorded testimonies of men who knew a poet personally; or the women poets' relationships with other poets.

Going back to my working hypothesis about the inclusion of women only—in a separate section or in a separate anthology—as a viable alternative, I must stress that we cannot avoid the fact that it was not a feminist anthological subject, but a traditional, patriarchally determined one that first included women poets in a separate section, and which, at last, gave some legitimization to "Feminine Poetry" in Latin American literature in the celebrated anthology edited by Federico de Onís.

As concluding remarks, we can consider two possible alternatives motivated by these representative examples. In the Hispanic world, to continue including women in a special section only perpetuates a practice initiated by patriarchal axioms of thinking; it means legitimizing women poets within the anthological framing contexts of poetry, but at the same time delegitimizing their integration in historical and aesthetic continuity and the development of poetic practice. A separate section marginalizes their work a priori from any thematic, stylistic, artistic, or aesthetic principle; it also presupposes an essentialist difference and allows the anthological subjects in the Hispanic culture to continue excluding women poets from the tradition, from the canon, and from the so-called masterpieces or exemplary texts of our culture. All these problems are equally valid in the production of anthologies "of women only." A gendered and biased politics of editing patronizingly accepts that there is such a phenomenon as "women's poetry" which is fundamentally "feminine." From this we can conclude that we should discard the working hypothesis I presented at the beginning of this essay, that anthologies or sections of women poets could be the solution. It is not viable at least in the Hispanic world, because to continue accepting the contradictory, double bind of being legitimized and delegitimized simultaneously is to collaborate with and to internalize the patriarchal axioms of exclusionary thinking.

Another alternative—a hypothesis to be tested in the future—can be an anthological subject sustained by a feminist consciousness working with framing contexts not limited to gender divisions, a construction of an anthology whose "third" would *dis-expect* a homosocial group of poets (male or female) and would agree with a nongendered, inclusive selection of poetry. Another way to change the anthological subjects in our Hispanic culture would be to bring forth new selections in which we also do a rethinking of— thus, questioning—the poetry by men already included in the anthologies of tradition, from *modernismo* to the present, especially in the more recent anthologies published in the 1980s. The feminist anthological subject I envision would realize and project new definitions and evaluations. Indeed, a feminist anthological subject is bound to be gendered as well, but at least this new discursive and cultural transmaterial event can contribute to undo the bare and still comfortably settled monologism of patriarchal poetry in the Hispanic world.

Notes

1. The reference to the "transmaterial" nature in verbal interaction is part of the current work that I am developing in opposition to the dichotomies that differentiate sharply between material aspects and the transmaterial properties of signification found in the work of, for example, Delgado.

2. El Modernismo; El Preciosismo Modernista; Colores y Palabras Antagónicas; Intimidad de Impresionismo; Erótica; Confesión y Mesianismo; Final del Cisne

Modernista; La Nacionalidad; El Paisaje de la Ciudad; El Paisaje en los últimos Años; Del Nacionalismo al Comunismo; La Vanguardia; Poesía Negroide; Poesía Amorosa; *Poesía Femenina;* El Culteranismo.

    3. These translations are the author's own.

Works Cited

Bakhtin, Mikhail Miklailovich. *The Dialogic Imagination.* Ed. Michael Holquist. Trans. Caryl Emerson and Michael Holquist. Austin: Univ. of Texas Press, 1981.

———. *Speech Genres and Other Late Essays.* Trans. Vern W. McGee. Ed. Caryl Emerson and Michael Holquist. Austin: Univ. of Texas Press, 1986.

Conde, Carmen, ed. *Once grandes poetisas americohispanas.* Madrid: Cultura Hispánica, 1967.

Culler, Jonathan. *On Deconstruction: Theory and Criticism after Structuralism.* Ithaca: Cornell Univ. Press, 1982. [Especially 43–64.]

Delgado, J. M. R. "Triunism: A Transmaterial Brain-Mind Theory." *Brain and Mind.* Ciba Foundation Symposium, 69 (New Series). Amsterdam: Excerpta Medica, 1979. 369–396.

Díaz-Diocaretz, Myriam. *The Transforming Power of Language: The Poetry of Adrienne Rich.* Utrecht: HES Publishers, 1984.

—. "Sieving the Matriheritage of the Sociotext." In *The Difference Within: Feminism and Critical Theory.* Ed. Elizabeth Meese and Alice Parker. Amsterdam: John Benjamins, 1989. 115–147.

Ferro, Hellen. *Historia de la poesía hispanoamericana.* New York: Las Américas, 1964.

———, ed. *Antología comentada de la poesía hispanoamericana.* New York: Las Américas, 1965.

Flores, Angel, and Kate Flores, eds. *The Defiant Muse: Hispanic Feminist Poems from the Middle Ages to the Present.* New York: The Feminist Press, 1986.

Foucault, Michel. *L'archéologie du savoir.* Paris: Gallimard, 1969.

———. "What Is an Author?" In *Textual Strategies: Perspectives in Post-Structuralist Criticism.* Ed. Josué V. Harari. Ithaca: Cornell Univ. Press, 1979. 141–160.

Onís, Federico de. *Antología de la poesía española e hispanoamericana.* New York: Las Americas, 1961.

Afterword
The Editor's Eros

Tom Conley

A convention cherished among literary historians generally opposes exegesis to interpretation. The division demarcates a boundary between the self or first person, the current writer, and that of the other, the third person or text issuing from another period. A generous soul, the exegete makes clear the voice of the third person muted by the ravages of time. Exegetes erase themselves or accede to an absent presence by assuming an identity with the texts they are reviving. By contrast, interpreters are narcissists; they reflect themselves and their time by virtue of an avowed attraction for given authors or problems characterizing periods and genres. The convention implies that the labor of exegesis tends to be more sacred, or selfless, than that of interpretation. Exegesis in fact rings of Christian virtue ("Jesus" interpellates us when we hear his name in *exegesis*), while interpretation connotes enterprise, a free agency of subjectivity, of mediation (in the sense of going-between, or of tertiary activity, in in*ter*pretation), mobile activities of hermeneutic barter of ideas in perpetual *negotiation*.[1]

Exegetical scholars generally are held to be immaculately scrupulous individuals who efface themselves from—but also *into*—the texts they resuscitate from darkness and bring into the light of day.

They generally bear an aura that places them, like orants, above interpreters who must, if they wish to accede to the status of editors, spend days and nights deciphering and glossing manuscripts and variants, learning paleography, living in the Vatican library, and living a polyglot life forged from the words of others. Interpreters wishing to become editors must prepare themselves for tribulations of the kind Saint Jerome encountered in the desert, or for the temptations Hieronymus Bosch arrays around Saint Anthony in the painting that hangs in the Flemish wing of the Prado.

The authors of this handsome collection of essays have succeeded in shattering this convention. The merit of the ensemble may be due in no small way to a collective refusal merely to entertain the opposition in order, by means of deconstructive method, as current idiolect goes, to "collapse" it. The authors do not, therefore, tell us that one term is merely in and of the other, or that the convention is invented either for heuristic purposes to stimulate or to reveal the real ideologies of editing. If the convention exists, the authors imply, it goes without saying that editorial practices fold interpretation into exegesis, and that in fact even the most sacred or rigorous editions of the Western canon are laden with self-fashioning designs. In the paragraphs that follow I would like to study how their feat is accomplished and to see how the authors alter our notions of the relation that editing holds with a canon, with production, and, more broadly, with ethics.

The nine chapters generally take up their topics as cases. The *Poema* of the *Cid*, Colin Smith tells us in the first sentence of chapter 1, "is a very special case." For Reinaldo Ayerbe-Chaux, the editions of Juan Manuel's writing constitute a dossier, a strongbox, or, as his title underscores, a "case" bearing the medieval writer's signature. Elias L. Rivers puts forward the contents taken from a historical "case" of Garcilaso's poetry, while Joseph V. Ricapito profiles the fortunes of the case of Spain's national *pícaro*. Pere Ferré displays an array of Romantic notions about poetry and resuscitation of the past where, "in none of these cases," did editors or readers of the *romancero* "rigorously establish a text." Susan Kirkpatrick tells us that in every instance where a writer is confined, both writer and editor are locked in a "deadly glass coffin," "made legible in a corpus," embalmed or mortified with editorial rigor. She puts forward women writers deadened, each in "a seemingly clear-cut case," including "the case of Carolina Coronado" or other women, in order to show that writers, if they change the lives of their readers, never have an erotically "legitimate place" for themselves.

When each of the authors brings forth materials in the frame of a *case* under study, called in question is the ocular privilege—a relation of denomination and domination—that comes with an editor's command over his or her archives; and, too, the ostensively slavish fidelity to his or her "master text," in which the former speaks for or through the latter. In every instance where the authors of this volume depict their topics as *cases* we can be reminded of the inflection that Freud gave to the substantive when he wrought his patients into the fictions of a *Krankengeschichte*, that the Standard Edition translates as "case-history." The truth that he unveiled through dialogue with his obsessional neurotics and hysterics became a matter worthy, as he understood the sense of case (from *casus*, or all that fall), of *destiny*, or whatever by *occasion* moved from a virtual or potential status into the hard fact of history. The case was thus an evidence of fate, of fortune fallen, or of the very object of his inquiry, the manifestation of the unconscious itself. The end of his research was contained in the history and imprint of the title he chose to place above each of his five great clinical narratives.

The fixing or fixating traits of the case histories in fact show us how the founder of psychoanalysis remains skittish about reducing his heroes—Dora, Hans, Schreber, the Wolf Man, and their attendants—to medical names or symptoms filed in cases. At the same time, however, the *Krankengeschichte* constitutes an argument for the poetic science that Freud saw himself founding and leading as if he were Moses. Chronicles of themselves, of Viennese time and of time immemorial, of Freud and his world, the case histories encircle contingent and eternal issues and, no less, collective and local praxes. We must recall how Freud tried to place a person he named Dora, a figure who defied him and, in doing so, enlightened him about the multiple urges and views of sexuality, into the confines of a case. A "case" of hysteria, Dora is tantamount to Pandora. Readers open the fateful box when they follow the story of the analyst discovering the laws of countertransference. Much as Freud tries to contain the woman he adores, Dora eludes his spell and ultimately "breaks off" the treatment. She slams a door in his face. From the experience Freud fashions a clinical autobiography that camouflages his longings for the patient who resists the charm of his expertise. Freud completes an authoritative but prismatic fiction—a founding moment in the history of the analytical cure—with appeal to theatrical conventions. The affair ends with the *deus ex machina* of an inconclusive postscript. When the clinical experience arouses and defies the analyst, as both name and figure, Dora and her *case* engage an erotic relation of the scientist to the languages of the world.

The same can be said of the nine essays in this volume. Each betrays an eros that comes with editing and its politics, and each follows an allure of its own relation with a specific body of texts. By doing so, the essays remind us that areas seemingly neutral or least invested with drive and tension are those most imbued with it. Eros can be, as the title of the volume implies, a basic component of any *politics.* The editor's task entails mediating relations that for various causes, of ideological or professional design, cannot be named. If indeed we can speak of a politics of editing, its field of operation and practice of decisions mark various codings of erotic relations to writing. This relation in turn is transmuted into the play of exegesis and interpretation, in other words, a mode of *dissimulation* that editors engage in displaying their relation to texts and institutions. Pere Ferré notes as much when he finds his own point of view in the words of Diego Catalán: "the 'document' masks the 'being' of the poem we are seeking to study" ("el 'documento' nos enmascara el 'ser' del poema que tratamos de estudiar").

Dissimulation is dissimulated over and again. Two symptomatic moments of the erotic and political labor of editing are made manifest in the two very different essays on Garcilaso. In the first, Elias L. Rivers traces the fortunes of editions that build and cast aura upon a monument of early modern poetry. To detect how Garcilaso has been read over four centuries, he insists that "the acoustic (and graphic) form of the material signifier is fully as important as the more conceptual and idealistic structure of the signified." From there he suggests that textual evidence will indicate how a history and anthropology of reading can be made of Spain since the Renaissance. On several occasions the author faces the awkward but delicious task of being obliged to cite himself—in the third person—as an element of the long history of Garcilaso's work ["(Rivers, *Obras completas con comentario* 19)"; "(Rivers, 'Garcilaso divorciado' 121)"; "in 1964, Elias L. Rivers followed the example of Keniston"; "Blecua's study was fully taken into account by Rivers in 1974 when the latter published a critical edition of Garcilaso's complete works"]. He appears to present himself neutrally, as one of many texts in an evolution of commentary. A scrupulous scholar, he uses the "he" to mask an object that Rivers would obviously treat as any in the Garcilaso corpus; any self-investment on his part, as revealed in the self-citation, would only be a bibliographical flicker in a greater *vie des formes* of a great *obra*.

When Rivers is impelled to crystallize the history he has sketched, he chooses a thorny editorial problem in Garcilaso's Third Eclogue. Rivers initiates a divided discourse—subject to examination of the acoustic and graphic form of the signifier—that begs the reader to apply the editorial method being advocated. The passage selected describes the death of the nymph Elisa:

> Near the water, in a flowery spot,
>
> she lay among the grass with severed throat
>
> as the white swan lies when he loses
>
> his sweet life among the green grasses.

> Cerca del agua, en un lugar florido,
>
> estava entre las yervas degollada,
>
> qual queda el blanco cisne quando pierde
>
> la dulce vida entre la yerva verde. (229–232)

Editors have contended that, among others, the scene of deploration in the flowers recalls Virgil's Fifth Eclogue, and also Sannazaro's *Arcadia*. Rivers adds that controversy over the *degollada* (decapitated, throat cut) brutalizes the pastoral atmosphere of the tradition inherited from the Virgilian tradition. Would *igualada* (equaled, leveled) be correct and thus less shocking than *degollada*? Does decapitation thrust the blade of history or castration into the timeless tenor of the eclogue? Apparently. "But Porqueras Mayo and Martínez López presented further arguments in favor of *degollada*, and Rivers in his 1974 edition accepted this reading. More recent gloss over the past sixteen years has shown that, he adds, a coextensive reading of both words is possible, but also that they may find their synthesis in *yugulada*. By combining the two readings (or collapsing the opposition), "we have the best solution to the problem of what the poet's final intention was," a statement Rivers then is impelled to undo by citing Olga Tudorica Impey and Mario di Pinto's discovery of the toponym "Val de la Gollada," which may situate Garcilaso's remarkable lines into a topographical cleft or vail near Toledo.

But where the editor states that emendations add to greater equivocation of violence basic to the innuendo of preciosity, Rivers appeals to a Freudian gesture in order to defer finality. Often Freud concludes his essays by asking for further study to resolve what remains unfinished. So does Rivers. "Future dynamics" will solve the problem. We must await the arrival of Science who will come, like Fate, to judge the final reading, but only at a moment *after* this moment of truth is established. Yet if the editor has become both the body of the poem and poet by means of total but *unnamed* identification with it, does not the choice—the *case*, the destiny of the selection—of Garcilaso's scene of the expiring nymph project the editor's death-drive into the writing of the poem? Is it not *Elias* who is transmuted into *Elisa*? Is the *locus amoenus* in the eclogue the cleft where a textual and editorial death is imagined by way of travesty, of transmutation, "cerca del agua, en un lugar florido," in the valley of the *rivers* of the pastoral and elegiac traditions? Thus read, the mute sound of the swan losing "la dulce vida entre la yerva verde" is also one of confused *verba,* or voice of poet and critic alike, lost or inexistent in the waves of sound echoing over the waters, but forever printed—metamorphosed—into a scene of a mirrored gaze of self-reflection. Elisa protracts the staging of an editor's revery of bodily transformation into the flowers and eros of an other, unnameable moment congealed in a timeless critical edition. The editorial scene staged before our eyes is one of a *scène d'écriture* filtered through the experience of Mallarmé's swans congealed in the ice of printed letters. It resembles a mystical transference of the "I" into the sign of a nymph mourned by the silent lament of the *cygne* or *cisne.* An erotic triumph of the editor's signature is written into the labor that is said to elucidate or fill gaps of knowledge.

Treating the same body of poetry from a political standpoint, Iris M. Zavala locates how and where Garcilaso has figured in a body of "master narratives" that an evolving State strategically administers to its subjects. The work, she argues, institutionalizes and represses. Yet the problem of naming that she encounters is no less richly problematic than that of Rivers, like Actaeon, happening upon himself as a nymph by the river of the eclogue. The three most recurrent substantives in Zavala's essay are *culture*, *hegemony*, and *I*. The first two tend to be synonymous, but the third has to mediate the other two by means of tracing the history of Garcilaso's editions. By appeal to *I*, Zavala studies an institution *in medias res* and, it appears, more directly than the author of the preceding essay. At the same time that a critique is made of repressive cultural production erected over the *Obras*, the *I* of the commentary must nonetheless inscribe itself in the history it is writing. Hence Zavala's name dominates the bibliography in order to gain agency or authority by which it can sustain itself. Yet it tells of a history from which it seeks to assume a distance. The bind entails choosing ways of being in and out of what is being told. Something cannot be named. To indicate what cannot, Zavala locates a tension of deixis in Wittgenstein: "There is nothing that can be said in the first person that cannot be said in the third." *I* can be *he* or *she*, or, as the French canon tells us in Rimbaud's *jeu de mots* in his "Lettre du voyant" (1871), "Je est un autre."[2] It follows that wherever the discourse addresses a third person, it also turns back to itself, as in the sentence following the paraphrase of the author of the *Tractatus:* "Lyric poetry was the agency for an emergent science of the constitution of the subject, made coextensive with that of language; there was an interplay between the language of the Empire and the unified and centered self." It appears that the essay has to unify and center itself according to the paradigms it castigates, and in this way *literally* symptomatizes a politics of editing seen from the standpoint of criteria of exclusion.

For the same reason it would not be wrong to turn the political bias of the editorial history, taken from the Frankfurt school, cast as "instrumental reason," against the authority that has fabricated it. As a collective, a "school," a syndicated center officially criticizing "cultural production," *they* incorporate themselves as a sanctimoniously neutral origin of a critique of "instrumental reason." The very formulation of the concept designed to counter hegemonic masterplots, when applied to the literary institution, betrays hegemonic strategies in the performance of its articulation.[3] Hegemony avers to be couched in every utterance, every citation; it becomes the jewelled money of every instance of discourse.

A means of rearticulating the political economy might be found in what Susan Kirkpatrick notes about editing Coronado and Avellaneda. In her eyes an effective editorial tactic entails shattering any agency that *essentializes* its object, whether in the articulation of textual apparatus, historical reconstruction, or bibliography. She opts for "textual fluidity over textual fixity," and contends that editing must pluralize the condition of any given text. She notes how language of any document can have "a fluid and never-finished existence," and implies that a work can reshape itself through the various sexualities of its readers. A text that offers an image of the male or female would thus have a fixating and limiting effect, whereas a reading or writing that works as minimally as possible with meaning, intention, or either original or final representation, will engage the *force* of writing that moves to and from or along the margins of social and literary institutions, and that hence cannot be fetishized as an "edition" or a "case."

Where Kirkpatrick offers solutions to the fixating, generally male-gendered acts of exegesis, her discourse becomes decisively erotic. It deals with engenderment as a way of exceeding gender. "The whole set of meanings that we can find in the early poems is made evident to us neither in the uneasy protests of the unedited poem [by Coronado] nor in the smooth, conventionally feminine surfaces of the published collection; rather, it is in *the conjunction of the two* that we can see how the poem is produced *in the push and pull* between the subordinated and the dominant" (emphasis added). The critic is telling us that a politics of editing requires us to work in and through the sublimations of attraction and of congress with the texts we read, and to embrace their form to promote modes of identification that cannot be fixed. The language she finds in these capital moments humbles those of the editorial history reviewed in the opening pages, and by its own form demonstrates where an editor becomes both an agent and a writer of literature.

A truism of the history of psychoanalysis dictates that sublimation involves rechanneling instinctual drives into artistic or documentary creation. For Freud, the emblem of the principle is drawn in the parabola of the career of Leonardo da Vinci, for whom the thrust of eros is channeled into the production of "timeless" and "great" works. For Jean-Paul Sartre, a card-carrying Freudian, we see that an initially erotic attraction to literature is displaced when transformed into political commitment.[4] In this respect Susan Kirkpatrick shows us how not to repress either the poetic or the political areas of editing, but to have the two work with and about each other.

Where erotic and critical elements are conjoined in her discourse, standards of measure are obtained. As in the reflection of Rivers into Garcilaso, Kirkpatrick's identification with Coronado as writing and movement indicates how strategies of fixation prevail elsewhere. Thus Ricapito's representation of Lazarillo as an answer to failed social institutions (the *pícaro* represented as a caseworker or clairvoyant sociologist working tirelessly over three centuries) gives the lie to the question that ponders if literature can aspire to anything other than dialogue with itself. It asks if only past literature can have symbolic efficacity. If so, literature must be disinterred in order to name problems that current conditions relegate to silence. Through its many editions Lazarillo must therefore keep an ideological hold on a *universal* public. When Evangelina Rodríguez tackles the difficult order of editing Golden Age theater, a genre of which the printed text, like a videotape, is only a partial object, she is led to look for terms that will "fix" what remains ineffable, or contain what cannot outlive the act of the performance animating movements of language and body. If indeed the element of chance and of fugacity of the dramatic texts cannot be located, her own theatrical gesture, traced in a brief apostrophe at the end of her reflection, tells us why. She appeals to foreign terms that serve to derealize, thus name, what resists language. They seem to have a timeless appeal: *tejne, clinamen, tessara, kenosis, demonizacion, askesis, apophrades*. Cast as they are from Greek or Latin, they are sought because, unlike Spanish or English, they appear to resist change, and appear adequate to the desire to control momentarily the "multifaceted character of dramatic manuscripts." Their fixity becomes thus a means and a hope—an esperanto—to sustain investigation.[5] The *allure* of the terms, however, becomes the ruse of their truth.

Pere Ferré comes to similar conclusions when he shows how the Romantics' task of "gathering and restoring" literature of times past points to a bogus and loathsome origin of scholarly positivism. In France, we recall, Sainte-Beuve established the paradigm for a century of literary botany when he realized that his creative talents were no match for those of Victor Hugo. When he saw that Alfred de Vigny had already arrogated for himself the role of the poet Moses leading the masses, he could resort only to science. A tradition of rigor was instituted over disillusionment and frustration experienced in the more compelling world of letters. Ferré takes the same perversion a step further by showing how, at the same time, a Spanish learned class claimed itself to be more sensitive, more lyrical, and more poetic than the masses out of which it was emerging, and how its labors of "restoration" institutionalized a drive to maintain, for the sake of capital, a staunch gap between the rich and the poor or the lettered and lower classes. Only through a battle for productive *contaminations* of voices of different classes, times, and origins, he argues, would a broader historical and literary perspective be attained.

The same theme inaugurates the volume, in Colin Smith's remarkable review of the fortunes of the *Poema de mio Cid* in which he shows how the work now stands in the middle of a battlefield. The *Poema* does not live in the sanctuary of a monastic library.[6] The poem was written to rival concurrent French *chansons de geste.* In crafting the reading, Smith comes to the threshold of another *scène d'écriture.* Now it is marked by the first-person shifter:

> If Spaniards have never tried to deny the imitation of French styles of architecture and decoration at this time in northern Spain, I see no reason why they should have doubts about the influence of French models on their nascent literature. In the case of the "Poema" *I have gone further,* arguing that it was the first Castilian epic, the initiator of a new genre, the work of a man who in the early years of the thirteenth century wished to provide his homeland—Castile, specifically Burgos—with a national epic to rival the best French chansons de geste. *I add,* not as a sop to any nationalistic opinion but as a considered aesthetic judgment on *a text that is a part of me* as few

others are, *that he triumphantly succeeded.* (emphasis
added)

The origin of a founding place that receives the *I* is located in the
other, but it is represented as a struggle for an identity gained by
contact with alterity or a stranger. A heroic, anonymous scribe is
transmuted into the editor who now battles new Rolands and new
Olivers metamorphosed in the name of French invasions from the
North, under the banner of Joseph Duggan. Hoisting himself into
his stirrup, Smith projects an illusory moment of original, founding
creation when the author, in the armor of a medieval hero, becomes
the identity of an editorial self, a scribe, who carries on a combat
raging since the inception of medieval literature and the Franco-
Iberian canon.[7] The origin of the *Poema* can thus be at once collective *and* individual, contingent *and* transhistorical. In the same
blow it inaugurates and perpetuates a founding battle, the same
conflict that Freud marshaled over and again to argue for his tenets
about the psychogenesis of human subjects. By reverting to the
scene of an origin, Smith productively contaminates fixed views
that attempt to resolve or mediate battle, whether in the view, then,
of "a scribe who was economizing on parchment," or now, as
Reinaldo Ayerbe-Chaux typifies the labor of the medievalist, in
"an editor . . . who has battled with the text" by retracing its myriad
"disturbances." Smith implies that any scholar—male or female,
medievalist or theoretician, exegete or interpreter—must find multiple sensibilities in mixed *tones* of discourse.

The same tones may be what Myriam Díaz-Diocaretz seeks when
she appeals to figures, drawn from Bakhtin, of *others* whose discourses resonate in given pieces of writing. Wherever a conflict of
voices takes place, rewriting virtually begins. Thus her "framing
context" of anthologies not only buckles the volume but also reproduces an arena of conflict not entirely unlike what Colin Smith
depicted as the carnage of medieval studies. For Díaz-Diocaretz,
anthology rings with the tone of *anthems* psalmodized in honor
of nations and of fathers, spoken above flowers collected in bou-
quets that adorn the dais where patriarchs speak at professional
conventions. The context of a battle for ultimate origins in medieval
Spain, located in the first—and founding—chapter of this collection, is reiterated by way of the economy of scholarly and popular

editions in modern times. Between one and the other an evolution of orientations, subjects, and genders is traced. Throughout many battles are waged. Everywhere everyone rightly seeks to revive— and to battle for—what conventions repress, in a vision that Reinaldo Ayerbe-Chaux casts in the oxymoron of "creative scholarly editions." The authors seek productive contaminations of styles; they make manifest a total identification with a textual other through pleasure taken in the denial of the self. In doing so they bend the barriers or "framing contexts" of disciplines inherited from ostensively "scientific" traditions, and thus bring forth the ethics of a sublimely erotic relation with signatures and language. Articulation of these unnameable confusions of drives and, as Freud would say, their "vicissitudes," marks the politics of editing.

Notes

1. Recent literature on the topic is rich. Using an apparatus taken from Foucault to ground his *Shakespearean Negotiations* (Oxford: Clarendon Press, 1988), Stephen Greenblatt underscores how much the great bard is a production of enterprise. Shakespeare's patient exegetes play roles no less invested than those of critics or editors marketing ideas and editions. Greenblatt avows affinity for concepts drawn from *L'archéologie du savoir, L'ordre du discours,* and "What Is an Author?" In this last essay Foucault, we must remember, used many of the distinctions— which still hold force—that Benveniste articulated in the first volume of the *Problèmes de linguistique générale* (Paris: Gallimard, 1966). Benveniste elaborates the tension between discourse and history (not unlike that of interpretation and exegesis) in terms of patterned dissimulations of shifters. To have the look of history, a discourse recounting events past avoids recourse to the first-person singular and writes in a preterite tense; or the enunciation of an object in the third person (*it, he,* or *she*) depends on the copresence of a masked *I* that is whispered to a witness, a reader, a spectator, or an implicit *you*. No discourse that aspires to representation fails to display these hinges of its underpinnings and, in turn, its ideology. Less recent literature emphasizes the relation between hermeneutics and capitalism. Norman O. Brown stressed that the trickster, Hermes, is engaged in an "acquisitive" way of life, in *Hermes the Thief: The Evolution of a Myth* (New York: Vintage, 1969 Rpt.), 80.

2. The economy of the statement has its most convex correlative in the media business of baseball. Since the era of free agency (literally, era of the "free subject"), the player (e.g., José Canseco, Roger Clemens, Rickey Henderson) gains "agency" by means of his agent who engages a bidding war with a team's management. Because single salaries have escalated to sums that would relieve burdens imposed on the national debt, be instrumental for repairing decay in the educational system, help the homeless, etc., crushing social contradiction becomes the *real* and forcibly unnamed subject of the news. For their interviews players are taught both to reduce and intensify the contradiction. To say "I want $5,000,000 per year for five months

of work" is tantamount to sacrilege. To mediate direct instancing of greed, the players are trained to use the *I* in the third person. Before bevies of camcorders, "José Canseco," says José Canseco, "will have to do what is right for José Canseco." The third-person *I* (sign of collapse into tautology, i.e., greed) *appears* to modify the preposterous terms of the scene. On a basal level scholars also play baseball. We are impelled to cite our proper names in texts so as to be repertoried and quantified in reviews of citations, indexes, and bibliographies. These in turn are used to gauge productivity and to influence decisions concerning promotion or increment of salary.

3. To the point, it can be added that for this reader a good deal of writing that mimes the style of the second and third generations of the Frankfurt school has the misfortune of using *tone* to display filial lines of filiation. Similar turns of expression multiply, wit (if any) becomes predictable, and most conclusions ponderous. Writing of this kind—and this can be extended to adepts of formalism, deconstruction, semiotics, psychoanalysis—displays an oedipal relation wherever it cites (and thus despite itself identifies with) the key words of a "master discourse." The diction shows that it is not ready to distort or rewrite what has been imposed upon it. Taken in this sense, following Zavala, it stands that any institution, be it Garcilaso, Adorno, or public and private universities in North America, leaves the imprint of "hegemony" upon its subjects.

4. See Denis Hollier, *Politiques de la prose: Sartre et l'an quarante* (Paris: Gallimard, 1982), recently translated into English by Jeffrey Mehlman as *Politics of Prose* (Minneapolis: Univ. of Minnesota Press, 1988).

5. Here we are reminded of what, in *La vérité en peinture* (Paris: Aubier-Flammarion, 1978), Jacques Derrida noted of Kant's relation to Latin. Where the philosopher treats the most ethereal, moving, and difficult topics that know no language, he attempts to fix his relation to them by use of Latin terms that give enduring structure to the vernacular context. Appeal to an older and ostensively permanent idiom betrays the fragility of what the philosopher seeks in his adventure with the sublime.

6. Nor do many medieval manuscripts. Douglas Kelly reports that French manuscripts of the twelfth and thirteenth centuries have suffered more decay over the past twenty years than, perhaps, over five centuries (personal communication). Students of medieval literature have become numerous, but especially so are the demands placed upon editors who have to encounter these primary documents. Manuscripts have been consulted and read as they never were intended to be. Their fate, if we can project contemporary dilemmas upon them, concretizes what we see happening in the global sphere: universal stress, pollution, overpopulation, destruction by way of ocular fascination.

7. The figure resembles Sartre's personification of the writer *engagé* in his postwar *What Is Literature?*. Whatever the affinity, this scene of writing shares much with what R. Howard Bloch has noted about the beginnings of French medievalism in the nineteenth century. The creation of a national literature happens to be the transference of battles between France and Germany onto medieval texts. Wilhelm Meyer-Lübke and the Neo-Grammarians were conquering the French language. By the time of the Franco-Prussian War, French scholars had to sound a call to arms. They instituted a national *chanson de geste* and pure spirit of medieval French literature to mediate the losses of Alsace and Lorraine. The Strasbourg oaths

are unearthed to reclaim the conflicted area about the city, implying that medieval studies are born of contemporary conflict displaced into philology and archaeological reconstruction ("The First Document and the Birth of Medieval Studies" 13). Smith alludes to Bloch's representation of the writing of medieval literary history when, apropos the *chanson de geste,* he speaks of a "nationalistic overlay imposed in our own times."

Works Cited

Benveniste, Emile. *Problèmes de linguistique générale.* 2 vols. Paris: Gallimard, 1966–1968.

Bloch, R. Howard. "The First Document and the Birth of Medieval Studies." In *A New History of French Literature.* Ed. Denis Hollier. Cambridge: Harvard Univ. Press, 1989. 6–13.

Brown, Norman O. *Hermes the Thief: The Evolution of a Myth.* New York: Vintage, 1980 Rpt.

Derrida, Jacques. *La vérité en peinture.* Paris: Aubier-Flammarion, 1978.

Foucault, Michel. *L'archéologie du savoir.* Paris: Gallimard, 1969.

———. *L'ordre du discours.* Paris: Gallimard, 1972.

———. "What Is an Author?" In *Textual Strategies: Perspectives in Post-Structuralist Criticism.* Ed. Josué V. Harari. Ithaca: Cornell Univ. Press, 1979. 141–160.

Greenblatt, Stephen. *Shakespearean Negotiations.* Oxford: Clarendon Press, 1988.

Hollier, Denis. *Politiques de la prose: Sartre et l'an quarante.* Paris: Gallimard, 1982.

Sartre, Jean-Paul. *What Is Literature?* New York: Philosophical Library, 1949.

Contributors

Reinaldo Ayerbe-Chaux. Professor of Spanish and Head of the Department at the University of Illinois at Chicago. Among his publications, the most important are his contributions to Juan Manuel studies such as *El Conde Lucanor: Materia Tradicional y Originalidad Creadora* (1975), and his editions of *Libro del Conde Lucanor* (1982), *Textos y Concordancias de la Obra Completa de Juan Manuel* (1986), and *Cinco Tratados* (1989).

Tom Conley. Professor of French at the University of Minnesota, recently a Fellow at the Institute for Research in the Humanities at the University of Wisconsin-Madison. Specializing in problems of text and image in French and Comparative Literatures, he has published extensively on Montaigne. Work in Hispanic areas includes *Surrealismo documental: lectura de "Tierra sin pan"* (1988) and "Broken Blockage: notas sobre la guerra civil en el cine de Hollywood," *Revista de Occidente* (1987). He has published *Film Hieroglyphics* (1991), and *The Graphic Unconscious: The Letter of Early Modern French Writing* is forthcoming.

Myriam Díaz-Diocaretz. Senior Lecturer in the Department of Comparative Literature at the University of Amsterdam. The author of *The Transforming Power of Language* (1984), *Translating Poetic Discourse: Questions on Feminist Strategies in Adrienne Rich* (1985), and *Per una poetica della differenza* (1989), she has also published four books of poetry, and has edited and coedited volumes on poetics, critical theory, and feminist studies, including *Hélène Cixous: Chemin d'une écriture* (1990). She is the founding editor of the international journal *Critical Studies,* the general editor of the series *InterActions* (Amsterdam: Rodopi), general editor of the series *Cultura y Diferencia* (Barcelona: Anthropos), and (with I. M. Zavala) general editor of the series *Critical Theory* (Amsterdam: John Benjamins).

Pere Ferré. Professor at the Universidade Nova de Lisboa, director of its Instituto de Estudos sobre o Romanceiro Velho e Tradicional, and coparticipant in the project "Description, Editing, and Analysis of the Pan-Hispanic *Romancero.*" His published works include an edition of traditional *Romances,* as well as various studies on the Portuguese and Spanish ballad. At present, he coordinates both a project on analytical bibliography of the whole Portuguese *Romanceiro,* and the critical edition of this balladistic corpus printed between 1824 and 1960.

Susan Kirkpatrick. Professor of Spanish and Chair of the Literature Department at the University of California, San Diego. She has written numerous articles on nineteenth-century Spanish literature and is the author of *Larra: El laberinto inextricable de un liberal romántico* (1977) and *Las Románticas: Women Writers and Subjectivity in Spain, 1835–1850* (1989; Spanish version, 1991). She is presently working on questions of gender in late-nineteenth-century writing.

Joseph Ricapito. Professor of Spanish at Louisiana State University. He has published extensively on Spanish Golden Age literature and culture, especially on the picaresque novel, and has published two editions of *Lazarillo de Tormes* (Madrid: Cátedra, 1976; Madison, 1987).

Elias L. Rivers. Leading Professor of Spanish and Comparative Literature at the State University of New York at Stony Brook (Long Island). Author of works on Spanish Golden Age poetry, especially a variorum edition of Garcilaso de la Vega. He has also written other studies on Cervantes and classical drama, and has authored *Quixotic Scriptures: Essays on the Textuality of Hispanic Literature* (1983).

Evangelina Rodríguez. Professor of Spanish Literature at the Universitat de València, Spain. Author of works on Spanish Golden Age theater and short novel and contemporary Spanish poetry. She has written on Camerino, Zayas, and Calderón, among others; has edited several Spanish classics, including Calderón (1983); and has published *La novela corta marginada en el siglo de oro español* (1979). She is presently Director of the Cultural and Artistic Patrimony in the Government of the Generalitat Valenciana.

Colin Smith. Professor of Spanish, University of Cambridge. He works in medieval literature and history, Golden Age poetry, and English-Spanish lexicography, and has been Hispanic and also General Editor of *Modern Language Review.* In addition to works mentioned in the essay in this volume, he likes to recall his half-share in the archaeological and philological venture of *Place-names of Roman Britain* (1979), and hopes to pursue similar studies of the Peninsula.

Nicholas Spadaccini. Professor of Hispanic Studies and Comparative Literature at the University of Minnesota. He has written especially on Cervantes, the picaresque novel, and Spanish Golden Age drama, and has edited several Spanish classics and coedited books of literary theory and criticism, among them *Literature Among Discourses, The Spanish Golden Age* (1986), *The Institutionalization of Literature in Spain* (1987), *Autobiography in Early Modern Spain* (1988), *The Crisis of Institutionalized Literature in Spain* (1988), *1492–1992: Re/Discovering Colonial Writing* (1989), and *Cervantes's Exemplary Novels and the Adventure of Writing* (1990).

Jenaro Talens. Professor of Literary Theory and Film at the Universitat de València, Spain, and since 1983 regular Visiting Professor at the University of Minnesota. He has published fifteen books of poetry, translated into Spanish a number of European classics, and authored many books of literary criticism and theory, among them *El espacio y las máscaras* (1975), *Novela picaresca y práctica de la transgresión* (1975), *La escritura como teatralidad* (1977), *Elementos para una semiótica del texto artístico* (1978), *El ojo tachado* (1986), and *Romanticism and the Writing of Modernity* (1989). He also edits the series "Signo e imagen" at Ediciones Cátedra, and has coauthored (with N. Spadaccini) *Through the Shattering Glass: Cervantes and the Self-made World* (forthcoming).

Iris M. Zavala. Professor of Spanish and Literary Theory at Rijksuniversiteit, Utrecht. She is the author of some twenty books, among them, *Rubén Darío bajo el signo del cisne* (1989), *La musa funambulesca. Poética de la carnavalización en Valle Inclán* (1990), *Unamuno y el pensamiento dialógico* (1991), *Una poética dialógica. Mijail Bajtin y su círculo y la postmodernidad* (in press, 1991), *1898. The Dialogical Social Imaginary* (in press). She has also published four books of poetry, two novels (a third, *El libro de Apolonia o de las islas*, is in press), and a book on critical fiction, *El Bolero. Historia de un amor* (in press). She directs several book series on theoretical problems and feminist theories for John Benjamins, Rodopi (Holland), Alianza Editorial (Madrid), and Anthropos (Barcelona). The Spanish government recently awarded her the Lazo de Dama de la Orden del Mérito Civil for her contribution to Hispanic Studies.

Index